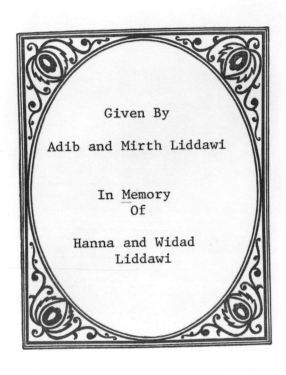

Given By

Adib and Mirth Liddawi

In Memory
Of

Hanna and Widad
Liddawi

MY FIRST FIFTY YEARS IN POLITICS

JOE
MARTIN

MY FIRST
FIFTY YEARS
IN POLITICS

AS TOLD TO

Robert J. Donovan

McGraw-Hill Book Company, Inc. New York • Toronto • London

To

The millions of Republicans—and to the many Democrats and Independents as well—who fought with me through the years to maintain the two-party system of government in the United States

MY FIRST FIFTY YEARS IN POLITICS

1

FEW OF MY CONTEMPORARIES have lived through such a long and revolutionary span of American politics as I have.

As a boy in North Attleboro, Massachusetts, where I was born and still live, I listened to Jacob S. Coxey recruiting his "army" of unemployed for the descent on Washington after the Panic of 1893. In 1896 I marched in a torchlight parade for William McKinley. Becoming a politician in my own right almost by chance at first, I began campaigning for office, in 1911, transported by horse and buggy or interurban. In those days politicians seldom had automobiles. A nickel got me to Seekonk on the trolley in ample time to address a meeting.

I served in the Massachusetts legislature with Calvin Coolidge; a close bond developed between us that endured unchanged throughout his years in the White House.

In 1925 I came to what was then the rather quaint, sleepy city of Washington as an elected member of the Sixty-ninth Congress and cast my first vote for Nicholas Longworth of Ohio for Speaker of the House of Representatives. Fourteen years later I was elected Republican leader of the House.

When Representative Allen T. Treadway, a Massachusetts colleague, nominated me for the post he said: "We are doing more than electing a floor leader. We are choosing a symbol of the Republican Party in this House." Many of my political friends and opponents would no doubt still agree that I have been a symbol of the Republican Party, though I strongly suspect that friend and foe would see this symbol in very different light. Nevertheless I still treasure those words.

1

Through the violent years of Franklin D. Roosevelt's New Deal my role of leader put me in the forefront of the opposition not only to many of Roosevelt's domestic spending programs, but also to measures, such as the lifting of the arms embargo, that threatened to drag us into war abroad long before Pearl Harbor did it for us.

The shattering defeats of Hoover, Landon, and Willkie made it far more difficult to keep the Republican Party alive and functioning than many remember in the prosperous times that shine upon the party now. The burden of keeping the party going in those days of adversity lay heaviest on our small but aggressive band of Republicans in the House. There were too few Republican Senators then to exert any decisive influence.

After the war the tide began to turn, and in 1947 I was elected Speaker of the House in the undeservedly maligned Eightieth Congress, during the Truman administration. Under the new succession bill which President Truman proposed and the Eightieth passed, I was for nearly two years first in line for succession to the presidency, as Speaker, since there was at the time no Vice-President. I served a second term as Speaker in the Eighty-third Congress in 1953–54, at the outset of the Eisenhower administration.

During the last fifty years I have been involved, I believe, more intimately and more extensively in Republican politics than any member of my party who holds public office today.

In 1916 I began attending the Republican National Conventions. That year I went to Chicago as a delegate from Massachusetts and finally voted for Charles Evans Hughes—an inauspicious enough start for a man who was eventually to preside over more national conventions than any other person in either party. I was in time to be the permanent chairman of the five Republican conventions that nominated Willkie, nominated and renominated Dewey, and nominated and renominated Eisenhower.

In 1936 I was Landon's floor manager when he sought the nomination at the Cleveland convention and became his Eastern campaign manager after he won it. Following Willkie's nomination in 1940 I was elected Republican National Chairman and in that capacity served as manager of his tumultuous campaign.

On at least three occasions, first in 1940, when I received forty-four votes on the first ballot at Philadelphia, then in 1944 and again in 1948, I found myself a dark-horse contender for the Republican presidential nomination. Each time the white horses were all too numerous and swift.

The denouement of my career came suddenly and, to me, unexpectedly—on January 6, 1959, at the conference of Republicans called in the House chamber to elect the party's leader in the House of Representatives for the Eighty-sixth Congress. For eighteen years I had been a candidate for reelection. No vote had been cast against me in such a conference since I first gained the post in 1939.

Having lived so long in the center of the political arena, I should have been wary, but I wasn't. I lived in a false sense of security in my established position as the leader. I had every reason to feel that I *was* secure. I had served my party honorably for a very long time. For twenty years in the House I had guided the party's course, often through perilous sessions. I was the only living former Republican Speaker.

Above all, in 1959 I had as leader a record of loyalty to President Eisenhower and of friendship for Vice-President Nixon that should have stood me well in time of need. I knew that if either of them merely spoke a word for me any revolt would be quelled. This was little enough to depend on in view of what I had done for them, sometimes to my own distinct political disadvantage. Indeed, I know of no one man who made more sacrifices for President Eisenhower than I did, without any personal profit whatever.

So I walked into the House chamber in January to face the challenge to my leadership from Representative Charles A. Halleck of Indiana without realizing the seriousness of the fight. By then it was too late. Now that it's all over I remember something Tom Dewey once told me at the Republican National Convention in San Francisco in 1956, the year Eisenhower was renominated. Before the balloting Dewey had made a speech chopping the Democrats to pieces.

"Tom," I told him, "if you had talked like that in 1948, you would have won."

"It's often easier to fight for someone else than it is to fight for yourself," he replied.

This is a lesson I should have heeded three years later, but, like Dewey, I defeated myself through overconfidence.

The story of my overthrow as Republican leader began in reality on the night of November 3, 1958, when returns from the Congressional elections came streaming in from coast to coast. The results were disastrous for the Republican Party. For the third consecutive Congressional election the Republicans had lost control of the legislative branch although they controlled the White House. Eisenhower had twice been elected President by landslides, but it was to be his destiny to share control of the government with the Democratic majority for six of his eight years in office. Nothing like this had ever happened before.

The 1958 election was not even close. The Democrats swept into power in Congress with the greatest pluralities since the pinnacle of the New Deal. Their margin in the Senate was so great that it assured them control of that body at least until 1962. Only by a superhuman effort will the Republicans be able to regain the House by then.

Often in the past defeat in an off-year Congressional election has presaged disaster in the ensuing presidential election, and some Republicans became immediately obsessed with fear that the party was doomed to return to the doldrums of the Roosevelt era.

A force akin to panic, it seems, spread through those Republicans in the House who had managed to survive, particularly the younger members. In their dismay over what had happened and their apprehension over what might lie ahead, they began to look for someone to blame for the calamity of election day. Many an eye lighted on me.

This situation was made to order for an ambitious rival, and Charlie Halleck was hardly the man to pass it by. It was, in fact, the hour he had been awaiting for years. When he felt absolutely sure of a majority, he moved in for the kill. I do not mean to imply that there was anything dishonorable about his decision to run for leader. That is the way of politics.

He had the most respectable backing. Without a doubt the White House crowd gave him all the encouragement he sought to run against me. These people did not have to initiate his candidacy. Charlie Halleck was aggressive enough to do that on his own, once he was reasonably certain that he had the votes to win. The vital thing for him was to know that high White House officials would give their blessing to his challenge, and on that assurance he had every reason to rely.

The President said that he was neutral. It was, however, a strange state of neutrality in which Eisenhower took no sides while his legislative liaison officials egged Halleck on. I was the President's leader in the House; I had made enemies in pushing legislation that he wanted passed.

If the President was going to remain impartial, he should have required the same impartiality of his subordinates. This is particularly true since the attitude of those presidential assistants who shuttle back and forth between the Capitol and the White House is regarded in Congress as reflecting the sentiments of the President himself. Ludicrously, some of them had come to believe that it was *they* that wielded the great powers of the presidency.

These subordinates were not impartial. I was too independent for them. They wanted someone who would cater to them. I would have no part of the notion that White House assistants could come around and dictate to Congress. In the years when the Democrats were in control I was among the loudest in criticizing Democratic members of Congress for "rubber-stamping" proposals from the White House. Now, simply because we had a Republican administration, I was not disposed to change my colors and ask Republicans who served under my leadership to leap blindly behind every suggestion trotted down from the White House. This attitude did not endear me to the President's staff.

I cannot moreover escape the conclusion that the course of events was influenced, at least passively, by Vice-President Nixon. He may have held himself correctly aloof, but the Vice-President was careful to do nothing to discourage his own followers in the House from supporting Halleck. Consequently, out of the fourteen-man Republican delegation from Nixon's home state of California, I was to get only a single vote.

The first distant rumbles of the approaching storm reached my ears in North Attleboro in the weeks after the election. Obtusely, I shut my mind against the notion that Republicans would reject me after all that I had done for the party, or that Eisenhower and Nixon would countenance it if they should try. I had given Nixon many a lift over the years when he was a rising young politician, and my files were fat with letters from the White House thanking me profusely for my help in getting the President's programs adopted:

Dear Joe: I think you know how much I have appreciated the loyal support and effective assistance you have given me during the last six months. Never once have you failed to come forward with your entire array of "horse, foot and gun" to make sure of implementing the party's program and the administration's plan. . . . As ever, D.E.

Dear Joe . . . what you and Sam [Rayburn] and the rest of the leadership did as a team in this difficult situation was very impressive to me, and I feel that the public ought to recognize how significant it was that the entire leadership pulled together so whole-heartedly and unreservedly on this crucial issue [mutual security appropriation]. Of course, I know how much effort you personally put into this fight, and I appreciate it very much. It was a tough situation you faced in the House, and I think you have every reason for personal satisfaction with the way you marshalled the boys on our side of the aisle. . . . Sincerely, D.E.

Dear Joe. . . . I seize upon this relaxation time to send you a note of appreciation and admiration for your splendid work this past session. . . . Sincerely, D.E.

Dear Joe: I congratulate you most sincerely on the passage of the reciprocal trade legislation in the House. . . . I am most grateful to you for all your hard work and for your continuous efforts on behalf of the administration. . . . Sincerely, D.E.

Et cetera. Little wonder I felt secure.

Moreover after each of the national elections for several years rumors had bobbed up in print that Halleck would oppose my leadership, which was not very surprising. Halleck had come to Congress in the first place hell-bent on running for President, Vice-President, Speaker, or whatever else opportunity might put in his way. Charlie is always available.

By the latter part of December 1958, the rumbles were growing louder, if not more convincing to me. Don Irwin, a Washington correspondent for the New York *Herald Tribune,* telephoned me in North Attleboro and asked for a comment on what he called an overt movement to unseat me.

"I am not the least bit concerned about this talk," I told him.

Then a friend called from Washington and was very serious about the situation. He said that he had just been talking to a man who had had legislative experience but was now high in the administration. This unidentified man had told my friend that a final decision had not yet been taken on whether "they" would wage a fight against me.

I returned to Washington before New Year's still undisturbed, though I soon discovered that Halleck had been in town and had been talking with three members of the President's staff—Jack Z. Anderson, Edward A. McCabe, and Gerald D. Morgan. Morgan, once assistant legislative counsel to the House, had been especially close to Halleck for years.

Another thing I found was that Representative Bob Wilson of California, to whom I had given a helping hand in his first campaign for Congress, was busy rounding up votes against me. Wilson had been one of Nixon's principal assistants in the latter's campaign for Vice-President in 1956, and I felt certain he never would have opposed me against the wishes of the Vice-President.

If at this point the Republican members had come to me and in sincerity asked me to step down because they felt that, having reached the age of seventy-four and being troubled at the time by a blood clot in my right leg, I could no longer carry the burden to their satisfaction, I would have bowed out.

There were several men whom I might have mentioned at once as being acceptable to me as leader. I would not have suggested Halleck, although he was seventeen years my junior. I did not consider him a man behind whom all Republicans could unite. I regarded him neither a popular choice nor a man who could provide the kind of leadership the party needed.

The toll of the years had removed a number of my staunchest old supporters from the House, and in the press of affairs I had never become as close to various of the younger and newer members as they and I might have wished. After a couple of years in Congress these men had begun to feel their oats. Many of the "Ivy Leaguers," as we call some of these young fellows, started dreaming of personal advancement through a change of leadership. Encouraged by Halleck and the White House people and plied with promises of patronage and preferment in committee assignments, they had taken to complaining that I was not displaying enough partisan aggressiveness. Bless them, I knew what it was to be in a political fight before they were born, and I had battled more Democrats than some of these fellows had ever seen!

There were some who resented my long and close friendship with Speaker Sam Rayburn, a Democrat from Texas. Among them were certain Northerners who didn't want to do anything for the South because, when put to the test, the South as a whole invariably turned against the Republican Party.

For me to have spent the first six years of the Eisenhower administration brawling in the House with Rayburn and Representative John W. McCormack of Massachusetts, the Democratic floor leader, would not have advanced the interests of the Republican party one iota.

In fact, it would have hampered the President's program, as can be well illustrated by an incident involving a bill sent up several years ago by the Department of Health, Education and Welfare. The Democrats did not like it very well, but with patience I won an agreement from their leaders to put it through without a roll call. Then to my dismay Halleck jumped up and lashed the Democrats until they cried in anger for one. They were in the majority, and, of course, the bill was defeated.

Another thing that my young Republican associates forgot was that my friendship with Rayburn enabled me to obtain for our side a good deal more patronage, such as jobs around the Capitol, than we, as the minority, ever would have got otherwise. Ironically, some of the men who had benefited most from this unexpected patronage were to vote against me.

A final circumstance that worked to my disadvantage in that first week of January 1959 was that in all my years as Speaker and leader I had never tried to build a personal faction in the House. I did not want one, and I never believed that it would have been beneficial to the party. Hence when the showdown approached, there were no particular Martin forces for me to rally.

Alf Landon telephoned from Topeka and asked, "What's all this stuff in the newspapers, Joe?" I told him that it looked as if there would be a fight, but that I could hold my own. "Well, I'll go to work for you anyway," Landon said.

He promptly got in touch with the three Republican members of the Kansas delegation. Later he called back and said that I could count on only two of them—Representatives Wint Smith and Edward M. Rees.

I believed also that I had Representative John Taber, of New York, the ranking Republican on the House Appropriations Committee, on my side. Taber and I were old friends. We had served in the House together since the times of President Coolidge. On Sunday, two days before the showdown, Taber came to see me in my office. He told me that when he had gone down to buy a railroad ticket at a ticket office in the Capitol, he had seen Morgan, McCabe, and Anderson with Halleck in one of the off-corridor hideaways. Taber went on to say that he never could bring himself to vote for Halleck. Together we looked over the list of the New York Republican delegation, which contained many of my personal friends.

"I've got to get at least half of New York," I observed.

"That's about what you'll get," Taber assured me.

I was sadly misinformed. I did not get half the New York delegation. Furthermore, shortly before the conference, or almost exactly forty-eight hours after our talk, Taber issued a public statement saying that he would vote for Halleck. The reason he gave was that Halleck would be willing to fight for the issues. Although he was an old friend of mine, Taber added, he believed that Halleck would offer stronger leadership.

I have formed my own opinions of why Taber turned against me, and, if I am right, they illustrate the kind of extraneous motives that play upon a situation such as we had at the conference to elect the party's leader.

I believe Taber voted against me because deep in his heart he was very angry at me on two scores. For one thing I had opposed him the year before on an immensely complicated measure called the accrual expenditures appropriation bill. With the backing of the Hoover Commission, the President had recommended it as an improved system of government accounting. Taber, no easy man to budge in such matters, objected to the bill. He counted on me to back him. However, the President wanted the bill, and as leader my loyalty was to him. This was but one of many cases where I estranged Republicans of my own persuasion by supporting the President against them, small thanks though it brought me from the White House in the end. Taber fought bitterly, and it was no easy job to get the measure through. Nevertheless we did it.

The second instance concerned the appointment of the House Minority Clerk. Taber wanted the job to go to a friend of his stepson. However, the Ohio delegation advanced the name of Harry L. Brookshire, who had been around for a long time. I did not interfere, and Brookshire was selected. This put Taber in a huff. He told me at the time, "You never do anything for New York"—meaning, of course, anything for Taber.

On these two counts I do not believe John Taber ever forgave me. Throughout the ensuing sessions I have encountered him in the cloakroom from time to time. He has offered no explanation. There is no compelling reason why he should. And what difference would it make anyhow? He says "Howdy." "Howdy, John," I reply.

2

ON MONDAY, January 5, 1959, the day before the conference, Charles A. Halleck of the 2nd District of Indiana, lawyer, war veteran, prosecuting attorney, legislator, formally announced his candidacy for the post of Republican leader of the House of Representatives. By that time he had received assurances that the great powers in the administration at the very least would not say *no*.

In the meantime Joseph W. Martin, Jr. of the 14th District of Massachusetts, blacksmith's helper, newspaper publisher, insurance agent, member of Congress, had made about every mistake it was possible to commit in the face of this development.

Still underestimating Halleck's threat, I called various conferences of Republicans in my office under the Capitol dome and as often as not invited members who proved to be the ringleaders of the movement against me—men, for example, like Representative John W. Byrnes of Wisconsin who were to fare very well under the Halleck regime.

I asked them to investigate what could be done to avert a fight that would divide the Republican Party, then accepted their offer to report back on Monday afternoon, by which time it would have been too late to do anything of consequence.

I overlooked the diligent activity of lobbyists of the automobile industry, the business organizations and the beef trust, who were scurrying all over town trying to line up votes for Halleck.

Finally, I squandered the vital hours of Tuesday morning by dutifully trudging to the President's weekly meeting with legis-

12

lative leaders at the White House. These had practically always been empty affairs, and on this morning as usual absolutely nothing was accomplished. I sat at Eisenhower's right hand at the Cabinet table, but he did not once speak to me, nor even look at me, as I recall.

The Republican conference was to begin at 2:30 P.M. Shortly before, I was somewhat shaken by a phone call from Representative Edwin B. Dooley, of New York, a younger man who had come to Congress a couple of years before. I had given him a gracious welcome and had treated him almost like a son. I helped him get his feet on the ground and lent a hand in getting him appointed to committees and to the Board of Visitors of the Merchant Marine Academy, a recognition that pleased him very much.

"Joe," he said, "I would rather cut my right arm off than do what I am going to do today, but I have to vote against you as leader."

I was stunned. "What is *happening?*" I asked myself.

Still I was confident that I had enough votes to win, and so I set out for the chamber. I found it rather laborious in those days walking through the corridors because of the blood clot. I limped a bit. I was conscious of the fact that I was looking rather run-down and tired, and I knew that this could have a bad psychological effect in the conference. But just in case the question of health was raised, I carried in my pocket a letter from Dr. Paul Dudley White, the Boston heart specialist who had treated President Eisenhower in 1955, saying that a physical examination had shown me to be in basically sound condition.

When I entered the chamber I took the leader's seat on the Republican side, as had been my custom for so many years. I was not in it long before I could see, as I had not seen in the previous weeks, what a carefully planned operation I was up against.

Representative Charles B. Hoeven, of Iowa, was presiding by virtue of his position as chairman of the House Republican conference. I had picked him for the chairmanship myself two years earlier. Hoeven proceeded to appoint a committee of counters, all of whose names were written on a piece of paper before him, without so much as consulting me.

At these conferences in the past Representative Daniel A. Reed, of New York, had always nominated me, but he was in the hospital now in his last illness, and I asked Representative Richard M. Simpson of Pennsylvania to make the nominating speech because he was reliable and dependable and had been my good friend. After he spoke, Representative Noah M. Mason, of Illinois, nominated Halleck. Here was indeed the climax of a long and often a very difficult relationship between Halleck and me.

Halleck had come to Congress in 1935. I recognized his ability early, and he was one of the younger men whom I personally brought along to positions of authority in the House. As leader I had given him the essential support he needed to become chairman of the National Republican Congressional Committee some years earlier. When I became Speaker in the Eightieth Congress, I backed him as floor leader. After we lost control in the 1948 election, I took over my old position as leader, and Halleck became one of my lieutenants.

Before one of the elections he came to my office and asked me to promise that if I should become elected Speaker again, I would once more back him for leader. I had refused to give this commitment so far in advance, because there was at the time considerable disgruntlement with Halleck in the ranks. Two or three other men had intimated that they might want to run for leader themselves. I told Halleck so, and it made him angry. As I recall the conversation, he said, "Well then, I withdraw my support for you for Speaker." "That's all right, Charlie," I replied.

As a matter of fact, I did support Halleck for leader when I became Speaker again in the Eighty-third Congress. Whether I was to remain Speaker through the following Congress depended, of course, on the outcome of the Congressional elections of 1954. Halleck has maintained—and the White House crowd has circulated his story—that I made a deal with him that if the party lost, I would retire, at least from a role of leadership, and let him remain as floor leader instead of reassuming the position myself.

This is not the case. When, following the Republican defeat in 1954, I was compelled to retire as Speaker, I returned to my old spot as floor leader, as I had done after the defeat of 1948, and again Halleck was forced to step aside. This did not go down well with him and, I gather, it did not go down well with the White House crowd.

Now all this was behind us, and here was Noah M. Mason, of all people, nominating Halleck in a speech that would have done credit to the Bourbons.

Even in the House of Representatives this ranked as irony of the first order. The whole philosophy that Mason was expounding was the antithesis of what the rebellious younger members stood for, or thought they stood for. Here was a man who opposed most of the things that Eisenhower advocated, especially in foreign policy—a man indeed whose speech implied that I had followed the administration's line too slavishly— nominating the candidate whom the President's staff was supporting.

After Mason's speech Hoeven moved things along so swiftly that, as I remember it, he did not even ask for seconding speeches. A motion was made to proceed in the usual way to vote for leader. Then Representative Hamer H. Budge, of Idaho, arose. He is another of what I call the last-ditchers, the extremists to whom the Eisenhower program has been anathema. He moved that the election be by secret ballot, something that was never done before. Yet this innovation carried, and I think the reason that it did was that many members who had pledged to vote against me were ashamed to register their choice openly.

On the first ballot the count was 73 for Halleck and 72 for me and 1 void because of illegibility, making the outcome in effect a tie. This necessitated a second ballot.

Before the tally on the first ballot had been announced, one

of my supporters, Representative Robert B. Chiperfield, of
Illinois, left for the day, supposing that business was finished.
When it came time for the second ballot we could not find him
and with two other of my staunch friends, Dan Reed and Representative Dean P. Taylor, of New York, away ill, I knew that
I was defeated. When the votes were counted on the second
ballot the score stood 74 for Halleck and 70 for me.

Before we adjourned I made a short speech. About all that
I could recall afterward was that I had taken some liberties in
paraphrasing a great address which we had listened to in this
same chamber eight years earlier.

"As General MacArthur said," I told my colleagues before
stepping down for good, "old politicians fade away."

An hour after I returned to my office Eisenhower telephoned.
He told me how much he had appreciated all that I had done
for him as leader.

"Regardless of what happened up there today, Joe," he said,
"I want you to know that I am most grateful to you."

This made me so angry I could scarcely hold back tears.

"Thank you, Mr. President," was all I could say. "Thank
you, Mr. President."

The next morning he was on the phone again.

"Notwithstanding what happened yesterday, Joe," he said,
"I hope you will continue to come to our leadership meetings on
Tuesdays and give us the benefit of your sagacious advice."

"I could not do that, Mr. President," I said.

"Why?" he asked.

"Because I am no longer the leader," I told him.

"You can come if I invite you personally, can't you?" he
urged.

"No, Mr. President," I said. "I cannot."

Later in the day Republican National Chairman Meade Alcorn called. He reported that Eisenhower and Nixon had told
him they would like to give a dinner for me. The place was to
be up to me, but Alcorn suggested the White House.

"Mr. Chairman," I said, "you believe in sending flowers to the dead."

That was the end of *that* dreary idea.

Then Major General Wilton B. Persons, who had replaced Sherman Adams as the Assistant to the President, came up from the White House and again raised the question of my attending the leadership meetings.

"If the President ever wants me," I said, "he is my President and I will respond with whatever assistance I can, but I am not going to attend the regular leadership meetings. Whenever there's anything I can do for you, I'll do it, so long as you keep these White House errand boys away from me."

Again the next day Bryce N. Harlow, one of Person's assistants, called. I have never regarded Harlow an errand boy. He was, and is, astute, tactful, and trustworthy, standing head and shoulders above the rest of the White House crowd. He said that the President was giving state dinners for the Speaker and for the Vice-President and would be pleased to have me attend one or both.

"I'm very sorry," I said, "but I plan to go to Nassau for a rest and will not be in town."

Later, when there was still considerable rancor in the air, Simpson told me that Nixon would like to see me.

"Well, I am here all the time," I replied. I suggested to Simpson that he and the Vice-President and Leonard W. Hall, former Republican National Chairman, have lunch with me in my office, which they did shortly. Nixon came in and shook hands with me cordially, and we all sat around my desk and ordered sandwiches, pie, and coffee. We gossiped about politics and the new session of Congress. Nixon talked at length about what he might do in 1960 (he made no reference to his own candidacy) to help the Republicans win control of the House again. As he went on I supposed that sooner or later, since he had expressed a wish to see me, he would get around to the subject that was on everyone's mind. But he came and went without ever mentioning a word about my defeat.

This was hardly typical of the response that I received from all over the country. James J. Farley telephoned to tell me he was sorry. Letters poured in—from Alf Landon, John Foster Dulles, Christian Herter, Henry Cabot Lodge, Lewis Strauss, Secretary of Labor James P. Mitchell, Earl Blaik, Patrick J. Hurley, Norman Vincent Peale, and many present and former members of Congress of both parties.

One of the most heartwarming of all was a telegram from Tallulah Bankhead. Her father was the late Speaker William B. Bankhead, my friend and one of my predecessors. I used to see her around the Hill when he was presiding over the House in the 1930s. Her wire was authentic Tallulah:

> DARLING MR. JOE, AS ONE GOOD DEMOCRAT TO ONE GOOD REPUBLICAN I AM SHOCKED AND HEARTBROKEN THAT YOU HAVE BEEN SO RUTHLESSLY DEPRIVED OF YOUR RIGHTFUL PLACE IN THE HOUSE. DISLOYALTY INJUSTICE AND INGRATITUDE HAVE NO PLACE IN EITHER PARTY IN SPITE OF YOUR DIFFERENCES ON MANY POLITICAL ISSUES MY FATHER HAD THE GREATEST RESPECT AND AFFECTION FOR YOU AND I ALWAYS AGREED WITH MY FATHER. MY LOVE AND BLESS YOU
>
> TALLULAH

Many months later I ran into Harry Truman at the Sheraton Park Hotel in Washington, and he asked, "What did you let those fellows lick you for, Joe?"

"I guess I couldn't help it, Mr. President," I answered. "They came up on me unawares. I wasn't ready for them."

"Well, it isn't going to help them in Sixty. I've been around the country, and I know."

Step by step I had worked my way forward from an obscure seat in the last row to the front of the House. Now in one stride I was for all practical purposes back again in the obscurity of the last row. It would be dishonest to say that there was not some bitterness and heartache and disappointment in this turn of fortune. The keenest hurt was the sting of ingratitude. In all the sensations that ebbed and flowed through me, however, I was never conscious of any feeling of regret that I had spent nearly fifty years in politics.

My defeat was part of the price I had to pay for remaining in public life so long. Everyone who stays in it loses sooner or later. But I never considered the price too high for the experience and the rewards of those fifty years.

As a young man I had drifted rather aimlessly into politics. Once in it, I did not intend to remain, but I was like The Man Who Came To Dinner. As I look back now it seems that politics was my destiny and that I could not very well have escaped it if I had tried.

3

MY FATHER, Joseph William Martin, Sr., who had come from a farm near Plainfield, New Jersey, and established himself as a blacksmith in North Attleboro, was a Grover Cleveland Democrat. I was born November 3, 1884, the day before Cleveland was elected for the first time. My father wanted to name me Grover Cleveland Martin. My mother, Catherine Keating Martin, an Irish immigrant, was a strong Republican and wouldn't hear of it. "Grover's a dog's name," she said.

Our family of eight children, in which I was the oldest of six boys, finally took on a completely Republican coloration when my father deserted William Jennings Bryan on the gold issue in Ninety-six.

All her life my mother was intensely interested in politics, and when Dewey campaigned through North Attleboro the week before the election of 1948, she admonished him—with more wisdom than any of us realized at the time—"Don't take it so easy."

Between my mother and myself there was a unique bond of affection. I never married. Until my mother died a widow in 1957 at the age of ninety-six I had lived with her all my life. For almost her last fifty years she was crippled by varicose veins and could seldom leave our white frame house on Grove Street, though she continued to do housework until she was eighty.

My mother had little formal education, but she was shrewd and witty, and a delightful conversationalist. Many people came to our house just for the pleasure of talking with her. In her invalid years she read newspapers avidly and absorbed so much information through radio and television that she often knew more about what was going on than I did.

My father's earnings, I believe, never exceeded eighteen dollars a week, which he turned over to my mother, who could get more out of a dollar than anyone I have ever known. She bought flour by the barrel and baked her own bread, which was necessarily the staple of our large family. As we children grew older and began earning money we paid "board," as she called it. Whenever she had some unusual expense she assessed us according to her notion of our ability to pay.

Her sense of right and wrong was very strong, and in a gentle way she was the boss of the children. In my own case, one of the consequences of her firm discipline is the fact that I have never smoked nor drunk. I dislike the taste of liquor anyhow. As children we were sent to bed at eight-thirty; we never would have dreamed of leaving the house without telling her where we were going and when we would return. This habit became so well fixed that even after I was a member of Congress I would report to her if I was going to run over to Fall River.

My mother and father were alike opposed to my going into politics. I remember how fully they both agreed with a family friend, George W. Cheever, a jewelry manufacturer in the town, when he admonished them one day: "Don't let that boy go into politics—he's too good a boy." Not that they objected to a political career as such. It was simply that they could see no future in town squabbles. When I was first mentioned as a candidate for the legislature they advised me not to run, but they never tried to stand in my way. Over the years they came to accept my career, and I am sure that my mother felt a deep pride when I was elected Speaker.

Through her I inherited a brogue, although she herself did not speak with one. My brogue has been a distinct political asset in Massachusetts. The Scotch thought it was Scotch, and the Irish thought it was an Irish brogue, and I was content to have each think as he did and take me for his own.

From my father I acquired another political asset. There are English Martins, French Martins, Spanish Martins, Portuguese Martins, Irish Martins—in fact, I saw *Martin* on a sign over a shop in Czechoslovakia. In a district like mine, composed of many strains, Martin is therefore a good political name. It even lends itself to useful adaptations, as I discovered in my first campaign for the Massachusetts state senate. A relative newcomer, I appeared before an audience of French-Canadians, and the chairman, who knew his business, introduced me as Joseph St. Martin. I received a rousing welcome.

The prophet of my high school class predicted that I would go to Congress some day. I am sure that neither he nor I realized to what a very great extent my youth was being spent in ways that gave me an extraordinarily wide personal acquaintance with the people of my district and put me in touch with some of its leading people. This was to bear fruit at the polls later on.

Because my family was poor, I began working outside school hours at the age of six as a newsboy and as a helper in my father's blacksmith shop.

In that long-forgotten world of the flaming forge I used to brush the flies off horses in summer while my father shod them. In winter, when I wasn't jotting down for him the names of the day's customers, I would sit on a keg of nails and watch him sharpen shoes so the horses could tread the icy streets. Among my favorite sights were the gypsy wagons that were brought in to be painted. Their interiors, decorated with historic scenes, were as gaudy as their exteriors of red and gold. The gypsies made their homes in these wagons, trekking from one town to the next to peddle wares and pitch their tents in vacant lots where they would read palms and tea leaves.

Practically everybody had a horse and a wagon or buggy then and patronized the blacksmith's shop as we patronize gasoline stations nowadays. People from every walk of life in the community streamed through my father's shop. If it was the gypsies today, it might be the banker tomorrow and the grocer the next day. Year by year, as I brushed away the flies and perched on the keg, my circle of acquaintances grew.

I made still more friends as a delivery boy for the North Attleboro *Evening Chronicle,* a respected newspaper that was to become practically a part of my life. Our world was much smaller and more intimate then than it is now. The population of the town was only four thousand, and it seemed that everyone knew everyone else. The men and women were more disposed then than they are today to give a young fellow a lift when he was starting out. No one bothers any more. People are colder, more indifferent than they used to be.

My paper route, which I built into the largest in North Attleboro, stretched up a hill where the nabobs lived. One of the matrons of this society was a Mrs. John E. Tweedy, who used to insist on bringing me into the house when I delivered her paper on cold winter evenings. Together we would sit and talk while the cook went for coffee and doughnuts. People don't have time for that sort of grace nowadays. Many years later I was able to repay Mrs. Tweedy's kindness with what I am sure she considered an enormous dividend. On January 20, 1953, as Speaker of the House of Representatives, I took her to the White House for the inaugural reception of the new President, Dwight D. Eisenhower.

Another who befriended me was a wealthy banker and businessman named Edward R. Price. One Christmas Day when I delivered his paper he invited me in and gave me a copy of Edward Everett Hale's *The Man Without a Country* as a present. The book made me nearly dizzy with patriotism. As it happened, I read it around the time when another brother was born. I begged my mother to name him Edward Everett, and I met with more success than my father had with his Grover Cleveland notions. Today my brother, Edward Everett Martin, is a member of the board of the Graybar Electric Company and the New England manager of that firm.

Another way in which my name became known was through a medium of fame peculiar to the small town of that day. I was a good baseball player. I was shortstop on the North Attleboro High School team and later played semi-pro ball in an intercity league, picking up ten dollars a game. All my life baseball has been one of my pleasures. I have known many of the true heroes of the game and have been involved in amusing experiences with some of them.

In 1940 the late Walter Johnson, the great pitcher for the Washington Senators, ran for Congress in Maryland, and I tried to help him. I am afraid my effort backfired. Since Johnson was an utterly inexperienced speaker, I got some of the boys to write two master speeches for him—one for the farmers of his district and the other for the industrial areas. Alas, he got the two confused. He addressed the farmers on industrial problems and the businessmen on farm problems, and he did not win.

Another time I hired Babe Ruth at the peak of his fame to play on the North Attleboro nine in a local game after the big league season. We paid him five hundred dollars. When the game was over I took him to the Elks Club and bought him a steak. He devoured it like a polar bear and asked if he might have another. The second disappeared as fast as the first. "Would you mind if I had another?" he asked. "Go ahead," I said, weakly, signaling the waiter. After the third he had a fourth, and I cannot imagine how many more he would have eaten if I had not finally hustled him out of the place. In manner the Babe was more like a boy than a man. In physique he was a curious specimen of giant on boy's legs. It was as if all the steaks he had ever consumed had gone into his chest, shoulders, and arms, with little nourishment left over for his legs.

After my graduation from high school in 1902 a well-to-do man in town, who was impressed by my prowess at shortstop, offered to help me through his alma mater, Dartmouth. College did not seem so necessary then as it does now, and as I had a newspaper job that interested me and enabled me to contribute some money to my family, I decided to postpone going to Hanover for a year. By the time the year had passed, however, I was absorbed in newspaper work. It looked as though I had a good future, and I felt that I should keep working and take some of the burden off my parents by helping put my younger brothers through college, which I did. Even when I was in the legislature, I was using most of my $750 salary as a state senator to help defray Edward's expenses at Dartmouth.

While I was still in high school, delivering the *Evening Chronicle* after hours, a feud sprang up between the management of the paper and some of the Republican businessmen of North Attleboro. Although it meant nothing to me at the time, the quarrel was to grow in intensity and was to lead years later to an important turn in my life. In my last year in school some of the disenchanted businessmen put up money to start a rival paper called the *Leader*. One of its principal financial backers was my friend Edward Price, who had given me *The Man Without a Country*. When he invested in the *Leader*, he said that I was to be given a job on the new paper. While I was still in school, therefore, I worked on the side as a copy boy, reporter, printer's devil, and handyman. I even used to clean the presses. When the commencement exercises were over, I moved into a full-time job there.

It soon became obvious, however, that the *Leader* could not make the grade. Shortly before it folded I was offered a job as a reporter for ten dollars a week on the *Sun* in Attleboro, four miles from my home, and I took it. This proved to be another lasting political asset. On my rounds as a reporter there I made a whole new set of friends. The prominent people of Attleboro became some of the strongest supporters I have ever had in my life. Indeed, their sons and daughters still vote for me. A key to my political success in a district which is now often carried by Democratic candidates for the other offices is that the people who were for me in the beginning are still with me, they or their descendants. I have kept my friends through the decades.

Long afterward, when I was struggling to stay in office against the high tide of the New Deal, I appeared at a dairymen's meeting in New Bedford. A delegate from Taunton, which is in my district, arose and made a great show of being a Democrat.

"I vote the straight Democratic ticket, except for Congressman Martin," he said. "I never saw him before tonight, but I have always voted for him because my father told me to, fifteen years ago."

After a few years in Attleboro, the *Sun* made me its North Attleboro correspondent, and in returning to my home grounds I picked up a couple of other clients by stringing for the Boston *Globe* and the Providence *Journal*.

I had not been back in North Attleboro long before a row, which generated more heat than light, erupted around the person of James W. Brehaut, the superintendent of schools. Like so many of the old New England town quarrels in which I was to become involved, it is difficult now to explain what this one was all about. The only thing I distinctly remember is that Brehaut was considered to be too high-handed a fellow, and many of the people wanted him dismissed. They were dead wrong. Brehaut was a good man and an excellent educator. But knowing no better at the time, I sided with my friends and became involved in a movement to elect a town school committee pledged to dismiss him.

Soon I found myself in the thick of town politics and was fascinated. Exploiting my ample circle of friends, I persuaded two men, Herbert J. Straker and Frederick S. Gilbert, to run for the committee on the Republican ticket. Then I went around to my Democratic friends and tried to get them to accept Straker and Gilbert on a bi-partisan slate. This they refused to do. They were sympathetic with our objectives, but they were not going to nominate the Republicans. However, they promised that if I would dig up the names of a couple of others who were against Brehaut, they would give them the nomination.

Nowhere in North Attleboro could I find anybody who would

bother to take the Democratic nomination, since it was a waste of time to run as a Democrat in that town in 1906. When I reported my failure, the Democrats startled me by saying that they would be happy to nominate *me* for the school committee.

There has never been any question about my Republicanism. I grew up a Republican simply because my family and practically all my neighbors were Republicans. The very air I breathed in North Attleboro was Republican, and it had never occurred to me to be a Democrat. Nevertheless I was determined that we were going to get a majority of anti-Brehaut men on the school committee. And I told the Democrats that if they wanted to give me the nomination, I'd take it. They did, and so the first time I ever ran for public office, it was as a Democrat.

No Democrat since has ever staged a stranger campaign. Rather early in life I seem to have developed the trait of living up to political commitments, even those that worked to my disadvantage. The first such instance occurred in the election of president of our senior class in high school. There were nine boys and eight girls in the class. We boys got together and agreed to vote for a lad named Philip R. Cook. Then, to my astonishment, the girls held a caucus and put me up as a candidate. One vote from the boys' side would have elected me. However, I considered myself bound by our agreement to vote for Cook. If his word is not good, what good is a man? I voted for my opponent, and he won by one vote.

Now I had got Straker and Gilbert the Republican nomination and I considered myself in honor bound to support them. Consequently, as the Democratic candidate I not only asked the voters to vote for my Republican opponents, but I voted for them myself. Even under these topsy-turvy circumstances—and this was something that was to give a boost to my political career —I got 535 votes, about twenty-five short of enough to have elected me. They were enough certainly to open the eyes of Republican leaders to my ability to get votes in North Attleboro. Happily, the fight against Brehaut fizzled out in the end.

Not long after this affair another town fight, the one that had been brewing since I was in high school, moved into the main ring. Although its ramifications are as hard to define now as those in the Brehaut quarrel, its consequences for me were much more substantial, because when it was all over I was no longer a reporter for the Attleboro *Sun,* but editor and publisher of the North Attleboro *Evening Chronicle.*

The paper had been established in 1870. At the time of which I speak, 1908, it had a circulation of nine hundred daily and sold for a penny a copy. I believe it was to become the last, or in any case the second-last, penny newspaper in New England. It was not, however, second to any in its Republicanism. In those days the *Evening Chronicle* was the Republican voice in North Attleboro, and in the nature of things it was closely aligned with the Republican organization. The publisher was Harry D. Hunt, a local Republican leader and, by appointment of President Theodore Roosevelt, the postmaster of the town. For a long time Hunt had been engaged in a political struggle for leadership. By 1908 it was plain that he was losing ground—he wasn't "taking the caucus," as we said. The faction that was opposing him contained many of the leading merchants of North Attleboro, and this put a great deal of pressure on Hunt. In the end he became fed up with the task of trying to run a Republican paper in the midst of this party feud. When his opponents suggested that they take the paper off his hands, he was ready to talk business. What it all amounted to, really, was that there was a transfer of political power from one Republican faction to another, and the paper went along with it.

The price Hunt was asking for the *Chronicle* was $10,000. A group of nine businessmen, eight of them Republicans, got together and put up $1000 each. Then they came to me and asked if I would subscribe a like amount and take the job of editor of the paper under the new management. I was twenty-four years old. As it happened, I had just about $1000 which I had accumulated through a combination of New England thrift and the succession of jobs that went back almost to my sixth birthday.

I had always been very careful with my money. I opened a savings account in 1902, and I still have it. "Never go in debt," my mother admonished me. I never have. Whenever I would buy a suit, the salesman would say, "Shall I put it on the books, Joe?" and my answer was—and is—always the same, "No thanks, I'll pay cash." I have never had a charge account.

In any case, there I was, an ambitious young fellow with $1000 in the bank, great enthusiasm for newspaper work, and enough experience to know how to put out a small daily. I accepted the proposition, and I never made a better investment. The paper prospered as its circulation grew to the present 4000 daily.

In time I began buying out the other interests. I never tried to force any of the other stockholders out, but over the years I purchased whatever holdings they or their estates wished to sell until, finally, just a few years ago, I acquired the last of the outstanding stock. In 1944 I extended my interests as a New England publisher by purchasing the *Sentinel,* a weekly in the town of Franklin in my district. As an investment I also acquired an insurance agency in North Attleboro.

My backers in the *Chronicle* transaction were men who were, as I have said, active in Republican affairs. I was attracted to their interests and began lending a hand to this drive and that. The first thing I knew I was organizing some of the young Republicans in the town. Our first meeting place was the soda fountain in Coady's Drugstore. Thomas F. Coady himself was a strong Democrat, but not such a fanatical one that he did not welcome our patronage. For the price of one soda apiece he let us sit as long as we wished on the high iron stools and talk about what we might do to make an impression on the regular organization. We even worked up a slate of young candidates at that soda fountain and entered it in the next town election. Our candidates did not win, of course, but these gatherings at Coady's were not a waste of time for me. Out of them came

some of my first personal political support. As the editor of the
Evening Chronicle, I was now beginning to exercise some influence in North Attleboro.

Increasingly I became involved in local campaigns, drifting
farther and farther into politics until in 1911, at the age of
twenty-seven, my friends put me up to run against the Republican machine candidate for the Massachusetts House of Representatives.

The outlook was uncertain. My opponent was a practicing
attorney and the former superintendent of schools, and tradition
favored older men then. Those were not the days of youthful
candidates. Not until women's suffrage and the return of the veterans after the first world war did the younger men come into
their own. At the time of my first campaign old-timers ran
county, town, and district affairs. Even to be a candidate for
the legislature then, one had as a practical matter to have been
the town clerk or the town treasurer or selectman for a long
stretch.

Nevertheless I plunged into the campaign with vigor. I had
no car, but I could make a circuit of North Attleboro, Attleboro,
Norton, and Seekonk on the interurban. Those places I could
not get to on the car line I visited by horse and buggy, making
speeches from the buggy—but only after I had unhitched the
horse. I didn't want to take any chances that some spy in the
crowd would set off a firecracker under the horse, leaving me
delivering my peroration flying down the road out of town. It
was that kind of campaign in spots. A fellow who was speaking
against me from a buggy of his own one night was grabbed and
pulled head over heels into the street.

Caps were the style in 1911, but I campaigned in an iron
derby to make me look older. Another lesson I learned for the
first time was not to be too upset over charges by the opposition. At Seekonk a fellow was haranguing a crowd not to vote
for me. He was saying that I was already the Republican boss
of North Attleboro and, if given a chance, I would become boss
of the whole state. This was unnerving until I overheard an old

farmer remark, "Well, that settles it. The young fellow's my man. If he can do as well as the speaker says he can, I'm for him. The man we've been sending to Boston all this time hasn't been worth the fare."

Enough of the voters evidently reached the same conclusion. I won, and in 1912 took my place in the Massachusetts House of Representatives, where I did not have long to wait for things to percolate.

My education as a legislator began with the very first bill I introduced. Hunting was a great pastime in my district, and many of my constituents wanted the season extended beyond the October 15–November 15 limit then in effect. A proposal to lengthen the period to six weeks seemed like a perfectly safe and simple debut for me. My innocence of the power of the Audubon Society and other conservation organizations could not have been more complete. Tossing that bill into the hopper had the effect of throwing a bundle of dynamite under a dam: I was swept over by the flood. The conservationists came at me from so many angles that I was soon fighting for my life to keep the hunting season from being shortened instead of lengthened. Only a frantic compromise with the Democrats prevented this calamity. We retained the month-long season, but changed the opening date to October 12, so the Italians, the Knights of Columbus, and others who made Columbus Day an important holiday could get out in the woods along with the rich fellows.

In later years in the legislature and in Congress I never again overlooked the influence of conservation societies. Indeed they seldom let one forget. They know how to stir popular agitation for or against measures they have a particular interest in, like the recent bill to protect the wild horses of Wyoming against hunters in cars or planes.

The conservationists favored this bill, of course, and I don't believe I have ever received more mail on any piece of legislation than I received on this one. From Newton, Massachusetts, alone, although it is not in my district, I received a thousand

letters in 1959 asking me to vote to protect the wild horses.
I did.

My first year in the Massachusetts legislature was the year
that a new city charter for Boston was up for consideration.
Like most reform projects supported by what we used to call
the Googoos—the good-government movements—it inspired
harsh opposition. Martin Lomasney, a powerful Democratic
boss of Boston, who was one of his party's leaders in the Legislature, solicited my support against the charter. I told him candidly that I would have to oppose him because my district was
in favor of the reform. In the end Lomasney had lined up what
seemed to him commitments enough to defeat the charter. When
the roll was called, however, he lost by a few votes. He rolled
out of the chamber like a mad elephant, and I had to skip to
keep from being knocked over.

"Joe," he snorted, "you at least were honest with me. If I can
ever help you, call on me. But I am going to take care of the
double-crossers!"

Years later, when it became necessary for the legislature to
redistrict the state because of an increase in the population,
Lomasney told the Democrats on the committee that was drawing up the new boundaries how he wanted his district laid out.
After that, he said he also wanted Joe Martin to be given the
best district possible.

Redistricting is an officeholder's nightmare because overnight
it can change the makeup of his constituency sufficiently perhaps to cost him the next election. The dread of everyone who
holds an elective office within a given district is that when the
boundaries are redrawn, as they are from time to time because
of population changes, he will lose a friendly town or pick up a
hostile one and that either way the vote will shift against him.

The truth of the matter is that redistricting goes to the heart
of democratic government. Indeed it can determine which party
controls Congress.

Consider the example of the South today. Republicans have
been gaining strength in many southern states for some years,

but it will be a long time before this strength is reflected accurately in the number of southern Republican seats in the House of Representatives. The trouble is that the legislatures of the southern states, being overwhelmingly Democratic, will not redistrict their states in such a way as to elect any Republican representatives. Whenever a congressman is elected, he becomes a potential candidate for senator or governor. And the Democrats in the South are not going to create any more potential Republican senatorial and gubernatorial candidates than they have to.

Tennessee, for example, has two Republicans in the House. On the basis of actual Republican strength in that state there ought to be at least three Republican congressmen, but the legislature gerrymandered Tennessee so that the Republican voters are bunched in two districts, leaving the rest of the House seats reserved for Democrats.

All sorts of machinations go on in this redistricting business. The political bargaining is endless. When I was in the Massachusetts senate, I was the chairman of the committee on election laws. The state was to be redistricted, and by virtue of my office I was the natural choice to head the redistricting committee. However, the leaders had someone else they wanted for that job. They told me that if I would take over instead the chairmanship of a committee to study consolidation of the various state commissions, I wouldn't have to worry about the new boundaries of my district. I took the job they wanted me to, and they took care of my district.

In redistricting as in all political affairs, personal influence plays its part. Years later, when I was in Congress, Bristow Draper, head of the Draper Corporation, textile machinery manufacturers of Hopedale, wrote to the Governor while Massachusetts was in the process of being redistricted, asking that Hopedale, which was in the so-called Worcester District, be shifted to my district. The Governor interceded with friends in the legislature, and when the new boundaries were drawn, Hopedale and the Draper Corporation were constituents of mine. This was entirely a personal whim on Draper's part. I knew nothing about his appeal to the Governor at the time he made it, and Draper never asked me for any special favor.

Gerrymandering is not the mischievous monopoly of any one party. If I happen to have stressed certain examples of it on the part of Democratic legislatures, I could no doubt cite just as many cases perpetrated by the Republicans. When I came to the House in 1925, for instance, every one of the thirty-six Pennsylvania seats was held by a Republican. One might have supposed that there wasn't a Democrat living between the Monongahela and the Delaware. Later there was a case in Pennsylvania in which the Republicans sacrificed one or possibly two Republican congressmen in a redistributing to make sure they would get a Republican state senator. Because of certain state legislation, including tax bills, the people who were doing the redistricting were more concerned over that one vote in Harrisburg than they were over one or two votes in Washington.

More recently, there was the example of California, whose districts had been laid out by a Republican legislature. In 1956, although Republicans cast only 47 per cent of the vote for Congress, they won seventeen of the state's thirty seats in the House. The Democrats recaptured three of these in their lopsided victory in 1958, and now that they have taken control of the legislature, we may soon see a permanent Democratic advantage established in a latter-day exercise in the art of gerrymandering.

The whole subject sometimes reminds me of a disturbance we had one day in President Hoover's office in the White House. In a redistricting of Massachusetts at that period one of our Republican colleagues, Representative Frederick W. Dallinger, got squeezed out. The state's delegation appointed Representative Edith Nourse Rogers and myself to call on the President and ask him to appoint Dallinger judge of the United States Customs Court. Dallinger was an able man and Hoover liked him. He assured us that he would make the appointment. When we rose to leave, Mrs. Rogers tripped over a wire, pulling the telephone off the President's desk. "That's the way with a woman, Mr. President," I said as I picked it up. "Give her a judgeship, and she wants the telephone too."

But matters such as redistricting were not yet of major concern to me early in 1912. Furthermore, I had scarcely got my feet on the ground in my first year in the legislature when the Bull Moose bellowed. Like many another Republican I was caught in the crossfire between the forces of Theodore Roosevelt and those of William Howard Taft. My dilemma was all the greater because, while my sympathies were with the regular Republicans, the sentiment in my district was predominantly Bull Moose. In the end I stood by my convictions and supported Taft. Only my personal popularity saved me in office.

One evening I was to speak at Norton. Before I went to the rostrum the chairman cautioned me, "If I were you, Joe, I wouldn't mention Taft's name to this audience. Just talk for yourself." Having taken my stand, I did not feel that I could follow his advice. For the full ten minutes that were allotted to me, therefore, I plumped for Taft, except at the very end when I said, "Gentlemen, I have served you this year on Beacon Hill. If that service was satisfactory, I'd welcome your continued support." Contrary to the chairman's warning, the audience rewarded me with warm applause. The next election day I was the only Republican who carried Norton, and for years afterward I was welcomed back with a reputation as an honest man.

It has been my observation that in politics a man who has the courage of his convictions survives longer than the man who shrinks from them. I recall that at about the time of which I am now speaking the Governor vetoed a wages-and-hours bill for the street railways of Massachusetts, the effect of which would have been to force all the companies to put on day and night crews. This was feasible in the cities, but in towns the size of North Attleboro the companies could not afford to hire so many men. Their practice was to thin out the crews in nonrush hours and assign the men who were laid off during the day to work in the evenings. This would not be tolerated today, of course, but it was accepted then. Accordingly, I voted to sustain the veto.

"I'm sorry you did that, Joe," one of my friends in the House said. "That will prevent you from ever becoming a senator. When you go into Taunton you will find labor is strong and will beat you."

"I had to vote my district," I replied. When the time came for me to run for Senate, I was nominated without opposition and elected by a large plurality.

The split in 1912 generated passions in the Republican Party the like of which I have never witnessed since, not even in the cleavage between interventionists and noninterventionists that occurred at the time of Willkie's nomination in 1940. The intense feeling in my own district was fanned during the campaign by visits of the rival candidates.

Taft came to Attleboro by train. As a state representative and a party regular I was made a member of the reception committee and was ushered aboard the train to shake hands with him. I was one of those who stood on the rear platform with the candidate when he addressed a crowd at the station. The thing that impressed me was the solidness of the man. His figure was rotund, and he had a massive head with a white mustache turned up at the ends. Above his broad forehead his hair was parted in the middle. He was larger than Roosevelt, but nowhere near so volatile. Taft was sound; Roosevelt was sound and fury.

T.R. came roaring into North Attleboro in a large open car waving a red bandanna, one of the symbols of his campaign. His followers along the route waved red bandannas back at him. His close-cropped hair was tousled and his mustache ragged. He flashed a dynamic grin in a manner that made it appear that he was biting the air. As a Taft man I stayed in the background, but not so far back as not to notice with some apprehension that the man who was riding with him was Dr. Joseph B. Gerould. Dr. Gerould was the man who had brought me into the world twenty-eight years before. On this score I had no objection whatever to his riding with Roosevelt and sharing the plaudits.

Furthermore he was an old friend and one of my partners in the
Evening Chronicle. But Dr. Gerould was also, as it happened, a
man who was running against me for the legislature that fall,
and the less attention he attracted the better I liked it. Fortunately, T.R.'s visit proved more exciting than damaging. The
results on election day must have given Dr. Gerould some second thoughts about the merits of his work twenty-eight years
earlier.

One of my first experiences in managing an issue on the floor
came in a rousing political fight of a particular kind we do not
see any more. The first year I was in the Massachusetts House
was the last year in which United States senators were elected
by the state legislatures. The Seventeenth Amendment providing
for the popular election of senators became effective on May 31,
1913. The final election of a senator in the Massachusetts legislature in 1912 was a Donnybrook Fair that went on for days and
took ninety or more ballots to reach a decision. The leading candidates were important figures in Massachusetts politics. Among
them were Congressman Samuel W. McCall, who afterward became governor; former governors Eben S. Draper and Curtis
Guild, and Congressman John W. Weeks, who was to become
Secretary of War in the Harding and Coolidge administrations.

The decisive fight was between Weeks and McCall, both of
them Republicans. Beforehand Weeks called on me in North
Attleboro to ask my support. My welcome was something less
than enthusiastic because in Congress he had effectively opposed
a man I was backing for postmaster.

"I don't think I will be with you, Mr. Weeks," I told him.
"I don't owe you anything. In fact, the reverse is true."

He went away disappointed. However, the closer we moved
to the election the more convinced I became that Weeks was indeed the best man in the field. When I returned to Boston I told
him that I had changed my mind and would vote for him. That
decision won me a good and influential friend, who was to return my support in generous measure, especially when he was

a power in the Coolidge administration and I was an unknown young member of Congress.

When the voting began Weeks invited me to serve on a team of five floor managers headed by Channing H. Cox, a future governor. My task was to try to lure votes away from opposing candidates. One of the methods was pyramiding—winning pledges of a switch to Weeks when his total vote reached a certain level. In other words I would try to get so many to join us when his vote reached eighty and so many more when his vote reached eighty-five and so on. The higher the level the easier it would be to get votes because then members would have greater confidence that they were going along with the winner. The early switches were the important ones to get but the hard ones to find.

Instinct, I suppose, led me to a member from the Berkshires, a shingle manufacturer, who probably knew a good deal about roofing but was very naïve about politics. He told me that McCall was his first choice, Weeks his second. On the first ballot he voted for McCall, who led the field but failed to get a majority.

"Well, your man didn't quite make it," I told him. "Now you can go for Weeks. Second ballot, second choice."

I hardly dared believe that he would bite for this, but when the roll was called on the second ballot he dutifully voted for Weeks. The McCall managers were furious at him for not sticking with his first choice, as is customary, until all hope was gone.

"I'll have to go back with McCall on the next ballot," he informed me.

"You'll be making a terrible mistake," I admonished. "The worst thing you can do around here, let me tell you, is to get a reputation for instability. If people don't know where you stand, you will never get anywhere in this House."

I could see that he was impressed by this argument. On the third ballot he again voted for Weeks. We recessed over the week end, and the first person I saw in the House on Monday was the shingle manufacturer heading for me in a state of excitement. "Here's trouble!" I thought mistakenly.

"Joe, I can never thank you enough," he said. "You've saved my career here. Look at the response from my district."

Over the week end, naturally, our side had got all the important people we could line up in his district to pat him on the back, and he had telegrams from bankers and merchants and the district attorney, praising him for his courage and consistency. He thought that he had done a great thing, and he stayed with us until Weeks was finally elected.

Long afterward my friend from the Berkshires came to me in great agitation over a bill to regulate the size of shingles. The industry simply *had* to have it. It *must* be passed. There is no describing how much it meant to him.

"You can call the shots on shingles," I assured him. We put the bill through for him, and so far as I know it is still the law of the Commonwealth of Massachusetts on the size of shingles.

In 1914, after three terms in the House (a term was one year then) I was elected to the Senate. It was there that I first became well acquainted with Calvin Coolidge, who by this time was the President of the Senate. After that he became lieutenant governor and then governor.

Our friendship developed gradually through small incidents, but it grew steadily and lasted until his death in 1933. Some time after I had become a state senator, Coolidge was backing a bill to lengthen the time that must elapse before one could claim payments under the workmen's compensation law, a modification that was unpopular with the factory employees in my district. I have always supported legislation that helped the working man. This has been a prime source of my political strength.

"Joseph," Coolidge asked me—he was the one man in my life who always called me Joseph, pronouncing it Jo-*seff*— "Joseph, can you vote for this bill?"

"Yes, Mr. President, I can," I replied, "but I won't."

He did not take offense. One afternoon when I was standing outside his office, he poked his head through the doorway and called me. "Joseph," he said, "go in and call the Senate to order and preside until I get there." This was his way of cultivating my good will and giving a little distinction to a young fellow.

Our friendship continued even after I dropped out of politics for a while and he became Vice-President of the United States. I called on him in the capital during a visit in 1921. A frugal man, who would have been horrified at today's free spending, he inquired where I was staying. I told him that I was at the Ebbitt House, which stood on the site now occupied by the National Press Building.

"That's good," he commended me. "It's only about a third of what you'd have to pay at these other hotels."

I did not dare mention that I had tried to get in the Washington, but couldn't.

He invited me to the Senate restaurant for lunch.

"I am going to have bean soup, Joseph," he said. "What will you have?"

I have never liked soup, and I was famished, but I replied, "I'll have a bean soup too."

When we had finished he insisted that I let his chauffeur take me sight-seeing, after which I was to drop around to his suite at the Willard and have dinner with Grace and him.

The chauffeur grumbled when we set off.

"Congress has just bought a new Cadillac for Harding," he said. "They offered Coolidge one, too, but he wouldn't take it. He said this old Cadillac was good enough for us."

After the Coolidges and I had dined together at the Willard, the Vice-President asked me if I would like to go to a movie. I said I wouldn't mind. He began leafing through the evening paper for the amusement page. As it kept eluding him, it became perfectly obvious that he did not have the slightest idea where it was and had probably never looked at it before.

"On second thought," I said as his search proceeded, "I'd just as soon sit here and talk over old times with you and Grace."

With some relief, I am sure, he tossed the paper aside and to my surprise asked his wife to fetch his golf clubs. I did not know that he was a golfer.

"These sticks are a little dirty, Grace," he observed with a faint air of suggestion that she should have kept them clean.

"Would you like to play a game tomorrow, Joseph?" he inquired.

"Oh, no," I answered. "I'm not old enough to play golf."

While this was a jest, it nevertheless was a true reflection of the attitude most of us had about golf then.

Outwardly Coolidge was shy and taciturn. Toward his friends, however, he could be surprisingly warm—even sentimental. He had a strong sense of loyalty. He was able. He possessed sound judgment. His word was good. He was well liked. He was a strong governor.

As time went on, I found myself in the role of one of his favorites, which was not only gratifying personally but was a great help to me politically when I came to Congress. I was very proud of the affection Coolidge had for me. During the 1922 campaign he went out of his way to drive to North Attleboro one night to make a speech for Senator Henry Cabot Lodge at a rally at which I was presiding in the high school. I learned afterward that when he left he rode all the way to Norwood, fourteen miles away, before he uttered a word in the car. Then all he said was, "I've driven over a hundred miles tonight. I made a speech that probably didn't change a single vote, but as long as Joseph Martin is happy, I am."

As a President, Coolidge was not brilliant by any means, but he exercised good, hard common sense and did not try to stir up trouble. He was content to try to give the people the kind of administration they wanted and was not forever worrying them with alarums from Washington. He was the man for his time and made an excellent President.

I served three terms in the state Senate, something no one from my district had ever done before. The Republicans had a rotation system in which the nomination alternated between the towns and the city of Taunton. However, the leadership was agreeable to my seeking a third term, though I wound up in a primary fight. An episode in that contest sheds a little light on how elections were won in Massachusetts in those days.

In the primary I lost the town of Berkley, with only one vote appearing in the Martin column, although three of the selectmen were among a number of persons—including the town committee—who had signed my petitions. The county Republican boss, who also held the job of county commissioner, descended on Berkley to see what was going on. What had happened was that my opponent, a Prohibitionist, had been to Berkley spreading rumors that I was a drunk. The boss not only set the boys right on this score, but he told the selectmen not to bother showing up when the commissioners were considering the next round of road improvements unless I carried the town in November. On election day it was my opponent who got only one vote in Berkley.

After six years in the legislature I returned to private life, at the end of the 1917 session. For one thing, I had never had any intention of spending my life in politics. For another, having once successfully bucked the two-term tradition for senators in my district, I had no desire to force the issue still further. Moreover, my newspaper was growing and I wanted to spend more time in North Attleboro.

I had not been home more than several months when, at the age of thirty-four, I volunteered to fight in World War I, and then almost immediately came down with influenza. By the time I was back on my feet the Armistice had been declared. The next few years at last gave me a chance to settle down and run the paper without any outside distractions. As far as I knew, I was out of politics for good. I had no plans whatever for getting back into the rough-and-tumble of Beacon Hill and town elections when a call came one day in 1922 from Frank H. Foss, the Republican State Chairman, who asked me to come to Boston to see him.

When I arrived, he informed me that he was having a terrible time over Senator Lodge's campaign for reelection. Three factions were at war within the state organization, and the only person they could agree upon as manager of Lodge's campaign, the chairman said, was myself. I told him I was out of politics now, but he was deaf to all my explanation about the necessity of my tending to business affairs. He warded off my objections with arguments about what a great figure Lodge was in the Republican Party and how important it was for the Republicans to hold that seat in the Senate and how dangerous the Democratic threat was becoming that year. In the end I had little choice but to agree to manage Lodge's campaign. That decision put me back in politics for the rest of my life.

The campaign was touch and go, and our funds were inadequate. At the start of the final week we had only $35,000. I ruled that not a single cent of it could be spent on anything but getting out the vote. In fact I set out myself to reinvigorate the local organizations. I would drive into a town and say to the chairman, "How many votes can you get out?" and he would reply, "Seventy." "Can you do a little better than that?" I would ask. "Yes, if I had a little money," he'd say. "How much?" I would ask. "Oh, if we had fifty dollars we might get out a hundred and fifty votes," he would say. "All right, you do that," I would answer and hand him fifty dollars and hurry to the next place to do a little more invigorating. Lodge, who was the grandfather of United Nations Ambassador Henry Cabot Lodge, won by a vote that was so close there had to be a recount.

Early one morning the next summer, in August 1923, Senator Lodge telephoned me from Nahant. "Harding is dead," he informed me. As I was then secretary of the Republican State Committee he asked me to meet him later in the day at Governor Cox's office in Boston to discuss what part we should take in the funeral of the late President and in the welcome to the new President.

When I arrived Lodge took me aside before we entered the

Governor's office. This wiry, nervous little man with the white beard was a smart politician. Outwardly he was often austere and cold, but I always considered him friendly and human. During the 1922 campaign I took him to the first one-arm lunch room he was ever in. He was fascinated with the place. Harding's death was a blow to him. He had powerful connections in the administration, and as long as Harding lived Lodge was the kingpin in New England. With Coolidge it would be a different story. Lodge and Coolidge had fought bitterly. They were on opposite sides of the League of Nations issue; more than that, they belonged to rival Republican factions in Massachusetts. Lodge realized what the change would mean to him. With a spirit of resignation he said to me before we went in to see the Governor, "Joe, the king is dead. Remember, we're all with the new king."

It took no exhortation to make me loyal to Coolidge. Before the next convention, in 1924, I traveled across the country with two companions, lining up delegates for him. The Republican Party had some colorful leaders in the West then. A man I particularly remember was Senator Joseph Patrick Sullivan of Wyoming, who assured us of his support of Coolidge. Sullivan had come to New York from County Cork in 1888. One day he dumped all the money he possessed at the window of a railroad ticket office and said he wanted to go as far west as his dollars would take him. The ticket-seller calculated that Cheyenne, in the Territory of Wyoming, was the best he could do for him. There Sullivan went and became a sheepraiser, then a banker, then an oil man and finally a United States Senator and the Republican leader of his state.

That fall of 1924 I took a flyer myself. I decided to run for Congress and entered the Republican primary against Representative William S. Greene, who had represented the district since 1898. I lost. After my defeat I was sure that I was finished with politics forever. Six months later I was in Congress. Greene died a week after the primary. A convention was held to fill the vacancy. I was nominated and set out without delay on my campaign.

The days of the interurban and the horse and buggy were well behind me now. One of the Republican leaders in my district had the agency for the old Monroe automobile. For $900 I bought a black touring car and took off over the bumpy roads to meet the voters at rallies and clambakes. As a minor political stratagem I used to buy only a few gallons of gasoline at a time so I would have occasion to patronize a greater number of gasoline stations and get to know the proprietors—or rather get them to know me.

A good part of my life, and a happy part, has been spent at clambakes. Traditionally, the clambake has been an important institution in New England, like the chicken dinner in the South and the Midwest. It has been one of the principal social gatherings at which politicians meet the people and the people become acquainted with politicians. Both parties have long used the political bake as a means of raising money for local campaigns. Not all clambakes are political clambakes by any means, but politicians like to go to both kinds.

Sad to say, this old institution, which goes back to the time of the Indians, who taught the white man how to bake clams, seems to be declining slowly. One reason for this is that clams are growing scarcer. But when I was a young man there used to be a famous political clambake every year at Rehoboth, in my district, which was attended by governors and United States Senators. A feature of the affair was a clam-eating contest, and one would have to consume a couple of bushels at least to win. Two plates were about the limit of my capacity. When I had downed that much on a day of campaigning, I would have to switch quietly to fish at the remainder of the bakes on my itinerary.

After the last one I would often have a long ride home over dark roads. An old Irishman named Thomas Nolan used to travel with me to keep me company. One black night we were driving along a lonely stretch when some ghostly figures emerged

from a wood and headed toward the car. It was a time in which
the Ku Kluxers were active, and when Tom saw the sheeted
figures descending on us, he went stiff with horror.

"Good God, Joe," he yelled. "The Klan is after us!"

I was more curious than alarmed. Slowing down, we discovered that these mysterious beings were fraternity brothers from
Brown University, in Providence, conducting an initiation.

In the 1920s, when automobiles and roads were crude by
modern standards, campaigning by car held more hazards than
it does now. In the 1926 campaign my Democratic opponent
was a woman named Minerva Kepple. Like myself, she used to
drive from town to town making speeches. One day when I was
spinning along near Somerset I came upon a car that had broken down. As I pulled alongside, I saw Minerva sitting at the
wheel bewildered and dejected. She was due at a rally in Somerset, where she was to deliver a speech that would no doubt beat
my brains in. I suppose if I had had brains worth beating in, I
would have left her there and gone on to have Somerset to
myself. But I said, "Come on, Minerva, I'll get you there,"
and I whisked her into town in time for her speech. I defeated
her without any trouble on election day. I have heard that in
later years she always voted for me for Congress. I believe
that has been true also of others I have defeated. If so, it is
one good fruit of the rule that I have always followed never
to wage a vicious campaign. I have always tried not to hurt an
opponent personally.

In my first race for Congress I won by some 9000 votes,
and on March 4, 1925, I took my place in the Sixty-ninth
Congress.

4

I ENTERED the House of Representatives in some awe of the great names all about me. The prominent men of the House at that time included Longworth and Bankhead; Ogden Mills and Fiorello H. La Guardia of New York; Theodore E. Burton of Ohio; Christopher D. Sullivan, the leader of Tammany Hall; Millard Tydings of Maryland; Cordell Hull of Tennessee, the future Secretary of State; Fred M. Vinson, who was to become Chief Justice; and Richard S. Aldrich of Rhode Island, the uncle of Governor Nelson A. Rockefeller. In the Senate were Henry Ashurst of Arizona, William E. Borah of Idaho, Walter E. Edge of New Jersey, Walter George of Georgia, Carter Glass of Virginia, Robert M. La Follette, Jr. of Wisconsin, George W. Norris of Nebraska, Pat Harrison of Mississippi, Hiram W. Johnson of California, Burton K. Wheeler of Montana, and Reed Smoot of Utah.

The men who were loaded with the coin of seniority were rather more aloof in those days than they are now. They were less reticent about letting a newcomer know that they were running the show. The large round table which is still an important meeting place in the House restaurant was reserved for the Speaker, the chairmen of the various committees, and perhaps a few senior members of the Rules Committee. Anyone serving his first term would have been completely out of place. I had been in Congress three years before I dared pull up a chair.

In spite of the great reputations, I soon discovered, as new members probably still do, that whenever a particular subject came up, there was always one or perhaps two members who were expert on it and could address themselves to it far more intelligently than anyone else. And very often these were members that one had never heard of until he came to Congress.

There were no microphones in the House then, and a speaker had to concentrate almost as hard on making himself heard as he did on what he was saying.

In older days, I was told, a member would not wish to make more than two speeches in a session. The country might be better off if we returned to that custom. During my own time in Congress I have witnessed a deterioration in political oratory. Speakers are less eloquent nowadays. More personal effort used to go into the writing of speeches. I remember one year, when we were holding a big meeting in Massachusetts, I went to the North Shore several days beforehand to call on former Senator Albert J. Beveridge of Indiana, who was vacationing, to ask him to speak. "I would not make a speech," he said, declining the invitation, "unless I had two weeks to prepare it."

After thirty-five years in Congress I have encountered about every kind of speaker that American soil yields. We used to call Representative James O'Connor of Louisiana the sunset speaker, because he made a speech in the House every day at sunset. And Representative William I. Sirovich of New York was the B.C. speaker. A physician who wrote several plays that were produced on Broadway, Sirovich set his speeches in a framework that went back centuries before Christ. When I first heard him he was back around 500 B.C. I used to say to him, "Can't you get us up to date a little faster?" But I do not think that during his years in Congress he ever progressed much beyond A.D. 100 as his starting point.

A Democrat was flailing away at some situation one day until the House was knee-deep in clichés. His trouble was that he had one cliché too many. "I say to you, Mr. Speaker," he shouted, "that politics make strange bedfellows. Especially since women got into 'em."

Another fellow was going on like that in the Senate one afternoon when I happened to drop by. The Senator speaking was blind. As I listened, Senator Borah leaned over to me and said, "What a pity he isn't dumb instead!"

I had not been in Congress long before my eyes began to bother me. Other members, I discovered, were affected similarly. The reason was that the lighting in the House chamber thirty-five years ago was very poor, and anyone who read there a great deal suffered eyestrain. Of course, there was no air-conditioning. Summers seemed even hotter in Washington then than they do now. Many of the committee rooms were ill ventilated, and members would sometimes come to the verge of fainting during long hearings. The installation of air-conditioning in the 1930s did more, I believe, than cool the Capitol: it prolonged the sessions. The members were no longer in such a hurry to flee Washington in July. The southerners especially had no place else to go that was half as comfortable.

The great difference between life in Congress a generation ago and life there now was the absence then of the immense pressures that came with the Depression, World War II, Korea, and the cold war. Foreign affairs were an inconsequential problem in Congress in the 1920s. For one week the House Foreign Affairs Committee debated to the exclusion of all other matters the question of authorizing a $20,000 appropriation for an international poultry show in Tulsa. This item, which we finally approved, was about the most important issue that came before the committee in the whole session.

From one end of a session to another Congress would scarcely have three or four issues of consequence beside appropriation bills. And the issues themselves were fundamentally simpler than those that surge in upon us today in such a torrent that the individual member cannot analyze all of them adequately before he is compelled to vote. In my early years in Congress the main issues were few enough so that almost any conscientious member could with application make himself a quasi-expert at least. In the complexity and volume of today's legislation, however, most members have to trust somebody else's word or the recommendation of a committee. Nowadays bills which thirty years ago would have been thrashed out for hours or days go through in ten minutes. An intricate $40,000,-000,000 defense appropriation will pass the House in almost a matter of hours. Any one part of it would have been a great issue when I first came to Congress and would have been debated for perhaps months.

In contrast to present salaries of $22,500 a year, members of Congress received $7500 then and had a single clerk and a one-room office. Mail was light. I doubt that I received in the beginning twenty-five letters a day until veterans' pension cases started piling up. It was not until the New Deal that the blizzard struck. Then letters rolled in at the rate of 200 a day and the total reached 500 at the height of big controversies.

My first office was in the basement of the old House Office Building almost next door to my friend, Representative La Guardia, soon to become New York's most famous mayor. He once said to me, "I wish you were a liberal. If you were, you'd be a great leader for us." Although we were poles apart politically, I liked and admired La Guardia. Many people complained that he was a radical; perhaps he was. That does not alter the fact that he did a great deal of good.

Except for him, I was surrounded almost entirely by southerners in the House Office Building. This got me off to a good start in making friends from the South who were to prove useful in the days ahead when, as Republican leader, I needed some Democratic votes to block New Deal spending.

In those days of Prohibition some of the boys used to gather in the offices of these southerners at night for little parties at which the host would bring out corn whiskey. The Eighteenth Amendment did not prevent conviviality on Capitol Hill. Many of the boys had their bootleggers; one of these practictioners who became known in the headlines as "the man in the green hat" was arrested with his wares in the House Office Building.

No one can deny the hypocrisy that some committed in voting with the drys and drinking with the wets, and one person who would have none of it was Representative James Ambrose Gallivan of Massachusetts. Gallivan, who had been a good second-baseman at Harvard, was a strong wet and despised anyone who voted dry. He kept a well-stocked bar in his office and with it a record of voting on the Prohibition issue. Whenever any member dropped in for a drink, Gallivan would first check his record—if he had voted dry, he couldn't get a drop.

Of all the men of that day, however, I think the most picturesque was Representative George Holden Tinkham of Massachusetts. He was one of the Brahmins, a life member of the Massachusetts Society of Mayflower Descendants, who had come to Congress in 1915. Short of stature, he compensated for his lack of height with a long black beard that for some reason or other reminded me of an African hunter. This was appropriate because hunting trips to Africa were his avocation. With a zest that would be the envy of most men he combined his love of hunting with a virulent hatred of Prohibition. This fusion of passions was represented on the walls of his apartment in the old Arlington Hotel in Washington, where he hung stuffed heads of hyenas and other ferocious or grotesque animals bred in the Dark Continent, each one named after some leader of the dry forces.

One evening when I was dining with Mrs. Charles Sumner Bird, Republican National Committeewoman from Massachusetts and a pillar of the Woman's Christian Temperance Union, and her daughter, the wife of Governor Bass of New Hampshire, they said they would like to see Tinkham's apartment. It was famous at the time. When we arrived Tinkham took over.

"This is Andrew J. Volstead," he said, introducing them to an ungodly-looking beast. "And this," he said, as they approached the next weird head, "is Wayne B. Wheeler, of the Anti-Saloon League. *You* will be interested to know him," he said to Mrs.

Bird. And so on around the room. To my great relief, Mrs. Bird, a constituent of mine, enjoyed the exhibit.

If there was one issue that aroused George Tinkham more than Prohibition, it was the rights of the Negro, and perennially he would introduce what was known then as a force bill— a measure providing that the representation of each state in the House should be based upon the number of its voters rather than upon its population. Because the Negro was disenfranchised in the southern states, the effect would have been to reduce the South's representation.

One day the southerners turned the tables and with western help wrote into a bill that was pending on the floor an amendment to exclude aliens from population figures used in determining a state's representation in Congress. This struck at New England and thus brought me into the act with no delay. I suggested to the Republican leaders that they further amend the bill with Tinkham's proposal, so that if the North could not count its alien population, the South could not count its Negro population. That is exactly what was done, and Tinkham was elated. Here was his fulfillment at last.

Of course, the inevitable happened. The very next day North and South got together and dropped both amendments. The leadership gave me the job of mollifying Tinkham. I did not have to look for him. He was looking for me, and he had blood in his eye when he approached.

"Now, George," I said, "I want to congratulate you on the great contribution you have made to your country."

This surprised him and offered me an opening to make a little speech to him. I gave it everything, saying something to the effect that "First you have put through the only force legislation that this House has passed since the Civil War. You have done what not even Henry Cabot Lodge could do when he was in Congress. Furthermore you have saved the North. If it had not been for your great proposal, we could not have stopped the South from reducing our representation in Congress." And so on.

He seemed less than enthusiastic. But that night I was in the Carlton Hotel, where Tinkham used to dine, and there he sat in the lobby proudly relating his great accomplishment in almost the same speech that I had delivered to him in the cloakroom.

Finally, Tinkham answered, to my own satisfaction at any rate, the ancient question whether bearded men sleep with their beards under the covers or outside. Late one night while walking home from a party, Representative Richard B. Wigglesworth of Massachusetts, who is now Ambassador to Canada, and I chanced by the Arlington and dropped in to say good-night to our friend. I knocked on his door and, although no one answered, the force of my knuckles swung it open. From the deserted living room we stepped into the bedroom. I turned on the light, and there was old Tink sound asleep with his black beard draped over the covers.

No one can fully understand the motives of any member of Congress without knowing something about the district he represents. My district—it used to be the 15th when I first ran but through redistricting has become the 14th—embraces a considerable part of the old Massachusetts Bay Colony and a segment of Plymouth Colony. The population is about 360,000.

In addition to the Attleboros, it includes Taunton and Fall River, which are also industrial cities. To the north it runs through spacious and hilly New England country, where the foliage turns a vivid scarlet and gold in October and people still put pumpkins on fenceposts and doorstoops at Hallowe'en. Through regions of dairy and truck farms one can wind for miles over roads with few traffic lights and no neon signs. Thin white spires of colonial churches mark the sites of neat and shaded towns. Many of the surrounding fields, which only recently sprouted rows of cornstalks, are now the abode of new young families living in small frame houses with television aerials and aluminum storm windows. Wellesley, Wheaton, and Stonehill Colleges are three of my proudest "constituents."

At Wellesley the district lies only thirteen miles from Boston. Wellesley and nearby towns like Wrentham, Sherborn, Dover, and Millis—all within commuting distance of Boston—are communities of wealth, taste, and not too many Democrats. The last can no longer be said of the more populous areas of my district.

The old 15th was a safe Republican district, but it began shifting to the Democrats thirty years ago. Prohibition pulled voters away from the Republican Party in large numbers. Furthermore, as many have forgotten, Al Smith, though defeated by Hoover, broke the Republican hold on the cities of the North. In the populous states he mobilized the new immigrants in politics and gave cohesion and strength to the Democratic Party.

Then too the textile mills began leaving New England for the South, and the high-tariff issue on which Republicans had capitalized gradually lost some of its effectiveness. By necessity and conviction I was a high-tariff man for years, favoring protection for the mills of Fall River and Taunton and the jewelry industry of the Attleboros against the competition of cheap foreign goods. In my early days, at least, labor as well as management demanded a protective tariff, and it would have been political suicide for a candidate to advocate anything else. As conditions changed, I recognized the necessity and desirability of international trade so long as there are safeguards against the destruction of American industries. After the war I supported the Reciprocal Trade Agreements program.

Almost a third of my constituents live in Fall River, which was one of the earliest union towns in the United States. The unions may not endorse me, but two-thirds of their members vote for me. The union bosses have never been able to convince their members that I was against the welfare of the working man. Indeed, I have always enjoyed strong support from the rank and file of labor, particularly in the old A.F.L. trade unions and among the textile hands and weavers and loom-fixers. It has been a personal rather than a strictly political following that has kept me in office despite the rising Democratic tide.

Over the years I established a reputation as a fighter for New England, and the voters have kept reelecting me because I have given them service. Every year that I have been in Congress it has been my practice to visit each post office in my district at stated times to make myself available to discuss their problems with the people. In one town poultry farmers might come in to complain about the cost of feed grains as a result of government price supports. In the next town I would find a committee from a Negro congregation waiting to ask my advice in a quarrel they were having with the minister. Once in Seekonk a woman came in to protest the absence of sidewalks along state highways. A week later she was killed walking on one of these roads. One old woman brought me samples of rock ledge from her farm in Maine and asked me to take them to Washington to be tested for possible commercial use. During the Korean war two women appeared at a post office I was visiting and appealed to me to have Dean Acheson removed as Secretary of State—an endeavor, as I shall recount later on, I undertook on my own initiative without the necessity of any prompting from lady constituents.

As a young Congressman I scurried all over Washington doing chores for my district. I beat a path to the National Rivers and Harbors Congress and to the War Department to see the Army Engineers about Taunton River and Fall River Harbor improvements. I hastened to the Interstate Commerce Commission to protest the discontinuance of two trains daily between Fall River and Middleboro. I turned up at the Navy Department to borrow a cutter for the Sea Scouts, and appointed young men to West Point and Annapolis. I introduced pension bills for widows of Civil War veterans in my district. I fought for appropriations for new post offices and more letter carriers. I appeared before the United States Shipping Board to advocate more shipping for Boston Harbor. I urged the use of Fall River granite in new construction at the Naval War College at Newport. I introduced visiting constituents to President Coolidge.

On behalf of the textile industry I worked for higher tariffs on cotton and wool products, and on behalf of the factories of the Attleboros I introduced a bill to repeal excise taxes on jewelry and silverware. I presented the case for a higher tariff on briar pipes before the House Ways and Means Committee. I asked the Tariff Commission to raise the duty on products of duck-farming to protect my constituents who sold feathers and down. I sought protection on eggs from China and shoes from Czechoslovakia. I opposed trade pacts with Great Britain.

In an Evacuation Day speech in Boston—the first delivered by a Republican since President Taft—I said: "Boston was evacuated by the British just 162 years ago, and they shall not be allowed to return now to drive American workmen from their benches." The South Boston Citizens Association presented me a shillelagh.

In 1925 I sponsored a bill to remit duties on a carillon imported by the Church of Notre Dame de Lourdes in Fall River. This was, in fact, the first piece of legislation I ever introduced in Congress. Heeding the advice of older men that a young fellow should not make too much noise when he came to Congress, I did not deliver my first speech until February 15, 1927, when I rose to oppose the McNary–Haugen farm bill.

"Mr. Speaker," I said, "as a representative of one of the largest industrial districts of the country, I want to record my opposition to the McNary–Haugen bill. No one sympathizes with the farmer any more than I do. No one desires his prosperity any more than I. . . . But I cannot vote for this measure which is a striking departure from sound economics. . . . This measure is a price-fixing bill—a dangerous path to tread. It is designed to increase materially the cost of living. . . . Why bring increased burdens to the millions of toilers for the simple purpose of making a political gesture to the farmer?"

It is little wonder that when I listen to debates on the farm program now a third of a century later I say to myself, "This is where I came in."

I was never a fanatic on any issue. I came to Congress eager to promote the welfare of the Republican Party. To me that was synonymous with promoting the national welfare.

Many people suppose that rivers-and-harbor legislation and the pork barrel are a Congressman's surest means of keeping a hold on his district. Before going to Congress I may or may not have shared this belief, but once there it did not take me long to discover the fallacy.

In 1928 a fire destroyed a large part of the Fall River business section. It occurred to me that it might inspire private owners to rebuild quickly if the federal government would step in and put up a new post office, even though the old one had not been damaged. I went to see President Coolidge about it. In discussing the extent of the damage to other property I mentioned that the Wilbur House had been destroyed.

"Wilbur House?" Coolidge mused. "Let's see, Joseph, that's the place where you had to step up a flight of stairs to get a drink, wasn't it?"

"That's the place, Mr. President," I replied.

Coolidge penned a note to Secretary of the Treasury Andrew Mellon: "Please see what you can do to give Joseph a Post Office." In no time at all I had the funds, which, I might reasonably have concluded, would make everyone in Fall River happy and, therefore, well disposed toward me on the next election day.

The first thing I knew I was in the middle of a sizzling fight in Fall River over the location of the post office. Louis Liggett, proprietor of the Liggett drug store chain, was then the Republican National Committeeman from Massachusetts and thus a man toward whom it behooved me to show some respect. He owned certain property downtown that he wanted us to buy. I considered the site inappropriate and opposed it, so for my pains I had the National Committeeman angry at me. In the end we decided to demolish the standing post office and rebuild on the same spot. This brought a howl from a great many people who were attached to the old building and thought it should be renovated.

Massachusetts building contractors were scrambling for the new post office, but when the bids were opened, who got the job but a firm in St. Louis! This caused vast local resentment. Then I was pressed by the granite people to have the new building done in Fall River granite. The builder used Indiana limestone. The post office was to extend through a block, and a tug-of-war developed among the merchants as to which of two streets should have the main entrance. While all this was going on, the contractor discovered that he had bid too low and couldn't make payments due some of the local subcontractors, who promptly came screaming to me about it.

The matter was straightened out somehow, and we got the post office up without its being a complete political debacle for me. Just as I was thinking that my troubles were over at last, one of the Republican faithful came to me in great agitation.

"This post office business has been the limit," he said, "but last night was the worst."

"What happened last night?" I managed to ask.

"I was coming up Bedford Street admiring the new post office," he said, "and who do I see is the night watchman?"

"Who *did* you see was the night watchman?" I inquired.

"The father of that Democrat who ran against you for Congress last year," he announced almost triumphantly.

This is the sort of pitfall one can get into trying to do something for the people back home. It was by no means the only case of its kind. When I was first elected to Congress, for example, I fell heir to the old Taunton River issue. For a hundred years my district had been interested in having the river widened and deepened to make it navigable for steamers.

Where my predecessors had failed I got the necessary legis-

lation through Congress, only to find it the biggest issue raised
against me in the next election. The railroads were angry because it threatened them with new competition. The gas company people were furious because they feared that they would
be put to great expense removing their pipes from the river
bed. The owners of a large stove company at Taunton were
frantic lest the widening of the river weaken the foundation of
their factory. And to top it off many of the voters were suspicious that I, who was to become a veritable symbol of economy
in government, was a big spender.

In my next campaign I had to go to considerable lengths to
convince the people that I was not, as the Democrats were
charging, an "expensive Congressman." My opponent was the
mayor of Taunton, Andrew McGraw, a physician. Badly as he
wanted to win, he never allowed his political instincts to interfere with his doctor's instincts. When we attended clambakes
together during the campaign he took great care in advising
me what dishes I should eat to remain healthy, in spite of the
fact that my health and vigor were being employed against him.

In the Republican ranks of the House I got off to a good start,
and as time passed and I achieved seniority by being reelected
every two years, I progressed steadily, if slowly, toward a
position of leadership.

As a newcomer in 1925 I supported Longworth in his bitter
but successful fight for Speaker against Representative Martin
B. Madden of Illinois, also a Republican. I did so at the request
of Coolidge and his friends. This was the first step in the right
direction, for it pays to be on the winning side in a contest for
the Speakership, particularly since the Speaker has a great
influence on appointments to committees. But almost more important to my progress was my good standing, not only with the
President himself but with the powerful figures from Massachusetts who surrounded him. One was Secretary of War
Weeks, whom I had supported in his fight for Senator and who

assured me when I came to Washington that I still had a
balance in his ledger. The very day I took office a messenger
arrived from the War Department with a wheelbarrow laden
with a set of Hinds' *Precedents*, which Weeks had used when
he had occupied my seat in the House. In all these years since,
I am afraid, I never got around to making use of his gift.

An even more influential friend in a way was Frank Stearns,
the man who had in my opinion made Calvin Coolidge. Stearns
was the wealthy head of R. H. Stearns & Co., a Boston department store. He had gone to Amherst College before Coolidge,
and it was a deep disappointment to him that Amherst, unlike
Yale, Harvard, and Princeton, had not produced a President of
the United States. This seems to have been in the back of his
mind as he spent his influence and his money helping Coolidge
become governor. When Coolidge entered the White House and
wanted someone he could trust absolutely at his side, he turned
to Stearns. For weeks at a time Stearns lived in the White
House. People nowadays do not think of Coolidge as one who
was the object of hero worship, but that comes close to describing Stearns' feelings. One day after a diplomatic reception he
said to me almost rapturously, "Oh, Joe, I wish you could have
seen the little man come down the stairs at the head of that procession!" Even during my early days in politics Stearns had
been eager to help me, and now that I was in Congress, he
made a practice of mentioning my name around the White
House to men of influence in Washington.

My friendship with the President brought me to the White
House oftener than most young Congressmen get there. One
morning when I was having breakfast with him, his shaggy dog
begged for a muffin and I gave it one, not knowing whether the
frugal Coolidge had observed me. The dog returned, and this
time I asked the President whether I might feed it a muffin.
"Give him *one* more," Coolidge said precisely.

I came to handle small legislative chores for the administration, and I was gratified to hear one day that when Stearns had

informed the President that he had turned over a certain job to me, Coolidge had remarked, "Good, then it will be done."

By a trick of circumstances, more or less, I landed in my first year on the House Foreign Affairs Committee. My predecessor, the late Representative Greene, had been a member of the Committee on Merchant Marine and Fisheries, but someone other than myself had been picked to fill this vacancy. Several Massachusetts newspapers had urged my appointment to the Post Office Committee, and I decided that I would ask for this assignment. On one of my first days in Washington, however, I happened to inquire of Frank Foss, who had come to Congress with me, what committee he aspired to.

"Post Office," he said. "How about you, Joe?"

I did not wish to stand in the way of my friend, the man who had recently been the Republican chairman in my state, so I replied that I was going to make a play for the Committee on Interior and Insular Affairs, the only other one I could think of on the spur of the moment. Foss made the Post Office Committee all right, but I never became a member of Interior and Insular Affairs. Instead, to my surprise, the Committee on Committees selected me for Foreign Affairs. Somewhere along the line a decision had been made to give the vacancy on this committee to Massachusetts. There were no other powerful contenders, a circumstance due partly to the fact that foreign policy did not seem so important then as it does now, and I was chosen by a margin of one vote.

Although a first-year man, I was cordially received on the committee, which was composed of some very substantial members of the House. Stephen G. Porter of Pennsylvania was chairman. Hamilton Fish of New York was on the committee. So were Charles Eaton of New Jersey, who went on to the chairmanship, and Tom Connally, the colorful Texan with the long white locks, who later became chairman of the Senate Foreign Relations Committee. Another member was Martin Luther

Davey, who afterward was elected governor of Ohio. I think, however, that the member who interested me most at the time, because of his personal history, was Representative Charles M. Stedman of North Carolina. I regarded him as a remarkable link with the past because he was the last Confederate soldier to serve in Congress. He had been a major in General Robert E. Lee's army and had been thrice wounded in the Civil War. He died in 1930, at the age of eighty-nine.

Although even then Foreign Affairs was one of the important committees of Congress, so few matters of consequence came before it in those days before Hitler, Mussolini, and Hirohito that membership was a sinecure. The $20,000 authorization for the poultry show in Tulsa was merely an example. We devoted just as much time to measures regulating opium trade or to programs for rebuilding American embassies in different parts of the world. The United States Embassy in Moscow was situated over a blacksmith shop. My vote in favor of a $20,000,000 embassy construction bill got me into hot water in Massachusetts, what with the Democrats yelping that I was more interested in sending money abroad than I was in helping the already growing line of the unemployed at home.

Before the second world war widened our understanding of life overseas, Congressmen often experienced sharp reactions in their districts to the slightest things they did that had a bearing on foreign countries or personages. Not all of these reactions were unfavorable, as I was to learn during the visit of the King and Queen of England in 1939. As one of the leaders in Congress then, I was on the committee to welcome the royal couple upon their arrival at the Capitol. Morning coats, striped trousers, and silk toppers were obligatory. The day before, however, Sam Rayburn told me that he did not have a topper and was not going to get one. "I'm just going to wear a derby," he said. I did have a topper, but since Rayburn had none, I decided that I would go along with him and wear a derby also. When I got to the Capitol the next morning, I found Rayburn's bald head grandly encased in a high silk hat, which someone had lent him. I would have had time to dash back to my apartment and grab my own topper, but I said to myself, "To hell with it," and appeared at the reception in my derby.

This became the big news photograph of the day, my receiving King George VI and Queen Elizabeth in a derby while all the other members wore toppers. The wives of the others were not pleased, but far from making me look foolish in the 14th District of Massachusetts, it turned me into something of a hero. Almost immediately I began receiving mail to the effect "Good for you, Joe. Glad someone down there has the gumption to stand up to the King of England and not feel he has to crawl into a high hat." "Thank God," wrote a doctor in Brockton, "we've got one independent man in Congress."

In spite of the dearth of great issues, I found that being on the Foreign Affairs Committee gave me a good deal of prestige. Borah was one of the respected voices in the country on foreign questions then, and although he was on the Senate Foreign Relations Committee, the public tended to confuse our committee with his, and people assumed that I sat at his right hand.

Much more important to my advancement than the Foreign Affairs Committee was my appointment to the powerful House Rules Committee in 1929. A seat had become vacant through the death of a member from Massachusetts, Representative Louis A. Frothingham. It was agreed that it should be filled from our state. The Massachusetts delegation was polled, and I was selected. "I was awfully glad to see you get on this committee, Joe," Speaker Longworth told me. It was a long step forward. I was on the escalator now, so to speak, and I continued to move as Longworth picked me as a member of his "cabinet," as his steering committee was called. We have no such body in the House now as this small, informal but nevertheless influential group. It was made up of leading Republicans in the House from each section of the country. The "cabinet" always met in the Speaker's office. It functioned extremely harmoniously as an organ of programming and high policy.

I had become a good friend of Longworth's. In the Congressional campaign of 1930 the Republicans won control of the House by a very narrow margin. Under the old rules, the Seventy-second would not meet until December 1931, more than a year away. In so long an interval a number of members would be expected to die, and with so slight a majority deaths could change the balance in such a way that the Democrats would get control and Longworth would be replaced as Speaker. Needless to say this was very much on his mind when, suddenly, one of our Republican members, who was in his seventies, married a woman of thirty. When the bridegroom entered the House one morning Longworth beckoned me to the Speaker's desk and whispered, "Say, Joe, you don't think that old boy is going to do me out of my job, do you?" Fate wrote a different ending. Several members of the Seventy-second did die before it met, and one of them was Nick Longworth. The seventy-year-old man with the thirty-year-old wife lived on. Longworth's fear had been justified, however. Because of the deaths, the Democrats were able to organize the new Congress and to elect Representative John Nance Garner of Texas as Speaker.

As one grows older time flows faster, and I look back now in disbelief at what a brief era the decade of the 1920s was and at the innocence which did not comprehend that one of the great watersheds of history was at hand. The thirty-year period that was then dawning has witnessed change on a scale that has never before been experienced in a single generation of mankind. Many of my old friends in Congress who died before the end of the Twenties would have been incredulous at the world their successors have had to deal with. It seems odd to remember now what a daring novelty even an airplane ride was for us.

Like a number of others in Congress I made my first flight with Charles A. Lindbergh. One of the things Lindbergh did to popularize aviation after he returned from Paris was to take Congressmen on short jaunts around Washington. Parachutes were strapped to our backs before we boarded, and we were told that if anything went terribly wrong, we were to jump out of the plane, count to ten and then pull the cord. One of the members was horrified by the instructions. "If there is going to be any jumping, I jump now," he said and wriggled out of his chute and left.

Lindbergh took us off the ground without a bump. Although this was my first experience aloft, I could sense that he was handling the plane flawlessly. It was reassuring just to watch his cool, professional manner. He was smiling most of the time. The plane had an open cockpit and a closed cabin, and Lindbergh suggested that the passengers rotate between the two, so that all could take a look at the controls. La Guardia was the first to ride up front. He bounced into the cockpit with a show of nonchalance that comes with familiarity. He had flown as an American military pilot in Italy in the first World War, and he did not want any of us to suppose that this sort of thing was new to him. I was the next to ride in the cockpit and found it exhilarating. The member who rotated into my place was terrified when the plane banked and frantically grabbed Lindbergh around the neck. That ended Lindbergh's experiment with seating Congressmen in the cockpit. From then until we landed the passengers were kept in the cabin.

In a way this otherwise uneventful flight was a fitting end to an era. Soon we were to be off on another flight, breathless and bewildering with loop-the-loops, nosedives, barrel rolls, vapor trails into the wild blue yonder, and crash landings. This time the pilot was not the earnest Charles Lindbergh, but the ebullient and exasperating Franklin Delano Roosevelt.

5

AFTER a lapse of nearly thirty years it is hard to convey the wrack and the distress through which the Republican Party passed in the Depression and the ensuing years of the New Deal. It was in this melancholy period that I came into a position of leadership not only of the Republicans in the House of Representatives but in the national party organization as well. Throughout most of these tempestuous years I lived, as the saying goes, at the eye of the hurricane.

Now, with the battles of the Thirties far behind us and the reforms forged in those controversies accepted as a normal part of our life, one cannot so easily understand what a wrench many of the innovations of the New Deal caused Republicans of my bent and background. American society as it had existed for a generation or so before the Depression was certainly not a perfect society, as anyone knew who had, like myself, lived close to the hardships of New England mill towns. Nevertheless it was a good society and, at its own peculiar pace, a progressive society. Above all, in a world that was flying faster than anyone realized into the clutches of regimentation it was a society that cherished the individual and fostered his enterprise.

Many of the experiments of the New Deal seemed to us certain to undermine and destroy this society; in that light they constituted a challenge that neither I nor many of my Republican colleagues could resist. We fought them with every weapon we could lay our hands on. If ours was a vehement opposition, it was not, on the other hand, a categorical opposition. The reforms I considered wrong or nonsensical—and

66

there were some of both—I fought. But there were reforms of another sort, such as social security, which I supported as wise and humane.

In the main, however, I lived by the proposition that the function of the opposition is to oppose. And as the fortunes of the Republican Party plummeted through the defeats of Hoover, Landon, and Willkie, opposition often took the desperate form of throwing up a sail in hope that somehow it would catch the wind of a popular reaction which would drive our party forward once again. I had to keep probing, probing, probing for the popular side of an issue. In the Roosevelt administration, let us not forget, the Republican Party was pitted against skillful and resolute politicians, whose interest—if any —in a healthy two-party system was not easy to detect.

We had to struggle to stay alive under the onslaught of this host. In our opposition to the New Deal programs, self-preservation often became an end in itself.

As I moved up the ladder of party leadership, my problem was compounded by division within the Republican ranks, especially as we approached the vital issue of isolation versus intervention. It took endless contrivance and compromise to keep my own forces together. I had not only to fight the New Deal but to ride with the hounds and run with the hares of my own party in the process. Much of the time I seemed to be engaged in a war on two fronts.

It is, I believe, a pity that President Hoover was not reelected in 1932. If he had been willing to make a concession on the legalization of beer and wine, he might have been. He might have survived the Depression if it had not been for the wet issue, which not only intensified popular sentiment for the Democrats but poured millions of dollars into their campaign. A number of Republicans discussed this problem with the President in the White House in that fall of 1932. I was one of them. I personally urged Hoover to come out in a campaign speech for legalization. He declined to do so. Hoover was not what I would call an ardent dry by any means. In fact, he stood by the mild plank in the 1932 Republican platform proposing submission of a constitutional amendment that would "allow States to deal with the problem as their citizens may determine." But when it came to favoring wine and beer, he had made commitments to the contrary, and he lived up to them.

More than anything else, then, it was the wet issue that crushed the Republican Party in that period. If Hoover could have overcome this and continued in the White House for another four years, I am convinced that he would have brought us out of the depression before we had to wait for a world war to do it for us. He would have done so without closing banks with loss to hundreds of thousands of depositors. And it would have avoided the expenditure of the billions that were appropriated under the New Deal, to say nothing of the expansion of the federal bureaucracy that accompanied it.

When I reflect on what happened in that election, my mind often wanders back to the day Franklin Roosevelt was nominated in Chicago. I was in Washington, where Congress was still in session, and strolled over to the Senate private lobby. A dozen Senators, including young Bob La Follette, were listening to the broadcast from the convention. The consensus was that in Roosevelt the Democrats had nominated their weakest candidate. The Senators said that he did not have an appeal to the mass of voters and wasn't likely to catch fire.

When he became President, I liked Roosevelt personally and admired—ruefully at times—his dynamic political skill. Of all our Presidents, he has been the shrewdest politician. Politically, he was much smarter than his party. He was a superb judge of public opinion and was wonderfully adept at creating a personal following. Like Eisenhower, he relied a great deal on personal charm, but his charm was more effervescent than Eisenhower's. He had a far greater relish for politics than Eisenhower has. Like myself, he was a practical politician. That is what politicians should be. During his years in office we met often. He invited me to many social as well as political gatherings in the White House. As members of the same trade we understood one another well, which was fortunate, because each of us seemed to have a keen appetite for public attack upon the other. Frequently there was nothing behind these attacks but the appetite. Except, of course, when Roosevelt had suffered some setback from which he wished to divert attention. In such instances he would as a pure stratagem take to denouncing me or some other likely Republican.

In spite of this, I must say that having a President of the opposing party in the White House put some sport in politics, which has necessarily been missing for me since Eisenhower took office.

Roosevelt had spent a good deal of his time in Massachusetts as a boy and was familiar with Buzzard's Bay and the north shore of Cape Cod. Like Grover Cleveland, Daniel Webster, General Leonard Wood, Joe Jefferson the actor, and many others, F.D.R. had fished in the waters in front of my summer home at Sagamore Harbor on the Cape. To exhibit his knowledge of the area he used to ask me "Are those Douglas firs still growing in front of the New Bedford waterworks?" or "Does that fine white house still stand at the intersection where the road from the Cape comes into Taunton?"

Much good-natured banter passed between us. One year he came to the Capitol to deliver his State of the Union Message. I was, as the minority leader, on the committee to escort him into the House chamber. I took my place outside the Speaker's room, where Roosevelt was waiting, because it was crowded with justices of the Supreme Court, members of the Cabinet and other dignitaries. Suddenly, I heard Roosevelt's voice calling, "Joe, where are you?"

"I'm right here, Mr. President," I answered. "I'm just a bit modest."

Roosevelt made his way to where I was standing.

"Joe, you'd better warn your boys to be on the lookout today," he said. "I've got a trap set for them."

"Thank you, Mr. President," I replied. "It is a generous foe who warns the opposition."

What Roosevelt meant was that he had some lines that seemed to make a great concession to the Republican viewpoint, such as might set our side applauding until he suddenly came to a "but," and then veered sharply in the other direction. The trap worked, and after the speech he told me with a booming laugh, "I got you."

"No, Mr. President," I corrected him, "you didn't get me. I didn't cheer at all."

The next year he confided to me before the speech, "There are no traps today."

"That's just because the election is over, Mr. President," I observed. He loved repartee of this kind.

At a White House conference one night early in the war he happened to remark during a discussion of our transport problems that one of the best harbors the Allies had was at Freetown. He had scarcely mentioned it when he swung around to me and, characteristically, said, "Joe, I'll bet you never heard of Freetown Harbor."

"Oh, yes I have, Mr. President," I replied.

"All right," he said, challengingly, "where is it?"

"On the west coast of Africa," I said, leaving him rather crestfallen, I thought.

"Well, *how* did you know that?" he asked.

"Why," I said, "because Freetown was the original name for Fall River, and there's still a place called Freetown in my district, so of course I knew they had a spot over in Africa called Freetown."

I think he was even more pleased with my answer than he would have been if he had caught me not knowing where Freetown was.

When Roosevelt returned from the Cairo and Teheran conferences the White House staff staged the usual flattering reception, dragging in busy officials from all over town. I used to say that in Hollywood one was paid to participate in mob scenes, but when Roosevelt came home from someplace, Congressmen had to pay their own taxi fare for the honor of greeting him. On this particular day I neglected to bring the ticket that had been issued, but with the help of Senator Francis T. Maloney of Connecticut, I talked my way past the guard by producing a club membership card for identification. Roosevelt was in high form, laughing, talking, and poking the air with his long cigarette holder. He was still dressed from his trip in a blue plaid checkered shirt and battered felt hat and, as I entered, he was remarking that he was surprised that they had allowed him into the White House grounds in such garb.

"And how did you get in here, Joe?" he called merrily.

"Oh, that was easy, Mr. President," I said. "I didn't have a shirt like that, so I used my Elks card."

Many times in the early years of the New Deal I sat alone with Roosevelt in his study on the second floor of the White House, rambling over topics of interest to both of us. It was a great pleasure to talk with Roosevelt. He was a fine conversationalist with a great fund of information and a relish for political combativeness in any form. He seemed to enjoy these talks with me because I had opposed him publicly and argued with him privately. One had to be on one's guard against him, however. He was a crafty speaker, who might devote two thirds of the time to matters far removed from Washington only to weave into the other third a skillful pitch for something he wanted from Congress.

One day I told him I needed a new road in the southern part of my district. He called in Louis McHenry Howe.

"Louis," he said, "call MacDonald"—Thomas H. MacDonald, head of the Bureau of Public Roads—"and tell him I am sending down a black Republican, and I want him to give him a road."

And I got it, which is more than I have got out of the present Republican administration.

Once in the late Thirties Stephen Early, Roosevelt's press secretary, remarked to me, "There's no man the boss has a

higher regard for than he has for you, Joe. There is no man he
would rather have with him." This was a curious observation,
I thought, and though I was pleased, I replied, "Too bad, Steve,
but I'm afraid that could never be."

Whether there was some hidden meaning in Early's words I
shall never know. But some time after that I was the guest of
Clare and Henry Luce at a party in the Waldorf-Astoria when
Charles Edison, a Republican who had recently become Secretary of the Navy in Roosevelt's Cabinet, approached me with
his wife and said he would like to ask me a question.

"Oh, yes," Mrs. Edison interjected. "Do tell us."

"Did Roosevelt offer you the job of Secretary of the Navy
before he gave it to me?" Edison inquired.

"No, he didn't," I said.

"Well, that's strange," the Secretary mused. "He said he
did."

In the years before the war I never heard Roosevelt lament the
burdens of the presidency. He loved life in the White House,
and no man ever had his heart in his job more. After the Japanese attacked Pearl Harbor and American boys began dying on
the battlefield, however, he spoke of the heaviness of his responsibility. My cordial personal relations with Roosevelt were
strengthened by the fact that many of his friends and associates
—like Steve Early and Louis Howe, who had married a Fall
River girl—were my friends. Basil O'Connor, who had been
F.D.R.'s law partner and was associated with him in the Georgia
Warm Springs Foundation, was a native of Taunton. When she
was an old lady O'Connor's mother, though a Democrat, would
call a cab on election day and go to vote for me for Congress.

Because of his charm, there was always a danger of being
taken into camp by Roosevelt. If I had to be on my own guard
against him, I needed to be doubly sure that he did not bam-
boozle some of my less wary colleagues. One evening that I
particularly recall he had attracted a group of Republican Congressmen around him at a White House reception. As he turned

on his radiance, I could see the face of one of my men from Ohio lighting up like the moon. As quickly as I could manage I took him aside.

"Get rid of that moonglow," I told him. "Remember what we're up against in this fellow. Don't swallow all that hokum."

My relations with Garner, who was now Vice-President, were also cordial, but in a different way. We had been friends for a long time in the House. As Speaker he had been a tough and clever operator. Once during a debate on an appropriations bill he vowed, "Every time those damn Yankees get a hambone, I'm going to get a hog." Like many of his similar cracks, however, I never saw this one in the *Congressional Record*. Members of Congress are privileged to edit the proofs before the *Record* goes to press, and Garner was adept at bowdlerizing his speeches.

As Vice-President, his sympathy for the New Deal soon faded, and he was not loath to speak his mind in the privacy of his office. "Come on over, Joe," he would say, "and we'll strike a blow for liberty." Striking a blow for liberty in his terminology meant sitting around and hoisting one. As his hostility toward the New Deal became more active, he was not averse to offering me a little subtle help now and then in my maneuvers as leader of the opposition. "Come on over, Joe," he'd urge, "and maybe I'll show you a few new tricks you could play." In truth, I went to his office seldom, but now and then he would slip me a tip that was of some use. I often met him socially. One night he gave a dinner for Roosevelt at the Washington Hotel. One of the entertainers was a sleight-of-hand artist, who won my lasting admiration by removing J. Edgar Hoover's suspenders without the F.B.I. chief's knowing it. This opened one of the rare gaps in my confidence in the alertness of the F.B.I.

With the coming of the New Deal in 1933 Representative Bertrand H. Snell of New York, who was the Republican leader of the House, made me his unofficial assistant (there is no official post of assistant minority leader), and this served to put me in the forefront of the battle with the Roosevelt forces from the outset.

In general I supported emergency relief measures that gave work to the unemployed. Thus I favored the National Recovery Act because it promised not only to create jobs but to produce a psychology of recovery. The N.R.A. parades throughout the country, in which bosses marched with workers, were a lively manifestation of this. It was only after I saw the wretched administration of the N.R.A., with whole industries being ruled by code authorities composed of men having little or no competence in the fields in which they exercised jurisdiction, that I turned against it. The N.R.A. came to typify in my mind the incompetence of government to run business.

As I have said, I voted for social security because I believe that the United States has an obligation to see to it that older people who have worked all their lives and thereby have helped build the country do not spend their last years in destitution. Although it was bitterly opposed by the American Bankers Association, I voted for the federal guarantee of bank deposits, one of the notable laws of the Hundred Days, which had strong Republican backing, particularly from Senator Arthur H. Vandenberg of Michigan, and the then Representative Jesse Wolcott from the same state, who is now chairman of the Federal Deposit Insurance Corporation.

Needless to say, I supported measures whose purpose was to check the political power of the administration. I had a great deal to do, for example, with putting through the Hatch Act, which prohibits federal employees from engaging in political activities, and with a bill forbidding labor unions to contribute to political campaigns.

I supported various measures which had the strong backing of business and which at the same time seemed sensible to me. Again, to cite another example, I played an important part in getting the Ruml pay-as-you-go income tax principle adopted.

Subsequently I came to have some doubts about the wisdom of pay-as-you-go taxes, yet I suppose this method is the most practical. The thing about it that has given me pause is that regularly withholding a person's taxes from his pay rather than requiring him to go out periodically and pay taxes tends to obscure the size of his tax bill in his mind. He concentrates on his take-home pay to the exclusion of everything else, including the amount being deducted for his taxes. Thus he grows indifferent to the cost of government. Under these circumstances it is often difficult to arouse the taxpayer to the need for economy.

Like other members from my part of the country, I opposed very strongly programs that either were directly harmful to New England interests or that favored other regions at the expense of New England.

Thus I fought the Agricultural Adjustment Act because the subsidies paid to southern cotton farmers came out of a processing tax levied on the textile mills of my district. I warned the administration that the A.A.A. would put us "on the road to Moscow" and I told the House: "Agriculture is not going to climb back to prosperity over the prostrate body of industry." The machinery of this bill, I said, would have bred an army of tax collectors and spies recruited from the ranks of deserving Democrats. In the end, of course, the Supreme Court held the act to be unconstitutional, as it did the N.R.A.

Similarly, I opposed the original wages-and-hours bill because it contained differentials permitting southern mills to pay lower minimum wages and thereby gave them an unfair competitive advantage over the northern mills. When, after some strenuous efforts on my part, these were eliminated, I voted for the bill.

I was against repeal of the Smoot–Hawley tariff bill and against the lowering of duties on products that competed with those of New England industries. I was opposed to giving the President broad powers to negotiate tariff pacts under the Reciprocal Trade Agreements bill. As I put it then: "I do not propose to let men who never saw my district determine whether or not those industries which have brought employment and livelihood to my people are economically sound. The group of college tariff theorists might deem it more important to sell cotton abroad than to continue the operation of a cotton, jewelry, woolen or shoe factory."

I favored the "Buy American" campaign. I remember telling a meeting in Brockton, Massachusetts, in 1938: "Last Flag Day the North Attleboro lodge of Elks wanted to have its members carry a small American flag in a procession but found it was impossible. They wouldn't carry a flag made in Japan, and none of American manufacture was available. The American flag industry had been destroyed."

I displayed a United States army officer's belt buckle that had been made in England.

"Think of it!" I said. "The buckles worn by our Army officers gave employment to British workers while thousands of our jewelry workers walk the streets."

The T.V.A. was another of the alphabet agencies that I opposed on similar grounds. My argument at the time was: "If the government dedicates the resources to building up the Tennessee Valley, we have a right to expect the public treasury to finance the making of New England and every section of the country attractive to industry also." "Would anyone," I asked, "expect me to vote for a measure to put northern money into the development of an industrial empire for the South?"

On this same principle I opposed reclamation projects in the early years of the New Deal. There was, I felt, enough land then under cultivation to meet the needs of the country for farm products. After I became Republican National Chairman in 1940 and had a chance to travel about and learn at first hand what some of the regional needs were and how the people felt about these projects, I realized that not all reclamation programs were wrong. After that I voted for those that promised to strengthen the national economy.

In most cases no doubt I fought the New Deal on issues that went against the grain of traditional Republican doctrine. One of these, emphatically, was taxes. The Roosevelt administration, it seemed to me, was using the power of taxation to underwrite pet theories and impose a new philosophy of government on the country—socialism. By collecting and spending huge sums the New Deal was causing centralization of power in Washington. When government money is being spent, the government is going to run the show.

Moreover, the New Dealers were being utterly inconsistent. On the one hand they were denouncing industry for failing to provide jobs; on the other they were levying punitive taxes that penalized thrifty and cautious companies. Business was prevented from accumulating adequate surpluses with which to expand its plant and provide the very jobs the government was howling for.

If the goal was to maintain and stimulate private enterprise, the way to do it was to keep taxes high enough to provide the treasury with the money needed to run the government but not so high as to eliminate corporation surpluses and thus destroy incentive. We had a young man in North Attleboro, I recalled, who started a jewelry manufacturing business with an initial investment of $100 and built it up to a point where it employed 1500 persons. Under some of the New Deal tax proposals he would not have been able to do so. In sum, my objection was that the administration was spending billions in taxpayers' money to stimulate recovery while at the same time it was discouraging through its high tax policies the expansion of business that alone could achieve permanent recovery.

This was the frame of mind I was in when, on Jefferson's birthday in 1934, Representative Clarence Cannon of Missouri asked the House for unanimous consent to make a commemorative speech. "Mr. Speaker, I heartily endorse this request," I said. "Any Democrat who believes in Thomas Jefferson nowadays should indeed be allowed to express himself."

Heavy federal spending and increasing centralization of government in an expanding bureaucracy in Washington were other aspects of the New Deal that I fought in a great many instances because they were repulsive to Republican traditions. I led the fight that defeated Roosevelt's proposal for a $3,600,000,000 lend-and-spend recovery program in 1939. I called it "the President's pork-barrel bill" and argued that it was intended not so much to prime the economic pump as it was "to prime the 1940 elections." "True-blue Americans," I said, "must not allow themselves to be divided by an honored party name which recently has come to be a shield for hateful isms imported from abroad." Over the years I was able, with southern Democratic support, to wage successful fights to reduce some of Roosevelt's proposals. Looking back now on the huge spending of that period, I am convinced I was right. It never did bring us the prosperity we groped for.

One year the W.P.A. came up with a request for funds for a dance program, which looked like a boondoggle. I got in touch with Representative Dewey Short, a Republican from Missouri, and said, "Dewey, when this W.P.A. dance appropriation comes up, why don't you give the boys a little vaudeville show?" He got the idea all right. When the debate began, he jigged down to the well of the House and put on a version of a W.P.A. dance recital that had Democrats as well as Republicans screaming with laughter. The appropriation was not approved.

In spite of our successes here and there in cutting New Deal appropriations, it is nevertheless clear in retrospect that federal spending was an abortive issue for the Republicans in the 1930s. I must say candidly that in the depth of the Depression, when the power of the government had to be used somehow to feed, clothe, house, and employ millions of people, the Republicans had no strong issue. Some of the recovery measures that came to be identified with the Roosevelt administration had been instituted under President Hoover. The outcry against government spending was a good old Republican tradition. It particularly pleased big contributors to the party. And it was a handy weapon to point at Roosevelt when we had no other. But when election day rolled around, it did us little good.

There was, I must emphasize, a fundamental difference between the political climate in which we attacked spending in those

days of deflation and low taxes, when no one would listen, and
the climate in which President Eisenhower made his effective
stand against the "spenders" in 1959. The latter was a time of
inflation and high taxes. People were vitally concerned about
the inroads being made into their wallets by rising costs of living, and they were susceptible to the argument that higher government spending would mean still greater inroads.

The power the Republican Party had held in Congress
throughout the Harding, Coolidge, and Hoover administrations
was reduced sharply, of course, by the Roosevelt landslide of
1932. In the Congressional elections two years later our numbers were whittled farther, and we reached bottom in the elections of 1936, the year Landon carried only Maine and Vermont.
From there we fought our way slowly upward again, and in this
period of gradually rising fortunes my role as a party leader
broadened. In 1936 I was chosen Republican National Committeeman from Massachusetts and presently became a member
of the executive committee of the Republican National Committee. In 1938 I was elected chairman of the National Republican Congressional Committee, which supports members of the
party who are running for the House.

None of our candidates had a harder fight that fall than I
did. The year 1938 was a time when the New Dealers were riding high, wide, and handsome. While Roosevelt himself was out
trying to purge Democratic members of Congress who had opposed him, his underlings were brazenly using the influence of
the W.P.A. to defeat me. The W.P.A. under Harry Hopkins was
a potent force in American politics in those days. Nine out of
ten times people will "vote their stomach," as we say, and the
W.P.A. was a huge employer, oriented in every way toward the
Democratic administration in Washington.

For my opponent the Democrats shrewdly picked Lawrence
J. Bresnahan, who had just resigned as director of the W.P.A.
in Massachusetts. The damage caused by the New England
hurricane that September offered the Democrats an ideal opportunity for getting voters' support. As nearly as I could estimate,

as many as 10,000 persons may have been added to the W.P.A.
force in my district. In one small town there were eight super-
visors for thirty-eight workers.

In an outrageous flouting of the rules W.P.A. trucks were
used to distribute Democratic campaign literature and take
employees to the polling places. Men and women on W.P.A.
were pressured into buying tickets for clambakes, whist parties,
and lotteries, all for the benefit of the Democratic campaign
fund.

I met the challenge head-on, making W.P.A. abuses a main
issue in my campaign.

"I'm the best Congressman in Washington," I would tell the
crowds. "The proof of that is that I can get more for my district
even in a Democratic administration than anyone else can.
Take these 10,000 extra jobs. You wouldn't have them if it
weren't for me. *I'm* the reason for these 10,000 jobs."

"And what do they do for you?" I would ask. "They give you
a lousy twelve or thirteen dollars a week. That's all you get."

In all honesty this was not bad money in those days for some
of those jobs, but at a time like that I couldn't allow the opposition to do all the demagoguing. I let them have their W.P.A.!

"What do they do for you?" I would demand of the workers.
"They make you work in the gutters, that's what they do. Are
you the foreman? Are *you* the boss? No, the boss is the son of
the alderman or the cousin of some big Democratic politician.
You know the fellow who spent thirty thousand dollars fixing
up that new night club in Fall River? His son is a W.P.A. foreman getting *twenty-two dollars a week!*"

I knew my district too thoroughly to be pushed around by
the W.P.A. I was well acquainted with the deep feelings of the
people in those hard times.

"Out of the pittance they give you," I would cry in outrage,
"they made you pay one dollar apiece for the Democratic campaign fund. The other day a woman came into my office in de-
spair because she didn't have any money for medicine for the

children. But she had to give a dollar to the Democratic campaign fund! One couple met me under a tree at night. They didn't dare risk having the W.P.A. foreman see them coming to my office. They didn't have money to buy the kids shoes for school, but they had to give a dollar to the Democratic campaign fund! They make you wear a campaign button. They brand you like they do the cattle on the Western plain. And they say this is America!"

I have rarely seen such intense interest in the outcome of a local election. When the milkman made his rounds on the day after, people would poke their heads out into the early morning air and ask him who won.

"Joe Martin by something like twenty thousand," he would answer.

The returns from the 1938 Congressional elections brought good news to the whole Republican Party. After six years of the New Deal, conservative sentiment had reasserted itself. The people had lost some of their enthusiasm for experimentation in Washington. There was less faith in pump-priming. F.D.R.'s popularity was wearing a little thin around the edges; the voters had repudiated his attempted purge of conservative Democratic legislators. Republican gains at the polls were dramatic. We increased our strength in the Senate by eight seats, and in the House we practically doubled our forces, climbing from eighty-nine to 169.

When the new Congress convened in January 1939, there was, however, a familiar face missing. Bert Snell, the Republican leader of the House, had decided not to run for reelection in November. For one thing he was becoming hard of hearing. But beyond that he was discouraged by the prospect for Republicans. His high ambition was to be the Speaker, and he knew that it would be many years before Republicans could win control of the House and elect their own man to this post. When he bowed out I immediately became the principal contender for his post as leader.

For a moment it looked as though I might be opposed by Representative James W. Wadsworth, Jr. of New York, whom I regard to this day as one of the most distinguished men of my time in Congress. His fellow New Yorker, Representative Walter G. (Ham) Andrews, who was also a good friend of mine, tried to enlist supporters for Wadsworth, but outside New York state he made little headway. Among the older men I had strong support from influential leaders like Representatives Leo Allen of Illinois and James Wolfenden, chairman of the Pennsylvania delegation in the House. And, by happy contrast with the events that were to terminate my leadership twenty years later, I had the enthusiastic backing of the new young members who had just been elected. They were well aware that the successes in the campaign had been scored under my chairmanship of the National Republican Congressional Committee. In the end the prospect of any serious opposition for leader evaporated, and in the caucus on January 2, 1939, Wadsworth joined in making my election unanimous.

I took over at a time when the political tide definitely was turning, although the trend was to be reversed again in a couple of years by the approach of war. In 1939, however, there was a far different band of Republicans in the House from any that the country had known since the Hoover administration.

Not only had the returns of 1938 raised our hopes for recapturing the White House in 1940, but the doubling of our number in the House put us in a position for the first time to offer formidable opposition to the New Deal. One hundred sixty-nine was still a minority, but it was no longer the impotent minority of the earlier years. Our morale was high and at last we were able to thwart the President on occasion, especially since many southern Democrats were in revolt against the New Deal and could be persuaded to join forces with us on certain issues.

It did not take us long to put the fear of God into the Democratic leadership. I instituted new discipline in our ranks. One of the forms it took was an elaborate new whip organization that I established, basing it on a system of key men representing each section of the country. It was their responsibility to know how the members in the House from their sections stood on every issue and to get them to the floor when a vote was coming up. By telephone and by fast footwork these whips were able within a matter of minutes to assemble practically our full membership. As a result, the Democratic leaders were disconcerted time and again to find that their forces, though more numerous on paper, were outnumbered by the Republicans present. Nineteen times in a row we defeated the Democrats on matters of varying importance.

Along with the whip organization, I appointed special Republican committees to study each major issue that was likely to come up so that we would be ready with our own case to present to the public and with our own recommendations, if this seemed warranted, to counter Roosevelt's. These committees held hearings, in all parts of the country, that aroused widespread interest. Said *Barron's* magazine, "In six short weeks Martin, as successor to the veteran ultra-conservative Bert Snell, has given the party what it lacked for several years—fight and fire, reasonably liberal leadership, unified action. . . ."

No doubt it will amuse some of my young latter-day critics to see me referred to as a comparative liberal, but that is because they were not acquainted with some of the old boys who were powers on our side of the aisle twenty-five years ago—men like Bert Snell, Dan Reed, and John Taber (all from New York), John Q. Tilson of Connecticut, and Robert Luce of Massachusetts. Those who knew what was going on had a clearer understanding of my at-least-near approach to the center of the Republican spectrum. Thus Albert L. Warner, then the chief of the New York *Herald Tribune*'s Washington bureau, described me in 1938 as "a moderate who has voted for a good deal of labor legislation and is sympathetic to social security reforms." Of course I did not consider myself a liberal then any more than I do today. And in view of my role as a Republican leader trying to hold different wings of the party together it is just as well that I was never known as a great liberal.

I had not been leader long before I had the disparate wings of our party in the House working together as a militant force. I used to assemble them in frequent conferences, give them "religion," and send them out on the floor fighting.

On some issues on which I needed help I would reconnoiter the field of the southern Democrats in search of votes. New England and the South, I have found, share certain traditions, which facilitated my quest. Both sections have, or at any rate had, a suspicion of federal subsidies and federal interference in state and local affairs. Both had been colonized by people independent in spirit, who had learned not to rely on help from others. From the beginning they had to stand on their own feet. By contrast, some other parts of the country were settled by homesteaders who were accustomed to looking to the government for help. In these regions, so it has seemed to me, there is not so strong a tradition against reliance on the federal government.

In any case when an issue of spending or of new powers for the President came along, I would go to Representative Howard W. Smith of Virginia, for example, and say, "Howard, see if you can't get me a few Democratic votes here." Or I would seek out Representative Eugene Cox of Georgia, and ask, "Gene, why don't you and John Rankin and some of your men get me some votes on this?"

Cox was the real leader of the southerners in the House. He was a good speaker and wielded considerable influence. He and I came to Congress the same year, and we became friends while serving together on the Rules Committee. After I was chosen leader he and I were the principal points of contact between the northern Republicans and the southern Democratic conservatives. A bushy-haired Georgia lawyer, Cox was a typical old-fashioned southern leader, who fought tirelessly for states' rights. His opposition to the New Deal was much more ingrown than mine, and he was ready to fight to any lengths to keep further power out of the hands of Franklin Roosevelt. In these circumstances, therefore, it was unnecessary for me to offer any *quid pro quo* for conservative southern support. It was simply a matter of finding issues on which we saw alike.

Sometimes I discovered—not only in the case of the southerners but with conservative northern Democrats as well—that the best way to combat the New Dealers was to put willing Democrats up to making the moves and delivering the speeches while we waited in silence to hand them our 169 votes on the roll call. We won a number of victories by this device, proving that wavering Democrats would often support a measure offered by one of their own party whereas they would balk if it was sponsored by a Republican.

By the end of the session we had succeeded, with the aid of the Democratic conservatives, in making substantial reductions in Roosevelt's appropriation bills.

Of course, we did not run the show. We could merely exert an increasingly strong influence of our own on legislation. The Democrats controlled Congress, and in most, though not all, major issues their power prevailed in the end. Still, 1939 was a year of revival for the Republican Party and of great personal gratification to me. In a poll of fifty-two Washington correspondents taken by *Life*, I was named as the ablest member of the House of Representatives. In 1940 Thomas L. Stokes wrote of me in his column: "It is no exaggeration to say that in [his] role he has contributed more than any other one man to the revival of the Republican Party."

If times had been normal, no one can say what might have been the Republican Party's destiny—and mine—in 1940. With Roosevelt now in his seventh year in office, we were approaching what ordinarily would have been the end of an administration, for in normal circumstances a third term would have been unthinkable. Within the Republican Party my prestige was high. Mark Sullivan was merely echoing what many Republican leaders were saying when he wrote in September

1939: "Mr. Martin is Presidential material of high quality. He has been the most efficient House leader either party has had in a generation." A Martin-for-President club was formed in Fall River, though I discouraged the idea. Among Republicans in the House a movement was started to support me for the nomination. Leo Allen told the press that many of the young midwestern and western members were for me. Senator Arthur Capper of Kansas predicted that I would be the nominee.

William K. Hutchinson, of the old International News Service, a confidant of Borah's, told me one day that he had asked the Senator about his preference for 1940 and had received the reply: "I haven't made up my mind definitely, but at the present moment I think I'd take Joe Martin." Kenneth F. Simpson, Republican National Committeeman from New York, publicly called me the uncrowned leader of the party and predicted that I would emerge as the nominee if there should be a deadlock in the convention. In the Emporia *Gazette* William Allen White wrote an editorial in January 1940 that fairly well summarized what was being said in scores of newspaper articles and editorials at the time:

. . . it may be said with absolute truth that no matter who has the lead in the presidential race now or in June, no matter how the favorite sons sniff the battle from afar and champ at the bit, the one real dark horse in this whole situation is Joe Martin. He is likely to be nominated if the balloting lasts more than two days in the Republican convention. He will make . . . if the dice roll right, a liberty-loving president.

The [Theodore] Roosevelt Club at its annual meeting in Boston unanimously indorsed me for the nomination.

One day a most unexpected offer came to me through the medium of Representative Robert J. Corbett, a Republican from Pennsylvania. He had sought me out to deliver a message from Miss Helen C. Frick of Pittsburgh, daughter of the late Henry Clay Frick, the steel executive.

"Miss Frick has never seen you," Corbett said, "but she has

read all about you and thinks you would make a good President. She told me to tell you that she would like to play a part in putting you in the White House. She would undertake to raise $125,000 for this purpose, and she said that you may have the first $15,000 any time you wish."

This was but one of many generous offers of help I was to receive from Miss Frick not only for myself but for the party when I was the Republican National Chairman. On this occasion I bade Corbett thank her and say that I would not accept her contribution because I was not a candidate.

Thus although I have never sought the presidency nor ardently aspired to it, many Republicans at that time were mentioning me for the nomination, and in normal circumstances something might have come of this sentiment. The word *normal*, however, had no place in the history of that period. Already in 1939 the seeds of defeat for the Republican Party a year hence were being sown by the militarism of Nazi Germany. And whether I wanted the nomination or not, whether under different conditions I could have got it or not, certainly it was put beyond my reach by the titanic controversies that erupted in the country over preparation for war and aid to the Allies.

My identification in the public mind with isolationism, although I have never considered myself an isolationist, made me unacceptable to the internationalist elements of the party. When the convention opened in Philadelphia, it was plain that this faction had the power to nominate a Willkie or someone else whose record was more in line with their own views than mine was.

6

On the cold afternoon of Sunday, December 7, 1941, I was talking with the late Clark Griffith, owner of the Washington Senators, in his office at Griffith Stadium between halves of a professional football game when the telephone rang. An assistant of Griffith's picked it up, listened, put it down and turned to us with a bewildered look.

"The Japanese are bombing Pearl Harbor," he said.

After the lapse of years I cannot separate the thoughts and emotions that swirled through me as I hurried downtown. One thing I do recall is that I had no doubts, no sense of regret or embarrassment about the path we Republicans had taken in the years that had preceded this day.

There had never in my experience been a time of such pressure, such sustained clash of powerful political and personal forces as occurred between 1939 and Pearl Harbor in the debates on preparedness, lend-lease, neutrality, the arming of merchant vessels, the draft, and the renewal of the selective service act four months before the Japanese attack.

In the starkest manner these issues placed many members of Congress in a classic conflict between local sentiment and the national interest.

Since it was my fate to be one of the most controversial of all the figures who played a part in the enactment of the legislation of that historic period, I ought to preface my reminiscences of it with a statement of the premises on which I acted.

To begin with, having lived through the repelling slaughter of the first world war, I was deeply opposed to the entry of the

United States into another war abroad. I believed that a second world war would change beyond measure the life of the people of the United States, as to a considerable extent it did. I was convinced that the American people condemned war, disapproved of entangling alliances, and loathed the thought of sending their sons to death and disfiguration on foreign battlefields.

As the leader of the Republicans in the House of Representatives I did not propose to adopt any course that might lead to my party's being held responsible for war.

I despised Hitler and Mussolini and earnestly hoped that the Allies would defeat them once the battle was joined. On the other hand, I thought it was alarmist nonsense and interventionist propaganda to say that a Germany victorious in Western Europe could leap across thousands of miles of ocean successfully to invade the United States through Canada or Latin America. While I was alarmed by the menace of Hitler, I did not think that a German victory necessarily would put the United States in peril of its life. I did believe that the United States must make itself strong. That was one of the reasons why, for example, I voted for the draft.

These were the fundamental concepts with which I approached the prewar debates. These were my underlying motivations. In frankness, however, I must go on to say that in my position I also had to think of the political effect of these events on the fortunes of the Republican Party and to act with that thought in mind.

By this I do not mean to suggest that I put political considerations above the national welfare. I hope that I never did. But the government of the United States is a political government. Even its minor acts have certain political effects. When in the midst of critical events it embarks upon great new policies, all the political components of the government are aroused. That is what happened with a vengeance in the pre-Pearl Harbor controversies. To have tried to eliminate political considerations from the upheaval in which the United States was transformed from a nation at peace to a country on a war footing would have been as unrealistic as to command geranium seeds not to grow in a hothouse. As a political leader in the thick of battle, it was inevitable that I should have responded to the political challenges that developed out of this ferment.

Certainly, one of these challenges was the ambition of Franklin Roosevelt. When we accused him, as most of us Republicans did at one time or another in those days, of being a "dictator," we were, of course, engaging in partisan exaggeration. But exaggeration of phrase only. True, we did not believe that he was a dictator in the Hitlerian sense. But we feared nevertheless that he would succeed in using the international emergency, as he had used the earlier domestic crisis, to extend and perpetuate his hold to such a degree that the Republican Party could not hope to return to power for a very long time. The vast new spending power conferred in measures like the lend-lease bill contributed to this danger. His craftiness in such camouflages as conducting political tours in the form of visits to war plants and Army camps only served to heighten our apprehension.

Furthermore, during those years Roosevelt had a heavy Democratic majority in both houses of Congress. His own party alone could have put through the measures he was proposing, but it did not. In fact, many Democrats consistently voted against their own President's program. They sensed that their constituents were opposed to the interventionist policies and voted accordingly, leaving us to make up the balance or suffer the consequences. In this situation the blame was laid to the Republican minority and sometimes to me personally. Roosevelt capitalized on this by trying to damage us with charges of obstructionism when members of his own party would not pull his chestnuts out of the fire. This was politics, and if he could play the game, so could I.

Six years of New Deal spending had not cured the Depression, and I had constantly to keep probing to make sure that more pump-priming was not being slipped past us in the guise of preparedness legislation. Turmoil in Europe was no justification for giving up our fight against statism and regimentation. We mistrusted the President's steady accumulation of great emergency powers. I thought, for example, that the broad authority conferred on him in the lend-lease bill was altogether out of keeping with our traditions of government. I believed too that by opposing such a grant of authority the Republicans might develop a strong issue.

Also, with respect to the realities of the situation we faced, Roosevelt was dissembling. He was trying as diligently as the Republicans were to avert the political consequences of a war-party label. Almost up to the time of Pearl Harbor he was saying not only in public but in White House conferences which I attended that the United States would not become involved in great military campaigns. About as far as I ever heard him venture privately was to express an opinion that the crisis might produce some naval skirmishes. In fact in Roosevelt's words I found my chief hope that we would be able to stay out of war.

If in candor he had talked differently, I do not know but what we might have voted differently. After the event, of course, a change of ways is always easy to reconstruct. Maybe we would not have done differently. In any case Roosevelt's request for virtual war powers without frank acknowledgment of the imminence of American involvement offered little inducement to the Republican leadership to change its course. Again, however, one has to grant that a public avowal by the President that American entry into the war was approaching would have inflamed some members to an even greater opposition than they were manifesting.

That leads us to the situation in the Republican Party. The great majority of the Republican members of the House were what the newspapers called isolationists. In the case of many this attitude sprang from conviction, from the deep wells in our national tradition that nurtured aloofness from foreign struggles. Others represented districts in which this sentiment was so strong that they could not have retained their seats if they did not reflect it in Congress. This was true of the Midwest, especially in the remarkably wide region including Illinois, Wisconsin, Iowa, Indiana, and even Michigan and Ohio, where the Chicago *Tribune* exerted an influence.

If I had been Demosthenes, I could not have reversed this powerful Republican sentiment in the House. There was no possible way of holding the Republican forces together except by accommodating it. To have tried to align the body of Republican Representatives behind Roosevelt's foreign policies, even if I had been of a mind to do so, would have torn the Republican organization in the House to tatters. And this at a time when Roosevelt was threatening to make the Democratic Party dominant in the United States for years to come.

We were in a bad way. The bandwagon boys and the people looking for defense contracts were gathered on Roosevelt's doorstep now. The loaves and the fishes were all on his side. The Republicans had been hit first by the Depression and now by this. Was there going to be a two-party system in the United States, or was there not? This was the question that stared me in the eye every day. Increasingly throughout this period my job became one of trying to hold the party together for survival. Much of my time was taken up mediating between the so-called isolationists and the Willkie interventionists. Often the former would demand that I oppose Roosevelt much more vehemently than I did, and at times this sentiment was difficult to control. Our party discipline in the House, which had worked so effectively against the domestic reforms of the New Deal, slackened under the foreign-policy quarrels. The Republicans were a party in the wilderness with scant resources to sustain us. As the battles over preparedness and neutrality surged back and forth in Congress, I was like a Confederate cavalry leader, living off the countryside and constantly looking for some opening that would guide us to political victory.

No Congressional leader could rely solely on his own resources in situations as complex and dangerous as these. It was only natural that I should have turned, for example, to the wise counsel of Herbert Hoover, whose knowledge and experience

gave him an unusual grasp of these problems. Another whose
advice I sought from time to time was Alf Landon. The guid-
ance I received from such friends, however, was in broad measure and not necessarily on specific issues.

Early in 1939 I opposed the measure providing for what was
popularly called the "fortification" of Guam, the southernmost
of the Marianas Islands, subsequently captured by Japan. This
item of $5,000,000 for improvement of harbors and airfields
caused one of the first fights in Congress over the isolation issue
in the pre-Pearl Harbor period. It was a most ambiguous piece
of legislation, which Roosevelt himself rather straddled. One
had difficulty deciding whether it was really a military measure
or some kind of pork barrel. Either way I was against it. Was it
merely for improvements not closely related to defense? If so,
I felt, as did many of my colleagues, that if we had $5,000,000
lying around for harbor work, there was some dredging right
here in our own American rivers that needed to be done. If, on
the other hand, it was in the nature of a fortification, then I
believed it would be provocative to the Japanese. In any case
I did not see how it could have strengthened our defenses. "Congress didn't want to add to the tenseness of the situation," I
explained after the appropriation was defeated in the House.
"Our people don't want to get too close to where the bricks are
flying."

After the war began in Europe in September 1939, Roosevelt was compelled by the Neutrality Act to issue a proclama-
tion embargoing arms for all belligerents. However, the President was determined to have the law repealed so that the Allies
could buy weapons in the United States. To this end he called
a special session of Congress for September 21. In an effort to
win bipartisan support for repeal he assembled in the White
House many of the leading Democrats and Republicans, including Landon, who was then the titular head of the Republican Party. I was opposed to repeal, and Roosevelt's disserta-
tion did not change my mind.

At the close of the conference he wanted a public statement

issued by the whole group. Someone suggested that he appoint a committee of those present to draw it up, which he proceeded to do. I didn't object until he named me as a member. Having no wish to put my name to any kind of statement that might in some way be regarded as a commitment on behalf of the Republican minority, I now dissented from the idea of having a committee.

"We have taken no action here, Mr. President," I said. "A committee would make it appear that we had debated this matter and were now handing out some doctrine on the subject. Why don't you just issue a plain statement yourself?"

"Oh, all right," Roosevelt said and without further ado jotted down several sentences with a stubby pencil. When he read the draft, I took exception to some phrase he had included on freedom of the seas. The way it was worded it looked to me as if Roosevelt was trying to slip in a subtle endorsement for repeal.

"Let's forget that part," I said. He scratched it out. Later when we were leaving, Landon said to me, "You certainly showed the value of your newspaper training on that one, Joe."

In the special session Congress went along with Roosevelt and repealed the arms embargo in a vote that followed party lines, Republicans dissenting. "I voted to retain the embargo," I explained at the time, "because I believed that a great majority of the American people did not want war and that dealing in implements of war is dangerous business and may prove to be our first step in entering the European conflict." My position would be exactly the same if the vote were taken today. Peddling arms around the world is an invitation to war, and I believe, for example, that we are simply sowing seeds of trouble by sending arms all over Latin America. I felt the same way about Roosevelt's request for authority to arm merchant vessels. For this reason, and because I did not believe it would be an effective measure in any case, I voted against it.

No single piece of legislation that has come before Congress in my lifetime has generated such pressures as the lend-lease bill. Indeed, if my own experience was any indication, these pressures eventually became self-defeating in the sense that they drove one ultimately to shun the clamor and listen to the voice of one's own judgment. The Republican Party was deeply divided. Landon and Hoover, for example, were opposed; Dewey, who was on their side at first, switched in favor of the bill. Willkie was, next to Roosevelt, its foremost champion.

When the bill came up in the House the first time, in February 1941, I voted against it, although my Republican colleagues and I were in the minority. It was not that I lacked sympathy with Britain's need for arms. It was obvious that a British victory would be in the best interests of the United States. I wanted to help Britain and I felt that we should help her, but in the American way, without upsetting the traditional balance between the legislative and the executive branches of our government. I would gladly have voted for a bill to extend her credits. I thought that $2,000,000,000 would have been an adequate amount. This would have purchased all the military supplies that American factories could have furnished the British in the ensuing year.

But if we in Congress had an obligation to an ally, we also had a duty to our own people. When I contemplated the broad discretionary powers that the bill conferred on the President, including the power to decide which countries' defense was vital to the defense of the United States, I believed that we were inviting the probability of our being drawn into war. Furthermore, as I said at the time:

"I am unwilling to give any President control of the public purse, which under the Constitution belongs to Congress. . . . The power to control the purse is the power to rule. If our form of government is to be preserved, that power should not be delegated to any one man. . . . Our task is to save Americanism."

It was my hope that when the bill went to the Senate, the broad powers I objected to would be eliminated. This was not to be the case, although certain minor improvements were made. These changes necessitated resubmission of the legislation to the House for final action. By now it was obvious that I could not get a measure to my own liking and also that the bill as approved by the Senate had decisive support in the House as well. While my original objections still stood, I decided to put them aside and vote for lend-lease after all as a contribution to national unity and the solidarity of the Allies.

"I realized," I said in a speech in the House, "that, Congress having determined to follow the policy set forth in the bill, it is the part of wisdom to act quickly. At least these amendments voice the apprehensions of Congress, and I sincerely hope that the President will use these enormous powers wisely. We have taken a step unparalleled in American history. There is danger at every step we take from now on."

The House stood and applauded my speech.

In September 1940, Congress passed the Selective Service Act for one year. I voted for it. In the summer of 1941, while the United States was still precariously a nonbelligerent, the measure came back to us for renewal for another year and a half. This time a large number of Republicans in the House, frantic over the drift toward war, were violently opposed and put a great deal of heat on me to take a stand against extension. It was perfectly clear that if I defied this sentiment and, as leader, voted for extension, the Republican organization in the House would have been torn to pieces. Not only that, but my support of the administration bill might have alienated a substantial number of Republican voters.

Once more I was faced with my old problem of holding Republicans together. By this time I had learned that a leader sometimes has to go along with the majority of his group for a way in order to bring them around to his course in the end. If one is leading ninety soldiers and eighty want to walk in one direction and ten in the other, one has to make some concession or at least give the eighty a feeling that one is in sympathy with them. That, in sum, is what I did.

A case could be made against extension in the form in which it was proposed. In the original act Congress had in effect signed a contract with the men who had been drafted for one year, as was acknowledged by respected members on both sides of the aisle. I believed that the United States government should honor a contract, whether it involved a new post office or a soldier. One year was one year. This year would not have been up until November. In that month only about 13,000 would be eligible for discharge, which would not have crippled the armed services. By releasing these men Congress would be keeping its word. An added reassuring element in the situation was that as draftees were released, they could be recalled immediately as reserves to maintain the country's strength. I would not have been opposed to a new eighteen-month draft for new men; it was the adding of eighteen months to the service of those who would have been in a year already that bothered me.

Then another aspect presented itself. There was widespread public opposition to extension of the draft. So long as I could feel sure that the national security was not being jeopardized, as I did in this case, my position as Republican leader kept me on the alert for an issue that might yet funnel the winds into our sails and blow us back again to the commanding position the Republican Party had enjoyed in the 1920s. Where I could capitalize on an issue without harming the country, I did. The draft-extension bill was such a vehicle. Yet it had to be handled deftly lest public sentiment turn against us in the end. This might have happened if the Republicans had defeated the renewal of selective service. The country might have become alarmed, and that would have enabled Roosevelt to play upon the sense of shock to our detriment.

The course I followed, therefore, was to court such popular sentiment as we could attract by opposing the bill, yet at the same time make no great effort to defeat it. I regarded it as one of those fights in which one comes out stronger if one loses than if one wins. Thus, while as leader I voted against it myself, I hoped that it would pass. When certain Republican members who were in doubt came to me for advice, I would tell them, "If I were you and it doesn't make any difference, follow your own preference on this." I did not knock myself out trying to get their votes.

When the voting began, I was taken aback by the large number of Democrats who, under pressure from home, were lining up with Republicans against the bill. As we neared the end of the roll call, with sixty-five Democrats voting against Roosevelt, I had the sinking feeling that I might have made a fatal miscalculation. Contrary to my wishes, the bill might be defeated after all.

Finally, by a hair's breadth, it was passed 203 to 202. If I had wished, I could have got that one vote; when a leader comes that close he can always obtain an extra vote. But that was not my strategy. We lost, but won. Selective service had been extended, but the Republicans had made a record of keeping faith with the men who had been drafted for one year.

As I rode down from Griffith Stadium after hearing the news of Pearl Harbor, I reflected how different everything would be now. What had occurred might have been avoided somehow, I was convinced. Only historians could decide in their own good time. The issues we had been living through so strenuously— the draft, neutrality, and all the rest—were dead and would never be revived in our lifetime. In the past they had been full of meaning for us, and I was satisfied with the manner in which we Republicans had met them.

When I arrived at my apartment at the Hay-Adams Hotel, across Lafayette Park from the White House, where I have made my home in Washington for many years, I received a message from the President to attend a meeting of the Cabinet and Congressional leaders at nine-thirty. Since I was at the time not only the Republican floor leader in the House but the chairman of the Republican National Committee, it was apparent that I would have to comment later. I drafted a statement, which was based upon the assumption that the President would ask Congress to declare war and which expressed my full support. I took the draft around to Henry P. Fletcher, then general counsel to the Republican National Committee, and he liked it. When I arrived at the White House, I was ushered upstairs to the President's study.

"It is not easy to be a President in time of war," Roosevelt said solemnly when the meeting opened. After informing us that he wished to appear before Congress at noon the next day, he gave us what news he had of the Japanese attacks. During the evening military and naval aides shuttled in and out with the latest details. While this went on for two hours or so, I waited and waited to hear the President say what he intended to propose to Congress, but to my astonishment the conference ended without any definitive statement.

Before leaving, I stepped over to Roosevelt and remarked, "Of course, Mr. President, this means war."

"Well, we'll know more about it in the morning when all the facts are in," he replied.

No doubt good and sufficient reasons prompted his evasiveness. Yet I could not help thinking in the midst of it all that here was a man who, having proclaimed so stubbornly that the United States would not enter the war, was now going to defer until the absolute last minute an acknowledgment that we were finally in it.

Naturally, his silence about a declaration of war momentarily pulled down the curtain on my carefully prepared statement about supporting the same. When reporters met me in the White House lobby, I rallied such talents as I have for the extemporaneous and said, "In the hour of great danger there is no partisanship. In that hour we all stand as one people in support of America." This may not have been literature, but it did not go unnoticed. "I thought you made a most excellent statement," Wendell Willkie telegraphed. And my prepared remarks did not go to waste, either. They formed the body of my speech in the House the next day supporting the President's request for acceptance of a state of war with Japan.

Momentarily, politics was laid aside. The chairman of the Democratic National Committee, Edward J. Flynn, and I ex-

changed messages pledging our respective parties to support
the war effort. Roosevelt telegraphed me his thanks. He put
great stress on the political truce and on a suggestion that the
two national party organizations might best function in the
field of civil defense. Indeed he made so much over such notions
that I suspected he was trying to give the impression that I
had agreed to discontinue all regular party activities during the
war. Any deal of this kind could have led to one-party government in the United States.

After talking it over with Senator Charles L. McNary of
Oregon, the minority leader of the Senate, I wired the President
back, making it plain that while we would support war measures, the Republican Party also would retain its identity and
would enter candidates in the 1942 Congressional election and
campaign on their behalf.

As might have been expected, the perfect truce did not last
long. In February 1942 Flynn declared that it would be a
calamity if a Congress hostile to the President's views was
elected. I retorted that Flynn "wants to liquidate the Republican Party and squelch all opposition."

From the outset of hostilities I gave the President my full support on the measures he proposed to hasten victory. This was
not always as simple and as politically safe as it might sound.

One morning during the war Speaker Rayburn called and
asked if I would come to his office. When I arrived I found that
he was waiting with Secretary of War Henry L. Stimson, General George C. Marshall, the Chief of Staff of the Army, and
Representative McCormack, the majority leader of the House.
After we took our seats and the door was closed, Stimson and
Marshall revealed to us the greatest secret of the war: the
United States was engaging in a crash program to develop the
atomic bomb before the Germans perfected one.

Marshall described the design of the bomb in some technical
detail. Stimson said that if the Germans got this weapon first,
they might win the war overnight. They told us that they would

need an additional $1,600,000,000 to manufacture the bomb. Because of the overriding necessity for secrecy, they made the unique request that the money be provided without a trace of evidence as to how it would be spent. No more extraordinary request was ever made to leaders of the House of Representatives, the trustees of the people's money.

My first reaction upon learning of the dawning atomic age was a feeling of horror that the Germans might beat us to a decisive weapon. Like Rayburn and McCormack, I agreed to use my influence to obtain an inscrutable appropriation. Since war funds generally were lumped together so they could not be analyzed by the enemy, our problem was to get the sums requested by Marshall and Stimson through the House Appropriations Committee. While Rayburn and McCormack went to work on Representative Clarence Cannon, a Democrat from Missouri, who was chairman of the committee, I won the assent of John Taber, the ranking minority member. Together we all slid the appropriation through the House without any breach of secrecy. The Senate went along.

This was the greatest gamble of the war. We had to take it in the interest of American safety. Yet if the bomb had fizzled into a huge grim joke, I would have been answerable to my Republican colleagues for having secretly put through a vast expenditure with absolutely nothing to show for it in return. At least we had the satisfaction, such as it was, of seeing the outcome of our gamble. The President never lived to behold what came of his.

In retrospect one must say that Franklin Roosevelt was an inspirational leader. Probably his party was the one which in the nature of things could have prosecuted the war the better. The poorer classes and the working people, for example, would have reacted unfavorably to a draft put through by the Republican Party. On the other hand, Roosevelt erred seriously and to the detriment of the country, I believe, in trusting the Russians excessively in the political negotiations at Yalta and elsewhere toward the end of the war. As for his domestic policies, the

New Deal did some lasting good, just as it did some temporary good by providing livelihood for many who needed it. Notwithstanding, Roosevelt's philosophy weakened our ideals of self-reliance, and we are poorer for it. To this day, I am sorry to say, it has encouraged too many people to depend on the government instead of on themselves.

7

In the momentous time encompassing the approach of war and the early stages of American involvement the most difficult period for me in the conduct of Republican affairs were the two and a half years following the nomination of Wendell Willkie in Philadelphia at the end of June 1940.

After the adjournment of the convention, over which I had presided as permanent chairman, Willkie gathered a small group of party leaders at his suite in the Benjamin Franklin Hotel. His purpose was to select a new Republican National Chairman who would succeed John D. M. Hamilton and who would also, as was the custom then, be designated as the campaign manager. There were many in the party who believed that Hamilton should continue as chairman, but Willkie was committed to the idea of a new face in the picture.

"Joe, who are you going to suggest?" he asked me.

"I haven't picked a man to suggest," I replied. Most certainly I did not want the job myself. For one thing I wished to concentrate on Congressional affairs at this critical time, and I told Willkie so. For another—and this I did not mention— I had no desire to jeopardize my standing with Republicans in the House by running the campaign of a candidate toward whom many of them were all but openly hostile. After we had discussed the problem inconclusively until almost 3 A.M., Willkie recessed the meeting until mid-morning. I departed with Alf Landon.

"Well, I'll see you at 10 A.M., Joe," he said.

"You won't see me, Alf," I replied, "because I am leaving

for Massachusetts at eight. Anybody they pick is all right with
me."

At that time I owned a cottage in Wareham, on Cape Cod,
which I used occasionally as a hideaway. It did not even have
a telephone. Worn out by the convention, I loafed on the beach
and with the help of sunshine and salt water tried to forget
politics. My idyll ended abruptly a few days later when Win-
field A. Schuster, a textile manufacturer and a member of the
Massachusetts delegation to the recent convention, descended
on me, exclaiming that Willkie had been trying frantically to
get in touch with me.

"We've been looking for you for three days," he said. "It
was only by accident that I ran into the chief of police in Wareham, and he told me you were here. They want you to be
national chairman—to head up the whole business."

"Oh, I'm not going to do that," I told him. "I have no desire
to do anything like that."

"Well, at least you wouldn't refuse to run down to New York
and have dinner with Willkie, would you?" he asked.

Of course, I could give only one answer to this question. I
returned to North Attleboro to toss some clothes into my bag.
In accordance with my life-long habit, I told my mother I was
going to New York.

"I have to have dinner with Wendell Willkie," I said. "He
wants me to become national chairman. I'm not going to take
it, don't worry."

When I arrived in Grand Central Station, Willkie was on
hand to meet me, along with two of his assistants, Samuel F.
Pryor, Jr. of Connecticut and my friend Sinclair Weeks of
Massachusetts, son of John W. Weeks and the man who became
Eisenhower's first Secretary of Commerce.

We took a cab to Willkie's apartment on Park Avenue, where
the candidate proceeded to offer me the post of Republican
National Chairman. With all the friendliness and candor I
could command I declined. I insisted that at such a time I
must devote my energies to Congress.

I would have been naïve to suppose that the matter would end there. Willkie simply would not accept my answer. He talked on and on, and whenever his powers of persuasion flagged, which wasn't often, Pryor and Weeks took over. Soon I had more than these three to contend with.

Willkie had arranged for the most concerted pressure to be put upon me. Landon telephoned from Kansas and told me that he personally wished me to take the chairmanship. A telegram or telephone call—I forget which—came from Helen Reid, of the interventionist New York *Herald Tribune*. She hoped that I would take it. Then a message came from Colonel Robert R. McCormick, publisher of the noninterventionist Chicago *Tribune*. *He* hoped I'd take it.

I realized very well, of course, what had happened. With the party torn asunder in a division that was rather aptly symbolized by the *Tribune* and the *Herald Tribune,* Willkie had been able to find no man other than myself whom the various factions could agree to accept as head of the Republican National Committee. He could not get the jigsaw puzzle of his organization together without me, but I had no stomach for being either the jig or the saw in this troubled situation.

"Sam and Sinclair have other engagements, but I want you to stay and have dinner with me," Willkie urged.

He and I went through the whole business all over again at dinner. He wanted me to be the chairman, to help him heal the divisions in the party, to provide a link between the candidate and Republicans in Congress, to give him the benefit of my experience in his campaign and so on. I maintained that my duty lay in Congress, that the Republican leadership in the House would be weakened at a critical time if I began scattering my energies all over the country. Indeed in every possible way that these conflicting points of view could be expressed by two men they were phrased by Willkie and me throughout that evening.

Finally, at eleven o'clock, Willkie said, "Let's go to bed, Joe. We'll have breakfast and talk it over in the morning."

I retired, wondering how I was ever going to get out of that apartment. After breakfast the next morning Pryor and Weeks returned and Willkie besieged me with a fresh store of energy. I have never known a man so hard to say *no* to. He had great midwestern simplicity and enthusiasm and a way of drawing a constructive picture of a situation that put one, myself in this instance, in an important place in the foreground. As he talked on, I became conscious of the fact that I *liked* Willkie. I also realized that I was not going to be able finally to reject his offer out of hand. I would require, I knew, some basis other than my personal desires for declining the chairmanship. In the end I said that I would accept it on two conditions. The first was that a physical examination must show that my health was up to the task. The second—and this I was sure would exempt me—I must get the approval of the other Republican leaders in the House. Willkie assented.

After taking a physical examination, which raised no barrier, I met with some twenty-five leading Republican Congressmen in the Republican cloakroom in the Capitol and told them my problem. To my surprise, they were overwhelmingly in favor of my accepting the chairmanship. These men, or many of them, still looked with suspicion on the Willkie movement. They were also dubious about some of the amateurs around the new candidate. A Martin rather than Willkie had been the choice of many of the Republicans in the House for the presidential nomination. They felt more at home with my views than with his. In the discussion of the chairmanship, they said that my presence at the head of the Republican National Committee would preserve the influence of what some of them called the regular Republican Party.

Moreover, many of them argued that if I did not take the chairmanship, it would go to Harold E. Stassen, and that was the last thing many of them wanted to see happen. I personally had no objection to Stassen. Although I have never believed that he would be nominated for President, particularly after he had tried but failed to make the grade in 1940, I always got on well with him. In the campaign that was beginning I was to find him an effective operator. Nevertheless he repelled Republicans in Congress. Partly this was due to his liberal views. In a larger sense it was a by-product of his unpopularity with the Republican organization generally. Republicans had a feeling that Stassen was out for himself only. Once a man creates that impression in a political party, he does not go very far.

When the meeting ended, I had no avenues of escape left. Willkie was waiting to hear my decision at a reception in the Willard Hotel that evening.

"Are you going to be with me, Joe?" he asked when I arrived.

"Yes, Wendell," I replied. "It looks as though I am."

"Like a member of the famed Northwest Mounted Police," Willkie said in making the announcement to reporters the next day, "I've got my man."

From that moment on, I was living on top of a powder keg. The world situation in the summer of the defeat of France and the Battle of Britain was explosive, and the dangers abroad exacerbated political passions at home. The conflict between the Republican Party and a Democratic President who was seeking a third term was uncompromising and bitter. Among Republicans themselves, as evidenced by my discussion with my colleagues in the House, division, mistrust, and personal animosities were rife.

The Old Guard Republicans resented the younger element around Willkie. The old-timers were suspicious that the Willkie people were trying to throw them out of their party posts, and in some instances their fears were fully justified.

These jealousies among individuals became magnified in conflicts between the Republican National Committee and the Associated Willkie Clubs of America (an organization headed by Oren Root, Jr. of New York), which had played a great part in getting Willkie nominated. When the Willkie clubs moved into the campaign to work alongside the National Committee, quarrels frequently developed over which organization spoke for the party.

As for Willkie himself, his experiences in Philadelphia, where he had had to overcome the resistance of the Old Guard to win the nomination, had cooled his enthusiasm for the regular Republican organization. Once in the stress of the campaign, I am told, he ranted in private that the organization was not giving him full support. The fact is that the organization supported him vigorously, and the 22,304,755 votes he received on election day, the largest number ever cast for any Republican candidate up to that time, were a proof of it.

Willkie was a man of strong likes and dislikes, and no doubt he treated some of the regular Republicans shabbily. Certainly in states like Indiana, where he had been reared, and Ohio, where he had practiced law as a young man, he had difficulties with the organization because Republicans there remembered him as a Democrat. An element in Willkie's troubles with the organization generally was that he tended to assume that Republicans would vote for him, and he concentrated his efforts on independents and anti-Roosevelt Democrats. In doing so he took positions on social reforms that rankled conservative Republicans, who recoiled at the notion of trying to out-Roosevelt Roosevelt. Furthermore, on certain deeply controversial issues like the selective service act, Willkie took one course and the majority of Republicans in the House took another.

Vexatious as all of this was, I think writers now tend to exaggerate the internal difficulties in the party during the Willkie campaign. No presidential campaign rolls along smoothly. Campaign machinery is too loose-jointed for that. But in retrospect troubles always look more glaring if the campaign ends in defeat, as Willkie's did.

There were no personal abrasions between Willkie and myself. He was always pleasant and affable with me. I also liked Oren Root and found him effective, intelligent, and cooperative. And to this day I disagree with those who considered the Willkie clubs an encumbrance. The Willkie clubs were a tonic that the Republican organization needed. They brought enthusiasm, aggressiveness, and color into the campaign—and they raised a great deal of money.

In trying to put our difficulties in perspective to this extent, however, I do not mean to deny the turmoil that shook the Willkie campaign. No one had to absorb more of it than the Republican National Chairman. Two thirds of my time was devoted to making peace among quarreling factions. There were days I was so exasperated that I told my associates I would give $10,000 to get out of the job.

First I would have to dash to Ohio to pull the regular organization and the Willkie clubs from one another's throats. Obviously the Ohio Republicans were not going to yield control of the organization to the Willkieites. I had to help work out an arrangement for allying the Willkie clubs with the state organization. Then I had to chase to New Jersey where the Willkie people were at odds with the organization in Hudson County. My task there was to get the two factions in line to keep the Hague machine from stealing Republican votes on election day.

Back in our Eastern campaign headquarters in the Commodore Hotel in New York some of the young Willkie hotheads were trying to freeze out former Republican National Chairman Charles D. Hilles, one of the best political minds in the party, because they considered him an Old Guard. I put a stop to this in a hurry by installing Hilles in an office near mine in headquarters. We had a good example of the short-sightedness of the Willkie amateurs one day when one of them came in triumphantly with checks totaling $5000. Hilles quietly took the checks back to the men who had signed them and returned with a total of $25,000.

After Willkie had announced my selection as national chairman, he flew to Colorado Springs to rest from the convention and to prepare his acceptance speech for the notification ceremony to be held in his native city of Elwood, Indiana, on

August 17. As the days passed, I became restive for some sign of a text of this speech, which would be perhaps the most important of his campaign. From Washington it seemed that Willkie was making slow progress, spending most of his time shaking hands and holding press conferences. Congress was still in session. Many controversial bills came to the floor, and a vote on selective service was approaching. In Colorado reporters were wangling comments from Willkie on pending legislation, which often portrayed him at odds with Republicans in Congress. These divergencies, in turn, were exploited by the Democrats to make it appear that a Willkie victory would mean government by a divided party.

To try to end this embarrassment and to get a look at the Elwood draft I visited Willkie at the Broadmoor Hotel in Colorado Springs around August 1. I urged him not to speak out on legislation every time someone asked him to. His precipitate statements, I argued, often put the Republicans in Congress in an unnecessarily awkward position.

"These legislative issues are Roosevelt's responsibility, not yours," I told him. "You're still on the outside. You don't have to comment on every bill. Don't voluntarily assume positions unless you have to. Wait and see how the questions come up in the campaign. There will then be some issues on which you will want to comment, but let's avoid these unnecessary conflicts as much as possible."

Some of those who have written histories of that period say that I begged and pleaded with Willkie not to come out for the original selective service bill. I didn't beg Willkie to do anything. I approached this subject entirely as a matter of political strategy. In so many words this is what I told him:

"The draft is a very unpopular issue. Naturally, people don't want their sons in uniform. The country is much opposed to war. Go slow on this thing. It is not necessary for you to take the initiative on selective service right now."

After all, Roosevelt himself was being cagy on this issue. It was not until August 2 that he came out for the selective service bill. Willkie made up his own mind what to do. In his acceptance speech he advocated "some form of selective service."

As the national chairman I simply could not hand the Democrats any such plum as a vote by me against Willkie on this issue. Furthermore the situation in Europe had now become so grave that it was obvious the United States had to prepare for an emergency. When the first selective service bill came up, I voted for it, as I have mentioned earlier. All told, 112 Republicans in the House voted aganist selective service and 51 voted for it. I believe the Republican vote against the bill would have been substantially higher than 112 if I, as the leader, had voted the other way.

As the campaign progressed, I continued to urge Willkie to be prudent on the intervention issue lest Roosevelt trap him out on a limb. Especially after Roosevelt's speech in Boston, in which the President with great political effectiveness promised the parents of America "again and again and again" that "your boys are not going to be sent into any foreign wars," I warned Willkie that F.D.R. might maneuver him into a position where the Democrats could tag the Republicans as the war party.

This issue illustrates the difficulties we faced in that campaign, which was crammed with more dramatic incidents than any other presidential election I have ever seen. Willkie's campaign opened at Elwood. That occasion, which attracted perhaps the largest political crowd in American history, a sprawling, sweltering assemblage of a quarter of a million people, was memorable as the closing scene of a grand tradition.

The history of the notification ceremony goes back to the early days of the Republic when men had to travel long distances on horseback to carry the first tidings of a nomination to the candidate. Even after the coming of the telegraph the ceremony of notification was continued, and it was both a colorful and an effective ritual in American politics. The tradition was quite deliberately struck a mortal blow in 1932 by Franklin Roosevelt, who, with a haughty show of turning his back on old ways, flew from Albany to Chicago to accept the nomination in the convention. The tradition of the notification ceremony succeeded in lingering through the Landon nomination and finally died in a burst of excitement and glamor at Elwood. I lament its passing. The notification ceremony was a useful medium for arousing interest in a candidate. It not only stimulated political activity throughout the state in which it was held but also provided a rallying point for the party nationally.

All roads into Elwood were jammed. In the outskirts early comers were living in their trailers. Buildings were hung with flags, bunting, and photographs of the candidate. Shipwreck Kelly sat on top of a flagpole advertising a brand of coffee. In the 100-degree heat, people consumed oceans of pop and beer, while perspiring bands played "Back Home Again in Indiana." Willkie, wearing a flat-topped straw hat, received an ovation when he arrived by special train at 12:30 P.M. with Mrs. Willkie and her mother. The parade moved through town behind the University of Indiana band. For an honor guard Willkie had the Summit Post of the American Legion from Ohio. He had once been its commander.

As Republican National Chairman and convention chairman and thus the official who was formally to notify Willkie that he had been nominated, I rode with him. While I was heartened by the spectacular size of the crowd, nearly everything else that happened that day filled me with discouragement. To begin with, I got my first look at the complete text of Willkie's acceptance speech only after my arrival. When I was in Colorado Springs he had finished only four or five pages. The sole influence I had in its preparation was to persuade him to soft-pedal the fact that his father was born in Germany. The summer of 1940 was no time to be trumpeting one's German ancestry. In Elwood, Willkie finally handed me the full text, typewritten, double-spaced, in ordinary pica type.

"Where's your reading copy?" I asked.

"This is it," he replied.

"Well, this isn't the way we do it in Washington," was all I could say in my disgust that his copy had not been typed, triple-spaced, in large letters so that he could read it without keeping his eyes glued to the page all the time.

The next discouraging development was a diversion of the planned route for a tiring visit to Willkie's old school. I objected. However, Senator James J. Davis of Pennsylvania, a native of Tredegar, South Wales, whose peripatetic career had included some years of residence in Elwood, had arranged this ceremony with an elaborateness that could not be shunned. So we went to the school, and when we got there the arrangements went awry. Willkie was almost crushed in the surging crowd. Everywhere he went he waved his arms like pinwheels, with the result that by the time he reached the park later in the afternoon for his acceptance speech, he was wilted.

As I feared, he had difficulty reading the speech from the small type. His performance was flat. Then the crowning blunder came at the end of the speech when the Willkie clubs, without my knowledge, piped in an appeal for funds to the tremendous radio audience. If ever such an appeal was out of place it was in a high-minded notification ceremony. Perhaps I should have amended my praise of this relic to say that notification ceremonies were effective when they were well managed.

When Elwood was ended, Willkie was as discouraged, momentarily, as I was. He vowed he was not going to deliver any more speeches over the radio. I urged him to make the most of his natural appeal to people by boarding a train and stumping the country. Miss Frick offered me the use of her father's gold-plated private railroad car for Willkie to travel in.

"Oh, that would never do," I declined with thanks. "Wendell is a man of the people now—he can't be campaigning in a gilded car."

After his campaign had warmed up and he had delivered a very successful speech in Tulsa, Willkie lost his aversion to radio. In fact I could hardly find enough money to buy him all the time he wanted on the networks. I made it my business to

stay close to national headquarters during the campaign to concentrate, as a national chairman should, on organizational work
rather than on speech-making. One of the few speeches I delivered was at a local rally in Pittsburgh. Among the Republicans who heard it was Henry Heinz, head of the H. J. Heinz
Co. Afterward he took me to a gathering of prominent businessmen in Pittsburgh and raved about my speech, in which, among
other things, I had said that Roosevelt in seeking a third term
was asking the American people "to abandon the Bill of Rights
and the constitutional republican system of government for
one-man rule."

"Why don't you give it on radio?" he asked. "That is the
most solid Republican speech I have heard in this campaign."

"We haven't the money," I explained. "Our radio funds must
go for speakers like Willkie and McNary"—McNary being the
vice-presidential nominee.

"How much would it cost to put your speech on the air?"
Heinz inquired.

I gave him an estimate—$15,000, as I recall. Thereupon
Heinz levied an assessment on each of his friends. "A thousand
dollars," he said to one. "Two thousand," he told another. "A
thousand," he asked a third. "I can't give that much," the last
said. "Well, five hundred then," Heinz replied, continuing his
solicitation. Within five minutes he had commitments enough
for me to deliver the speech on radio later in the campaign.

At campaign headquarters in New York I used to hold periodic
off-the-record press conferences. In one of these, when we were
going over almost as many topics as Mr. Heinz's fifty-seven
varieties, a question came up about the possibility of America's
entering the war. A reporter commented that the United States
could not go to war without an act of Congress. I replied that
while an act of Congress was necessary to declare war, the
country could conceivably become involved in war without a
formal declaration.

The reporter asked permission to quote my remark. However, I stuck to the rules and said that I could not be quoted. In the discussion we got talking about a rumor that was then circulating to the effect that after the election the United States would send part of the fleet to the Philippines. I said that this was only a rumor in Washington and that my reference to it was still off the record. I did not, as the world was soon to be told by the President of the United States, advise reporters that they could print the rumor on their own responsibility. Indeed to the best of my knowledge no story was ever printed out of that press conference.

As a result of it nevertheless I became involved in a row with Roosevelt, who used this press conference as a pretext for suddenly getting out and waging an old-fashioned political campaign, something he had loftily indicated earlier that he would not do. He would be too busy with world events, he had said, to "have the time or the inclination to engage in purely political debate"—except, of course, carefully leaving himself an out: "I shall never be loath to call the attention of the nation to deliberate or unwitting falsification of fact. . . ."

As the fall wore on, Willkie's campaign began to worry Roosevelt. The President took to searching for pretexts to justify open barnstorming. I say open because he already was campaigning covertly in the guise of Commander in Chief making inspection trips to war plants and military installations. On October 18 he announced that he would deliver five political speeches around the country, with whistle stops en route, of course, to reply to "deliberate falsification of fact." My press conference, or so he said after setting out, was one of the targets for his shafts of truth.

"Your President says this country is not going to war," he told the enlightened citizenry of Buffalo.

Since there were, in my belief, no stories printed about the conference in question, how did Roosevelt know about it? How did he learn what I had discussed off the record with reporters? On my own authority I cannot answer these questions. It is true, however, that some time after the President had commenced his attacks, attributing to me an act "more dangerous to our peaceful international relations than anything that has ever been done in Washington by this government," some of the reporters who had attended the conference came to me with an explanation. How they obtained their information I do not know. They said, speaking with distinct disapproval, that one of the reporters who had been present at the time and who had long been personally friendly with Roosevelt had communicated to him in some way or other the substance of my remarks. Whether the reporter or Roosevelt or his speech-writers made up the false statement that I had, as the President charged publicly, said that the newspapers could spread the rumor about the fleet on their own authority I have no way of ascertaining.

By this time the campaign was sizzling. No episodes recall the hot temper of those closing days better than my own experience with Henry A. Wallace's preposterous Guru letters and Roosevelt's classic thrust at me and my colleagues, Representatives Bruce Barton and Hamilton Fish, Jr.

Some years before, Henry Wallace, who in 1940 was Roosevelt's running mate, had been attracted to a White Russian named Nicholas Konstantinovich Roerich. This theosophist had assorted occult projects that fascinated Wallace, who presently entered into a weird correspondence with him, addressing Roerich as "Dear Guru." Wallace's letters contained, among other strange things, cabalistic allusions to "the Flaming One" or "the Wavering One" or "the Mediocre One," by whom he seems to have meant Roosevelt. Similarly, he mentioned "the Sour One," who seems to have been Secretary of State Hull, and "the Roaring Lion," assumed to be Winston Churchill.

Late in the 1930s, as I understand it, photostats of this correspondence fell into the hands of certain newspaper publishers and Republican officials. It was not until after the Democrats had nominated Wallace for Vice-President, however, that a movement was set on foot to put these letters to political use. Paul Block, publisher of the Block newspapers, took a suite at the Waldorf-Astoria during the campaign and invited a number of other publishers as well as myself as Republican National Chairman to discuss the wisdom of publishing the letters. The purpose of making them public, of course, would be to create a public shock that would serve to defeat Roosevelt and Wallace.

The publishers present were about equally divided for and against publication. This left the matter more or less up to me. A number of considerations crossed my mind. It was late in the campaign. Roosevelt and Wallace would have had little time to have answered to the issue posed by the letters. For this reason the voters might conclude that the Republican Party was resorting to a last-minute smear. In this connection I remembered certain speeches that Republican orators had delivered late in the Roosevelt–Landon campaign of 1936, attacking Roosevelt on social security. These speakers had said that the administration was preparing regimentation so complete that American workers would be compelled to wear metal tags comparable to the police cards that many Europeans then had to carry. For the Republicans this produced a bad political reaction in an electorate that was on the whole enthusiastic about social security. I did not wish to take a chance that the Guru letters might now somehow make Roosevelt the beneficiary of fair-play sentiment. Furthermore I didn't know anything about this fellow Guru. Maybe he had a great many more followers than any of us realized. Why kick away their votes? Everything considered, therefore, I decided that the Republicans would not use the letters. That put an end to the matter.

In the case of a great many people who remember the Roosevelt–Willkie campaign, the thing that seems to stand out most in their minds twenty years later is an incident that I took very lightly at the time. This was Roosevelt's famous line about "Martin, Barton and Fish," which he spoke in a talk at Madison Square Garden on October 28, 1940, and repeated in the Boston Arena two nights later.

I listened to the broadcast, either from Madison Square or the Arena. On the radio I heard the partisan audience merrily take up the chant of "Martin, Barton and Fish." It was an extremely clever performance, one that swayed the crowds. Yet, perhaps because I was sufficiently hardened to political life by that time, I felt no particular resentment over it. To me it was just one more campaign stunt. The Democrats had their tricks, and we had ours.

I never discussed it with Roosevelt afterward. I have since read that his speech-writers, Judge Samuel I. Rosenman and Robert E. Sherwood, hit upon this line with its meter of "Wynken, Blynken and Nod" while drafting the speech attacking the Republican voting record in Congress. They sold it to Roosevelt as a gambit for ridiculing this record. Naturally, it suited the President's purposes. It was a potshot at me as Republican National Chairman. It spattered Bruce Barton, the Republican candidate for Senator from New York that year. Finally, of course, it derided Ham Fish, who, as the Representative from Roosevelt's own district up the Hudson, infuriated the President by his opposition to the administration's foreign policy.

The day after the Madison Square speech I issued a mild statement calling Roosevelt's attack "a bit unfair." Recalling that Roosevelt had wanted Congress to go home in June, I said, "Since then most of the defense money has been appropriated and the major part of the defense laws were passed. Had Congress adjourned in June as Mr. Roosevelt desired, we would not even be started on our national defense program." That evening I was on the platform at a Republican meeting at Westbury, Long Island, and heard Barton denounce the President's remarks as "silly and ridiculous."

Martin, Barton, and Fish, if I may borrow a phrase, had always been good friends. Fish had served on the Foreign Affairs Committee with me. He was more extreme on the isolationist question than I was, yet not so extreme as some. I had known Barton for many years. His father was a minister in Foxboro, the town next to mine in Massachusetts. Roosevelt's attack lent a new bond to our friendship. Afterward whenever we three would meet one another here and there we used to refer to ourselves as "members of the firm." Nineteen years later when I was overthrown as House leader, one of the first letters I received was from Barton, who had long ago returned to the advertising business.

"It saddened me to read that you had been promoted out of the active leadership," he wrote. "But in my memory you will always be the leader, and I shall always remember the kindness and wisdom with which you tried to guide me in my brief service in the House. . . . I wish I could persuade you to relax and take up golf, card playing and whiskey. These are all wonderful medicine for old age. But I am sure the best medicine for you is the remembrance that you are still number one in the hearts of hundreds of men who have served under your leadership and will always think of you with affection."

Willkie was, I have heard it said, jolted by the "Martin, Barton and Fish" speeches, but he never mentioned the subject to me. Throughout the campaign Willkie, like practically all political candidates for every office, was optimistic. The large crowds, the tremendous enthusiasm that he encountered in all parts of the country sent his hopes soaring. Yet at the end he obviously was tortured by doubts.

Five days before the election I was in my two-room suite at the Commodore Hotel when he entered, strode through the sitting room into the bedroom and flung himself on the bed. He had been utterly prodigal in his expenditure of energy in the campaign, and he looked exhausted.

"Joe, how are we coming out?" he asked.

The prospect was not good, but I could not bring myself to tell him, except indirectly.

"We've got a chance to win, Wendell," I answered. "It's a very close race. There are twelve or fourteen important states —states like Wisconsin, Illinois, New York, Indiana, Ohio, Iowa—that hang in the balance right now. They are going to be decided by a small margin. If we get what they call that last week's pay-up, we can win. If we don't, we won't."

He did not say much.

"The difficulty that we're really under," I concluded as gently as I could, "is that we've got to take all of them."

Willkie kept fighting to the end. As has been my custom for fifty years, I spent election night at the *Evening Chronicle* office in North Attleboro. I talked with him by telephone at the Commodore very late, perhaps around midnight.

"It doesn't look as though we're going to make it, Joe," he said.

Willkie would have been a good President. While some of my fellow Republicans remained dubious, particularly because of his views on foreign policy, I did not feel concerned about him. Indeed, among Republicans there was too much emphasis on his foreign policy at the expense of his domestic policies. Willkie was sound. He had a great potential for leadership, and he would have given this country a sane administration.

In retrospect, however, I do not believe that he, or any other Republican for that matter, had a chance in 1940 once France fell. That was the thing that beat Willkie. True, the Republicans made some mistakes. One of them was that we did not exploit the third-term issue more effectively. We might have done better here and there. Notwithstanding, the collapse of the Allies made Roosevelt's election a certainty no matter what Willkie did. The fall of France and the imminent danger to Britain filled the American people with a fear of switching administrations. "Don't change horses in the middle of the stream" was never a more potent argument in American history than it was then. Not even the third-term issue could prevail against it.

We have become accustomed to saying nowadays that the party which seems best able to preserve the peace is the party that will win. But there are times, and 1940 was one, when the party that seems best able to prosecute a war is invincible. In the last analysis the people trusted Roosevelt's experience in coping with the situation that confronted the country.

8

INEVITABLE though it may have been under the circumstances, Willkie's defeat had a shattering effect on the Republican Party. Trouble hounded us everywhere.

The Republican National Committee went broke as many big contributors froze up, fearing that if the Republicans could not win with Willkie, the party was through. The national headquarters in Washington was evicted—by the C.I.O.!

Bandwagon boys who had gaily leaped aboard when things looked rosy now skulked away in the hour of discouragement. Even worse, men and women who had backed Willkie with wild zeal in the campaign turned coldly on him and tried to read him out of the party when he supported Roosevelt's foreign policies. I fought these efforts to a standstill. The party would have been finished if it had expelled Willkie.

In the demoralization following the election, eastern money, the "fat cats" of the Republican Finance Committee, the crowd from the National Association of Manufacturers tried to move in and seize control of the Republican organization. As national chairman I refused to yield to their dictation. For Republicans to have allowed these interests to emerge as the party symbol would have been an act of political suicide.

In the year after Willkie's defeat the Republican National Committee never had a thousand dollars in the bank. Debts piled up. For the most part our credit was no good. Fortunately, the railroads, the airlines and the telephone company did carry us on the books so we were not completely isolated from the country. I could go to a meeting, let us say, in Omaha, and

121

charge the fare to the national committee. But beyond that there was no expense money. If local organizations whose cities I visited did not pick up the hotel bills, I had to pay for them myself, even though I was serving as national chairman without salary. Whenever out-of-town Republican officials visited Washington, singly or in groups, I had as a matter of courtesy to take them to dinner and, of course, pay the tab. Before long I was out of pocket several thousand dollars.

For my pains I was attacked from all sides. I was too isolationist. I was not isolationist enough. I was a Willkieite. I was an Old Guard. A howl went up when I brought Frank E. Gannett, the publisher, and Clarence Budington Kelland, the writer, into the national committee headquarters as members of my staff. "Perhaps a wronger choice could have been made by Mr. Martin," the *Herald Tribune* fumed, objecting to a man of Kelland's isolationist views in the position of publicity director for the committee, "but we can't think just how."

If Republicans had been willing to spend their money as freely as their criticism, we would not have had the kind of troubles we did. There had to be some assistants at the national headquarters, yet I had no money to hire any, except a few stenographers. Gannett and Kelland came to Washington at their own expense and worked hard without salary. The critics were too busy criticizing to bother about details like this.

The telephone company may have been willing to carry us on faith, but the landlord was not. The rent on our offices at 718 Jackson Place came due every month and somehow had to be paid. Then the building was put up for sale. We had no money to buy it. One of the pillars of the party outraged me by suggesting that the Republican National Committee close up its Washington headquarters altogether and rent a single room in New York.

"That would be liquidating the Republican Party," I said, "and we are not going to liquidate it while I am chairman."

The C.I.O. bought the building and presently put us out because they wanted our space. I found an old brownstone up on Connecticut Avenue, which could be rented for three years for a total of $33,000. I signed the lease, assuming this obligation as a personal liability. This is one of the things I have had in mind in speaking of my services to the Republican Party. In those dark days the sole contribution of some big businessmen consisted in asking me to put through legislation for an eighty-hour workweek, or something of that nature.

After working all day at the Capitol, I used to spend my nights at the national committee trying to keep up with the work there. Late one evening in 1942 I got a long-distance call from a political friend in West Virginia, a disenchanted Democrat, who told me that if the Republicans only knew it, they could elect a United States Senator in his state that year.

"The Republicans around here," he said, "are so accustomed to being beaten that they take it for granted."

It is a commentary on the morale of the Republican Party in that period that it took a call from a Democrat to alert us to an opportunity to pick up a seat in the Senate. Acting on his advice, I went to West Virginia and stirred things up. The Republicans pulled themselves together, nominated Chapman Revercomb, and when November came around, he was elected.

Throughout these bleak years I could, fortunately, still count on financial support from some of the men and women who have remained loyal in good times and bad. Joseph N. Pew, Jr. of Pennsylvania, head of the Sun Oil Company, is an outstanding example. In his dedication to the preservation of the Republican Party he has given millions. Yet in all the years I have known him and have been close to him in campaigns and other party activities he has never asked me for a single favor. When almost no one else was giving any money his contributions kept coming in; without them the party might have utterly dried up for lack of funds. Of course, there were others. Helen Frick was one. H. Roy Cullen, the Texas oil man, was another.

The Republican Finance Committee was an altogether different story. This group was dominated by eastern money and the ultra-N.A.M. people. Even during the campaign there had been foreshadowings of trouble with this crowd. The Finance Chairman was Ernest T. Weir, head of the Weirton Steel Company. For a number of reasons, one of them being the fact that Weir had been involved in nasty labor disputes, some leading Republicans advised Willkie that he was an inappropriate symbol for the party and should be replaced. This opinion carried weight with Willkie. When he came to me about it, however, I persuaded him to abandon any idea of dismissing Weir as Finance Chairman. It struck me as an unnecessarily harsh thing to do. It would have caused all sorts of dissension in the middle of the campaign.

When the campaign ended in defeat, however, this crowd closed in on me. First they squeezed off money, and then as a condition of relaxing the squeeze they demanded what amounted to control of the Republican National Committee. They thought that they ought to run the party. I told them I did not think they should. Finally, some weeks after the election Weir came to town and asked me to drop around to his room at the Mayflower. After I arrived and we had talked for a while, he said that the Finance Committee members felt I should resign from Congress and devote my time to the national committee. That was their approach. A more improbable suggestion could hardly have been made to me. My whole heart was in Congress. I said there was no chance whatever that I would give up my seat. That being the case, Weir said I should resign as national chairman. Now I had no great desire to remain as chairman, but Willkie and other leaders were urging me to continue, so I was not going to make any commitments to Weir to step out of the chairmanship.

Weir then came to the heart of the matter. He said that the men who put up the cash in the party should have the decisive influence in its councils.

"I don't agree with you, Mr. Weir," I told him. "I think the men and women who put in their time and effort and get elected and the people who work in the precincts contribute just as much as the man who gives a thousand dollars."

In the best of circumstances this question of the proper realm of influence of persons who contribute money to a political party is a difficult one. In the case of those who have natural qualifications and suitable backgrounds for political leadership the problem is simplified, of course. But people who do not have these qualifications are not entitled to special consideration simply because they have contributed money. The assumption is that they made their contribution because they believed in the aims of the party and wished to advance them. Thus the contribution is a means to an end and not an end in itself requiring some special concession to the giver. Still, as a practical matter the line is not easy to draw.

At the time of my conversation with Weir I was in a rather chilly frame of mind toward the breed of contributors, common to both parties, who give money just to be in the show, to get invited to White House dinners and social affairs, but who disappear the moment the party loses. These are the people who treat money as a substitute for work. Needless to say one has to recognize them, because money is a necessity. But one does not have to turn the party over to them.

Weir complained that I did not consult him enough.

"Who do you go to for advice?" he asked me.

"I consult people who know something about politics," I replied.

"Who are they?" he wanted to know.

"Oh," I said, "men like Senator McNary, Styles Bridges, Carroll Reece. Men of that character. The experts—people who specialize in politics."

"Well, you never talk to me," Weir said.

"I was not aware that you were a political expert particularly, Mr. Weir," I answered.

Weir was angry. He resigned in April 1941, but the freeze on money continued through the 1942 Congressional elections, when the national committee had only $125,000 for the campaign. At that Republicans won 209 seats in the House and might well have picked up enough more to have taken control if only we had had more money to spend.

In my difficulties with the Weir group my colleagues in the House stood behind me and so did Willkie. In fact, speaking at a private luncheon in the Capitol one day, he made the remark, "The thing I like about Joe Martin is that he has the guts to tell those fat cats to go to hell."

Needless to say, I made some lasting enemies in opposing domination by the finance people, but I have never regretted my course. Where would the Republican Party have gone with these interests as the symbol of its leadership? They were too extreme in their conservatism. They had no appeal to the common man. Willkie was wise in steering clear of them to the extent he did, and so, when he became a candidate, was Eisenhower.

While many of these difficulties could not have been foreseen in their specific shapes and forms, it took no clairvoyance for an experienced politician to know that defeat for the third consecutive time in a presidential election would cause bitter recriminations within the Republican Party. Just as I had not wanted the office of Republican National Chairman when Willkie offered it to me at the start of a hopeful campaign, so now I had no desire to keep it in the throes of defeat. But just as I had no excuse for refusing it then, I could find no justification for relinquishing it now. In each case the pressure on me was very much the same. In the beginning no one else could be found whom all factions could accept as chairman. Now no successor could be found who was acceptable to all factions. If I had quit in the midst of the post-election dissension, the quarrels in the party would have been exacerbated by a fight between the pro-Willkie and anti-Willkie forces over the selection of a new chairman. Acutely aware of this danger, Willkie appealed to me to stay on. So also did twelve Republican governors, as well as McNary, Landon, and Dewey, who was now looming as the possible new leader of the party. More than any of these, however, it was an old-timer, Will H. Hays, who persuaded me to remain.

Hays, better remembered now as the "czar" of the motion picture industry, was the greatest organizer the Republican Party has seen in my lifetime. As Republican National Chairman in 1920, he played a vital part in Harding's victory. He was Postmaster General in the Harding administration. By 1940 he had gone with the motion picture industry, but he still maintained a lively interest in Republican politics. After Willkie's defeat he called on me at the Hay-Adams Hotel. A small man with the energy of a hydroelectric plant, he came in looking dapper as usual.

"Joe," he said, "the logic of the situation makes it imperative for you to go on as chairman. In the next Congressional elections you and your House Republicans are going to be the target. That's where the challenge will lie, and you can meet it better from here."

After thinking it over, I consented to remain as chairman through the Congressional elections of 1942 and was reelected unanimously.

Following his defeat, my personal relations with Willkie remained as friendly as ever. Even so, in that stirring year between the presidential election and Pearl Harbor we often found ourselves on opposite sides of the fence on vital issues involving neutrality and aid to the Allies. Willkie's ever-growing conflict with the viewpoint of the majority of Republicans in the House on these matters made my own task as the Republican floor leader all the more difficult. Indeed I had something of a problem remaining in favor with the House Republicans after I had served as Willkie's campaign manager.

His standing with this group, never high, diminished steadily as his support of Roosevelt's foreign policies increased. Republicans in Congress were particularly incensed over a comment he made at the Senate hearings on lend-lease. Senator Gerald P. Nye, a Republican from North Dakota, who was an uncom-

promising foe of the President's policies, was challenging Willkie about a speech he had made in October. In it he had remarked that if Roosevelt's record of honoring pledges was any
guide, the United States would "be at war by April 1941, if he
is elected." Now when Nye threw this back at him, Willkie
declared, "It was a bit of campaign oratory." The Republicans
did not like that reply in the least because it undermined all the
criticism that had been made of the President's foreign policy
in the campaign.

While I recognized and respected Willkie as the titular head
of the party, I could not as a practical matter operate as House
leader by consulting him concerning the position Republicans
should take in Congress.

Directly after the election Willkie got off on the right foot
with the whole country, Republicans included, with his Loyal
Opposition speech. On Armistice Day, six days after his defeat,
he addressed the American people in a national radio broadcast
from the Commodore. His thesis was that in the crisis that was
overtaking the United States the minority must retain its standing in the government. But this minority must not obstruct. It
must play the strong, constructive part of the loyal opposition.
This speech earned a great reception throughout the country.
If Willkie had stopped there, his place in the Republican Party
would have remained high. Against my counsel, however, he
did not stop there, and the political consequences were exactly
what I predicted to him they would be.

Early in 1941 he conceived the idea of visiting Britain. The
Roosevelt administration fell in with it and virtually made
Willkie seem the President's personal representative. Willkie
dropped by the Hay-Adams one day to ask my advice about
the trip.

"Well, I wouldn't take it," I told him. "What are you going
to get out of it? You can't do anything over there."

"I can see the debris from the bombing and conditions of the
war," he said.

"Well, sure, you can see *that*," I agreed.

"Anyhow," he persisted, "I'm going."

"I wouldn't do it," I argued futilely. "You stand in pretty well now as the head of the loyal opposition."

There were times when Willkie could be completely boyish about things, and this was one of them. The prospect of the trip was as big and shiny as Christmas morning under the tree.

"All I can say," I concluded, "is that Roosevelt is just trying to win you over. This won't be well received by the Republicans."

When Willkie, all within the space of five days, endorsed the lend-lease bill and, in preparation for his trip, called on the President, my prediction was well on the way to fulfillment. Step by step Willkie became more deeply involved in support of Roosevelt's policies, and with each step his role as titular leader of the Republican Party grew more precarious.

That Willkie was acting with sincerity and patriotism there cannot be the slightest doubt. Certainly he was not supporting Roosevelt because he admired him. On the contrary, he had little use for Roosevelt personally, and he never abandoned his disapproval of Roosevelt's domestic policies and philosophy of government. Although it may have destroyed his own influence in the Republican Party, Willkie supported Roosevelt's foreign policies because he thought they were for the good of the country. In doing so he laid the groundwork for the bipartisan approach to foreign policy that began during the war and flowered after it. This is Wendell Willkie's monument.

When the Republicans celebrated their annual party festival on Lincoln's Birthday in February 1941, Willkie, just back from England, began reaping the political harvest that I feared. Taft declared that the man who had been our candidate for President less than four months before "does not and cannot speak for the Republican Party." Nye called Willkie a "betrayer" of the party. In Des Moines the Young Republican National Federation, many of whose members had belonged to Willkie clubs during the campaign, threatened to condemn Willkie's trip and repudiate him as the Republican voice on questions of foreign policy. This would have been intolerable, and to head it off I issued a statement in Washington saying that I would "regret" it if the Young Republicans considered any resolution attacking Willkie. The statement had the effect I hoped it would.

Several days later Republicans from sixteen midwestern states met in Omaha, ready to castigate Willkie for his stand on lend-lease. I sent Robert McIlvane, who was then my secretary, to the conference to deliver to the leaders my personal request as national chairman that they refrain. With some grumbling about "gag rule" from Washington they complied. Then another midwestern conference opened in Indianapolis in March, in much the same frame of mind. This time I attended in person and defended Willkie as the rightful leader of the party and the man who held the esteem of the rank and file. After all, Willkie had brought new voters into the Republican column in 1940. Where would they have gone if the party had repudiated him almost before the echoes of the campaign had died away?

That same month, shortly after the Indianapolis affair, the Republican National Committee met in Washington and unanimously reelected me national chairman. In my speech I said that Willkie must be considered the titular leader of the Republican Party. I have never thought too highly of this business of titular leader, whatever it means. In fact, I don't think it really means a great deal of anything. Titular leader is a newspaper creation as far as I know, a sort of brass ring for the defeated candidate to grab at during the ride. Certainly, the titular leaders, whether they happen to be Wendell Willkie or Adlai E. Stevenson, do not necessarily exert much influence over a party. In Willkie's case, however, I did believe that his status in the party had to be preserved for the good of the party itself. It fortified him against the efforts of hotheads to read him out of the party, an act which would have been a dreadful spectacle for Republicans. After the national committee meeting, agitation against Willkie subsided for a spell.

Willkie had his eye on 1944. Some of his friends wanted him to run for governor of New York in 1942 and, like Cleveland and the two Roosevelts, use Albany as a springboard for Washington. The Gallup poll showed at the time that among all prospective Republican gubernatorial candidates—including Dewey, who was still District Attorney of New York County—Willkie was substantially in the lead.

However, Willkie had an absolute blind spot about the political importance of the New York governorship. He looked down on it. He wanted to go into the White House and had no patience with steppingstones. One of the paradoxes of this attitude was that while he did not wish to be governor, he did not want to see Dewey elected either. He disliked Dewey personally and realized that he was a potential rival for the presidential nomination. While I was still national chairman Willkie invited me to have dinner with him in Washington one evening. At the table he surprised me by asking, in effect, if I would organize a stop-Dewey movement in New York. Specifically, he wanted me to pick another good Republican candidate as an alternative to Dewey.

"Joe, I wish you'd get me a candidate for governor of New York," was the way he put it. "If you get me a candidate, a good candidate, I'll stump every street in New York for him."

It was out of the question for me to interfere in New York.

"There's only one way to do this," I told him, "and that's to run yourself. If you got elected governor, there would be nothing to stop you in Forty-four. It's the path that leads to the White House."

"I don't fancy that job," Willkie replied disparagingly. "You wouldn't want a man of my stature there."

"If you want my honest advice," I said, "it is that the only way you can stop Dewey is to run yourself."

Willkie clung to his own course, which led him to a dead end. Dewey was nominated, and inevitably Willkie had to support him. When Dewey was elected, he and not Willkie was on the inside track to the nomination.

A month after the election, the Republican National Committee met in St. Louis. Again I was under some pressure to run for another term as chairman, but this time I was calling the tune. I thrust my letter of resignation into the hands of the secretary and instructed him to read it. The instant he had finished, I walloped the table with my gavel and said, "Without objection the resignation is accepted. We will now proceed to the next order of business." This was the election of a new chairman. Into the contest poured all the old rivalries and ideological cross-currents that had had the Republican Party in turmoil for years. In recent times no election of a Republican chairman has heated up such a cauldron of personalities and philosophies as that one did.

A fine old cast of Republican characters was engaged, onstage and off. Offstage, for example, was my friend, Colonel Robert McCormick, whose Chicago *Tribune*, whether one liked it or not, had kept the Republican flag flying in the Midwest in the dark days of the 1930s when few other mastheads appeared above the ruins for us to look to. The colonel was one of the authentic enthusiasts of conservative Republicanism at a time when many kindred spirits were wavering. He might have been more effective if he had been somewhat more temperate. No one could fault his patriotism, however. Once when he was in New York for some Willkie fund-raising activity, I went with him in a group to the Links Club on East Sixty-second Street. As he walked through the club he glared at portraits of princes, dukes, lords, and assorted royalty.

"Where's Lincoln?" he asked crossly. "I don't see George Washington either."

McCormick was a man who was hard, not to say practically impossible, to argue with. But he had an immensely practical side to him. When I was visiting in Chicago once during the Al Capone era, he drove me through town in a limousine that had I am certain, bullet-proof windows and carried two bodyguards.

At his office was a Great Dane that looked as if it could have eaten both of these operatives with capacity to spare for McCormick and myself. In the years that I knew him the colonel had one overshadowing passion—a true, glowing hatred of the New Deal.

Onstage, the characters in St. Louis on that first anniversary of Pearl Harbor included Senator Robert A. Taft of Ohio; Harrison E. Spangler, Republican National Committeeman from Iowa; Werner W. Schroeder, Republican National Committeeman from Illinois; and Frederick E. Baker, a thirty-five-year-old public relations man from Seattle.

Although the maneuvering became rather complicated, the plot was fairly simple. Colonel McCormick was supporting Schroeder. Schroeder also had the backing of Taft. Willkie, who kept in touch with events from New York, opposed Schroeder. He considered him an isolationist. Willkie was for Baker. While I had no strong personal favorite, I thought that Spangler would be the best choice, and I was prepared to use my influence for him. He was less objectionable to each of the contending forces than any other candidate. Thus he seemed best able to preserve a measure of peace between the Willkie and the Taft wings of the party.

On the night before the vote a reporter from the *Tribune* came to my hotel room in St. Louis, saying he had a message from McCormick.

"What is it?" I inquired.

"The colonel says," he told me, "that if Schroeder isn't elected tomorrow, there is going to be a third party in America."

"Well, I don't believe that will happen," I said. "Mr. Schroeder is a very able man, and there have been times when I would gladly have supported him. But I am afraid that at this time I cannot do it, notwithstanding my great admiration for Colonel McCormick."

With war clouds rolling over the country, I felt that Schroeder, however much I admired the man and his abilities, would not have been the best chairman for the party because of his distinctively German name and his association with McCormick.

At Taft's request I dropped into a meeting he had called to try to put his candidate over.

"Joe," he said, "we've got forty-four votes here for Schroeder. It takes fifty. You can give us the rest, if you will."

"Yes, Senator," I said, "I could, but I won't. I don't think it's advisable."

The next morning before the committee met I ran into Spangler in the lobby.

"Harry, are you going to be a candidate today?" I asked.

"No," he replied. "I wouldn't have a chance."

"Have you got a man who could nominate you?" I inquired. "Can't you get someone from your own state?"

"Well, maybe so," he told me.

"I can get a fellow to second it for you," I assured him. "You scurry around and see how many votes you can get. This thing may deadlock."

In the short time remaining before the vote, he worked one side of the street and I worked the other, concentrating especially on certain groups that are customarily responsive to the national organization. When the first ballot was taken Schroeder and Baker each had forty votes and Spangler had fifteen. On the second ballot Baker gained a bit—forty-three votes as against thirty-eight for Schroeder and fifteen for Spangler. A third ballot then might have put Baker over. I moved for a recess, and I got it.

Then I rounded up the leaders of all factions for a little sermon on party harmony. I reminded them that things were not looking too good for the Republicans at the moment and that a split over the national chairmanship would only make matters worse. I tried to get across the idea that with all our factional troubles, it was a time for compromise and that, if this was to be the case, Spangler would be the best candidate. With Baker having shown surprising strength, it was not too difficult to persuade Taft to support Spangler, especially since the Iowan was known to be a Taft man himself. And the Baker people could see that it would be very difficult to elect their man without help from Taft or Spangler or myself. So in a little while we had some party harmony. Baker and Schroeder withdrew. The national committee meeting was resumed. Baker and Schroeder, who had fought each other through two ballots, walked down the center aisle arm in arm. And Spangler, who had not intended to run at all, was elected national chairman.

"Not a victory perhaps," Willkie commented, "but it averted catastrophe."

Willkie, as I said, was looking ahead to the next election. One day in 1943 he telephoned an old University of Indiana classmate named Lloyd Balfour, who owns a jewelry factory in Attleboro and who is a friend of mine. He asked Balfour to intercede with me to manage his campaign. Balfour got in touch with me and quoted Willkie as having said, "Tell Joe that if he'll run my campaign, he can name anything in the world he wants." As Republican leader in the House I had had troubles enough overcoming the effects of one Willkie campaign. I could not risk another. Pleading the press of Congressional business, I declined Willkie's offer. He made a try for the nomination anyhow, but was knocked out in the Wisconsin primary.

Our paths crossed only occasionally after that. When the Dewey–Roosevelt campaign was under way in the fall of 1944, Willkie and I had an appointment to meet in New York in mid-October. On October 8, several days before I arrived, he died suddenly of heart trouble. By a peculiar fate Wendell Willkie and Al Smith died within four days of one another. Indeed, separated in time by only a day or so, they lay in state on opposite sides of Fifth Avenue, Smith in St. Patrick's Cathedral and Willkie in the Fifth Avenue Presbyterian Church. I remember thinking how strange it was that two of the most vivid, dramatic, gusty, individualistic, mercurial performers on the stage of twentieth-century politics in America should suddenly have made their exits almost together. Men of dissimilar background, each had brought his career to a brilliant climax only to suffer harsh defeat from which neither could make his way back to the heights. Yet each left a mark on the American canvas that will last for a long time.

Names like Al Smith and Wendell Willkie evoke memories of some of the most tumultuous political conventions ever held, and at this point I therefore digress to relate my own experiences in some of the most exciting moments in the political history of the last forty-five years.

9

THE DAY WAS JUNE 7, 1916. The place was the Coliseum in Chicago, a drab pile whose grim turreted façade had been transplanted piece by piece in 1888 from Libby Prison in Richmond, a notorious place of incarceration for captured Union officers during the Civil War.

Outside, the rain was falling in torrents and a violent wind blew umbrellas inside out. Indoors, 12,600 men and women were assembled in the huge auditorium, which was completely draped in red, white, and blue from the floor to the high arched ceiling. Behind the rostrum was a large sounding board, used in those days before the electric amplifier to carry a speaker's voice to the farthest corner of the hall. Above the board was an oil painting of Abraham Lincoln, draped with an American flag. The speaker was Charles Hilles of New York, chairman of the Republican National Committee.

"The hour of eleven o'clock having arrived and a quorum being present," he was saying, "the convention will be in order. Paraphrasing a remark made by the late President McKinley, this is a year, whatever may have been true of past years, when politics is patriotism and patriotism is politics. Therefore, the audience will please rise and sing two verses of 'America.' "

Along with the thousands of others, as a delegate from Massachusetts I rose and sang. With this effort, such as it was, I began a participation in Republican national conventions which, with only one interruption, was to continue quadrennially for forty years or more.

As the permanent chairman, Warren G. Harding, a Senator

from Ohio who looked every bit the part, addressed us in vibrant tones: "Subsistence is the first requisite of existence, and we have the higher American standard of living because of the Republican protective policy which makes of Americans the best-paid workmen in all the world." Senator Harding reminded us of the Republican split in 1912 and bade us heal our division now.

The division of which he spoke still existed in the Massachusetts delegation, as it did in many other organisms of the party. Several Massachusetts delegates were pledged to Roosevelt, though the majority, including myself, remained unpledged. When I reached Chicago my impression was that Roosevelt never could be nominated but that since his support would be invaluable in the campaign, he might by timely action be able to swing the convention to a candidate of his own choice. Many others felt the same way.

In our rooms in the Congress Hotel we waited tensely for word from the Bull Moose headquarters in the nearby Auditorium Hotel. Now and then groups of Progressives would invade the lobby of the Congress to sing "Teddy, You're a Bear," a song written by Ring Lardner. However, hours and even days passed without a word from Roosevelt.

On the first ballot most of our delegation cast a favorite-son vote for Senator Weeks. When the result was announced, Charles Evans Hughes led, with Elihu Root running second, but no one had a majority. On the second ballot most of us stayed with Weeks. Hughes gained. Boies Penrose of Pennsylvania moved for an overnight adjournment. The next day, the final day of the convention, Roosevelt suddenly announced his choice in a message that was read from the platform in high drama.

"In view of the conditions existing," the former President wrote, "I suggest the name of Senator Lodge, of Massachusetts. He is a man of the highest integrity, of the broadest national spirit and of the keenest devotion to the public good."

The consternation into which the Massachusetts delegation was thrown upon having the name of one of our most distinguished citizens, indeed a member of our own delegation, unexpectedly placed before the convention in this manner is indescribable. Frantic conferences were called on the floor right in the middle of the third ballot.

"Massachusetts," the clerk called.

"We ask that you pass Massachusetts for a moment," Samuel McCall, head of the delegation, replied.

"No, no, no," many of our delegates shouted.

"The chair will wait on Massachusetts for a moment," Harding ruled.

We huddled around McCall and argued the question of suddenly supporting Lodge. The closer we examined the situation, however, the more impractical it looked to try to put Lodge over now. The convention had gone too far. After all, he had not been a contender before, and with the third ballot in progress Hughes was already in a commanding lead. By this time most of us, myself included, had decided to vote for Hughes as the man best suited to the task of reuniting the party. Finally, McCall caught Harding's attention and announced our decision. He said:

"That [Roosevelt's message] was the first time the delegation knew of the proposed action. While we should be very glad to support the brilliant son of Massachusetts whose name has been presented by Colonel Roosevelt, yet there is no temptation presented to which the delegates from Massachusetts may yield because the action of this convention has already been clearly indicated, so I announce the vote of the delegation. Massachusetts casts one vote for Weeks, three for Roosevelt and thirty-two for Hughes."

On this third ballot Hughes was nominated. Roosevelt's intervention, delayed no doubt because he still hoped to get the nomination himself, had simply come too late to help Lodge. If he had spoken earlier perhaps the result would have been dif-

ferent. In that case I for one would have voted for Lodge, but
now it would have been a folly damaging to the party. Lodge
was destined, it seems, to be unlucky at conventions. He still
might have reached the presidency through the 1920 convention if it had not been for another stroke of misfortune or, more
exactly, of misjudgment.

The most surprising experience I had in Chicago in 1916 occurred not on the floor of the convention but in the Congress
Hotel in the middle of the night. Because we were known to be
sober fellows, another young delegate and I were assigned a
room on the corridor occupied by Lodge and other senior members of the delegation. I returned home alone one evening and
retired early, only to be awakened after an hour or so with the
light on and a buzz of voices around a table. Three men were
playing cards. Two of them, Eben S. S. Keith and Jack Bradley,
both manufacturers of railroad cars in Massachusetts, I recognized instantly. On the third man I had to do a double-take,
but I had seen his photograph so many times that I would have
known him anywhere, even in my room in the middle of the
night. He was Diamond Jim Brady. Keith and Bradley had
found my unlocked room a convenient place for a late poker
game and had hauled Brady along with them. All three apologized for waking me, but I didn't mind particularly. Brady,
although much more quietly dressed than I would have expected, was wearing in his tie a piece of jewelry that was worth
losing some sleep to behold, a stickpin in the form of an ex-
quisite American flag made of precious stones.

"That's a beautiful diamond pin you've got there," I remarked.

"I had three of them but gave two away," Brady said. "You
are welcome to have this one."

"Oh, I wouldn't think of it," I replied in astonishment.
"That's too valuable a pin for me."

This was about the extent of the conversation. After another half-hour the game broke up. Diamond Jim waved to me

as he walked out the door. I went back to sleep and never saw him again. He died the following year.

In 1920 the Republicans met in the Chicago Coliseum again. After "The Star-Spangled Banner," Albert E. Brown, director of singing for the Republican League of Massachusetts, called upon the crowd: "Now please let's give three cheers and a tiger for the greatest country on earth, the United States of America. *Hurrah! Hurrah! Hurrah!* for the United States! *Tiger!"* And we all gave three cheers and a tiger.

How long ago 1920 was! Former Senator Chauncey M. Depew of New York, was still among us, regaling the convention with recollections of talks he had had with Lincoln. And there was much excitement when a camera was brought in to take moving pictures of the convention scene. "This is one of the afflictions of being in public life, having our pictures taken for the movies," said Senator Lodge, the permanent chairman. The women's suffrage amendment had been ratified that year, and during the nominating speech for Harding there were cries of, "The girls are in politics now as well as the boys."

I was not a delegate in 1920. I had gone to the convention as a friend of the Massachusetts delegation, and I watched with fascination as Hiram Johnson, General Leonard Wood, and Governor Frank O. Lowden of Illinois fought each other inconclusively through the first four ballots. That brought us to the end of the fourth, or next-to-last, day of the convention.

The following morning I arose at six o'clock and took a walk before breakfast, as I often did in those days. Heading down Michigan Boulevard, I ran into my friend John Weeks, who was emerging from the Blackstone Hotel. Weeks had been defeated in his candidacy for reelection to the Senate in 1918, but he remained a power in the Republican Party. All that night, although I did not know it at the time, he had been in and out of certain smoke-filled rooms in the Blackstone.

"Good morning, Senator," I greeted him, "shall we be going home today?"

"That is what we have been debating all night long," he replied wearily.

Then he grew cryptic. He said that no decision had been reached, that Lowden and Johnson and Wood were to be given another chance to break the deadlock, although he conceded that any such outcome was improbable. If the deadlock was not broken, he ventured, a compromise would be sought. He said that Coolidge, whose name had been placed in nomination the preceding day by former Speaker of the House Frederick H. Gillett of Massachusetts, still had a faint chance. Coolidge's best showing had been made on the first ballot, when he received thirty-four votes. After that his strength had declined. Massachusetts, my friend told me, should keep working for him.

After Weeks had gone through all these preliminaries, however, he looked at me and said, "I think it will be Harding."

That opinion was sufficient for me. Bidding Weeks good-bye, I retraced my steps to the Congress Hotel and to the Florentine Room that had been Harding's headquarters. The only person there at this hour was a janitor, and he was taking down the Harding pictures.

"Can I have a button of the next President of the United States?" I asked him.

He gave me what was, I suppose, a sympathetic look. "Anyone who thinks this man is going to be President can have all that's left," he said, and offered me the last handful.

Several hours later the balloting was resumed. On the fifth, sixth, seventh, and eighth ballots the stalemate among Wood, Lowden, and Johnson continued, with Harding rising on the respective ballots from 78 to 89 to 105 to 133½. On the ninth ballot the handsome Senator from Ohio shot into the lead with 374½ votes. On the tenth he was nominated with 692⅕, and I was the only member of the Massachusetts group who was equipped to pin on his lapel the button of the Republican candidate for President.

The cheers of "Hurrah for the next President," "Hurrah for Ohio," "Hurrah for the Mother of Presidents!" had scarcely subsided before the convention turned to nominate a Vice-President.

The first to be nominated was Senator Irvine L. Lenroot of Wisconsin, and those aware of what was going on in Chicago knew that the Republican Senators, who were running that convention, had tapped him as Harding's running mate. They knew aright, but as events were soon to prove, they did not know everything. The truth was that the delegates, seething with resentment over senatorial domination, were on the threshold of revolt, and it needed only the nomination of a vice-presidential candidate other than Lenroot to set the rebellion loose.

Some time before the nominating speeches Wallace McCamant of the Oregon delegation came to the Massachusetts headquarters to seek out Lodge. As a result of a primary, the Oregon delegation had come to Chicago instructed to vote for Lodge. In my hearing McCamant asked Lodge's permission to place his name in nomination for Vice-President—under a President who, it was destined, was to die two years after his inauguration. Knowing very well that the Senators had tapped Lenroot, the luckless Lodge refused to allow his name to be offered.

McCamant went before the convention anyhow, but the words he spoke were not the words he had intended to speak.

"Mr. Chairman, ladies and gentlemen of the convention," he said, "when the Oregon delegation came here instructed by the people of our state to present to this convention as its candidate for the office of Vice-President a distinguished son of Massachusetts, he requested that we refrain from presenting his name. But there is another son of Massachusetts who has been much in the public eye in the last year, a man who is sterling in his Americanism and stands for all that the Republican Party holds dear. And on behalf of the Oregon delegation I name for the exalted office of Vice-President Governor Calvin Coolidge of Massachusetts."

To the amazement of those of us from Massachusetts, the convention went wild. Coolidge's weak showing in the balloting for President had been taken as a sign that it would be useless to nominate him for Vice-President. Indeed, before the nominating speeches began, W. Murray Crane, one of the Massachusetts leaders who was close to Coolidge, had passed the word, "Don't put the Governor up. He's been beaten once, and he doesn't want a second defeat." That was why Massachusetts did not nominate him. Crane was a former Senator himself, and he knew what arrangements had been made. Yet here was the convention now whooping it up for Coolidge. Of course, loud cheers can sometimes mask fundamental weakness, but these were different.

"Coolidge is going to be nominated," I told a woman seated next to me. "The cheering for the other fellows was in the galleries. It's the delegates who are cheering now."

One ballot was all that was needed. Coolidge received 674½ votes. Lenroot wasn't even close with 146½. For candidates who would appeal to voters the convention had nominated an ideal ticket in Harding and Coolidge, as the election was to prove.

For the next twenty years Republican conventions, although colorful and interesting gatherings that brought together the leading men and women and the main currents of thought in the party, were cut-and-dried affairs when it came to the nomination because of the dominance of certain candidates.

At the 1924 convention in Cleveland everyone was for the renomination of President Coolidge. I attended as secretary of the Massachusetts delegation. Thus I was in charge of all its arrangements and the arbiter of such mighty issues as whether Mrs. Edwin S. Webster, wife of a partner of Stone & Webster, the engineering firm, who was so infatuated with the maroon-colored Massachusetts badges that she wanted two or three extra, should be given them. These badges cost a couple of dollars apiece so we hadn't brought many extra ones along. However, my ruling was firm: "Her husband contributes $5000 a year to the party. For heaven's sake give them to her."

The age of radio had now overtaken the Grand Old Party, and the convention was broadcast over a nationwide hookup. John Philip Sousa was there to direct the band playing his "The Stars and Stripes Forever." "The Long, Long Trail" was still the popular song for group singing between speeches. The orators were still calling Harding a martyr to the service of his country. Copious use of verse in convention speeches was still in vogue, and Representative Theodore Elijah Burton of Ohio was applauded as he intoned:

> Oh that there might 'mongst
> Propagandists be
> A duty on hypocrisy,
> A tax on humbug
> An impost on dreary platitudes
> A stamp athwart the mouth
> Of everyone that ranted.

Addison G. Proctor, eighty-six-years old, of St. Joseph's Michigan, the last survivor of the convention that nominated Lincoln at Chicago in 1860, was one of the speakers. He told us in a fine piece of understatement: "In the nomination of Lincoln, it seems to me, we builded better than we knew."

Dr. Marion L. Burton of Michigan delivered the nominating speech for Coolidge—"This hour is fraught with solemn obligations." When the chairman asked if there were any other nominations, the air was filled with shouts of "No, no, no!" Coolidge was chosen on the first ballot, and Charles G. Dawes of Illinois was selected on the third ballot for Vice-President to complete the ticket.

Immediately after Dawes was nominated I left the hall and ran into Senator James E. Watson, of Indiana, who was getting out of a cab. Watson hoped to get the Vice-Presidential nomination himself. He was no more modest than anyone else from Indiana; modesty isn't a characteristic bred in that state.

"How's it going, Joe?" he asked.

"Well, we've just nominated the Vice-President," I informed him.

"Who?"

"Dawes."

Without another word he climbed back in the cab and drove off.

Kansas City was the site of the 1928 convention. On the way out, the Massachusetts delegates were still puzzled by Coolidge's announcement in the Black Hills the summer before that "I do not choose to run for President in 1928." At one of the stations a telegram was put aboard our train, from whom I cannot recall, asking if we would poll our delegation to ascertain how many would be willing to vote for Coolidge if he were a candidate for renomination. We did, and about thirty-four out of the thirty-nine said that they would support him. Before we reached Kansas City, however, another telegram arrived telling us to forget the whole thing. To me all this meant that a movement was on foot to capture the convention for Coolidge. However, within the several hours that elapsed between these two telegrams Pennsylvania declared for Hoover, and that insured that the Republicans would have a new standard-bearer.

Some believe that Coolidge's statement in the Black Hills was in fact a maneuver to get the nomination and that he was chagrined when he was dropped from consideration. As one who knew him well, I believe that he would have accepted renomination if it had been offered. But I do not believe that he hoped for it or that he was disappointed when he did not get it.

In any event, we rolled on across the prairies happily unaware of the catastrophe for the Republican Party that lay just over the horizon, scarcely a year away. It was 1928. Everything was fine. Depression was the last word in our vocabulary as we entered Convention Hall in Kansas City. Madame Schumann-Heink sang "The Star-Spangled Banner." Nicholas Murray Butler was in his heyday as a delegate from New York. Resonantly he introduced a resolution to amend the platform so as to repeal the Eighteenth Amendment and return the problem of liquor control to the states, but unfortunately for the party it was shouted down.

Secretary of Commerce Herbert Clark Hoover—"America's greatest administrator in human welfare," in the words of the nominating speech—had the nomination clinched before the first delegate arrived in Kansas City. Frank Lowden, with 74 votes, was the closest rival as Hoover galloped to victory on the first ballot with 837. The nomination for Vice-President, however, was a more complicated business.

Powerful leaders of the party wanted the second place on the ticket to go to a Massachusetts man, specifically to former Governor Channing Cox, who was endowed with a superb mind and a persuasive voice and was still young. Senator David A. Reed of Pennsylvania and others approached our delegation. They assured us that they could deliver 460 votes for Cox and asked if we could produce 60 more, which to all intents and purposes would have put him over, 545 being sufficient for the nomination.

This proposal, however, handed us a practically insoluble problem, because Governor Alvan T. Fuller took the understandable position that if any citizen of Massachusetts was going to be supported by the state's delegation it was he and not his predecessor. Yet to the liberals, like Hiram Johnson and Borah, Fuller was repugnant because the year before he had declined, upon the advice of a learned committee, to pardon Sacco and Vanzetti. In view of the distinguished character of this committee, which consisted of President Lowell of Harvard, President Stratton of the Massachusetts Institute of Technology, and Judge Robert Grant, I do not see how the Governor could have followed a different course.

With Cox thus blocked and Fuller unacceptable, the leaders began turning to Senator Charles Curtis of Kansas. If they could not get a man who could deliver Massachusetts to the Republicans, they at least wanted someone who was likely to carry the doubtful state of Oklahoma. And they believed, cor-

rectly, as events were to demonstrate, that Curtis was such a
man because he was one eighth Indian, being a direct descend-
ant on his mother's side of two famous chiefs—White Plume,
chief of the Kansas Tribe, and Pawhuska, chief of the Osage
Tribe. The streets of Kansas City already were clattering to
the hoofs of hundreds of mounted "cowboys" hired by the
Curtis forces to demonstrate for him when his name was placed
in nomination. One of the seconding speeches was delivered by
his daughter, Mrs. Leona Curtis Knight, a delegate from Rhode
Island. Curtis was nominated on the first ballot and became
Vice-President under Hoover on March 4, 1929.

The 1932 convention in Chicago, which renominated President
Hoover, I did not attend because with Congress remaining in
session my duties kept me in Washington. However, I was
back on the scene in Cleveland in 1936, this time as not only
a delegate-at-large from Massachusetts but as Governor Landon's floor manager.

The New Deal was the consuming issue. Never—before or
since—have I seen a political gathering so completely absorbed
by one subject as that convention was by Franklin Roosevelt,
his associates, and his projects. In the very first address of
the convention, that of Senator Frederick Steiwer of Oregon,
who was temporary chairman, the delegates were put on notice
that "Our purpose here today is not only to adopt a Republican
platform and to nominate a Republican President—a deeper
and thoroughly American purpose is to start the drive to put
an American deal into the place now usurped by a self-styled
'New Deal.' "

We scorched the walls of that building with our pronounce-
ments upon the New Deal: "Re-man the citadels of liberty"
. . . "monstrous, reckless propaganda machine" . . . "economic freedom" . . . "Siamese twins of bureaucracy" . . .
"tyranny" . . . "un-American" . . . "coddles agitators" . . .
"lavish spending" . . . "unconstitutional dictatorship" . . .
"arrogant individualism of Franklin Delano Roosevelt" . . .

"New Deal spoilers and wasters" . . . "never known the necessity of meeting a payroll" . . . "Thou Shalt Not Steal" . . . "socialistic experiments" . . . "Aubrey Williams" . . . "Tugwell" . . . "Wallace" . . . "Ickes" . . . "plowed under the land of plenty" . . . "boondoggled" . . . "Reciprocal Trade Agreements Act" . . . "N.R.A." . . . "A.A.A." . . . "theory of the old world" . . . "planned economy" . . . "economic blunders" . . . "New Deal pump-primers" . . . "America is in peril" . . . "Valley Forge."

The last was what we were to remember and was not in any sense meant to convey what Roosevelt personified.

A demonstration for Landon burst into the aisles before John D. M. Hamilton, who was to be the new Republican National Chairman, was halfway through his nominating speech. The band mournfully played "Three Long Years," and marchers sporting sunflowers carried banners reading UP WITH ALF— DOWN WITH THE ALPHABET . . . LAND LANDON WITH A LAND- SLIDE . . . THE COOLIDGE OF THE WEST—THAT'S WHY WE LOVE HIM.

Landon was the logical candidate for several reasons. At that particular time Republican strength was centered in the East. We were hopeful at least of a big vote in New England, New York, and Pennsylvania. Yet we had no outstanding candidate in the East. Landon's record as governor of Kansas was excellent. And it looked as though, if we were to have any chance at all, it would come through nominating a man who might recapture the West and add it to whatever votes we could garner in the eastern states. In the Massachusetts primary that spring I supported Landon, an easy winner as it turned out. By that time I was a recognized Republican leader in Congress, and Hamilton, who was managing Landon's campaign, asked me to take the job of floor leader at the convention. It proved to be a fairly simple one. On the first ballot Borah got nineteen votes; Landon got the remaining 984 and the nomination.

That night Hamilton, former Senator Hiram Bingham, of Connecticut, and a dozen other Republican leaders from all parts of the country, including myself, met in the Hotel Hollenden to consider a candidate for Vice-President. Two names soon predominated—Frank Knox, publisher of the Chicago *Daily News,* who wanted the nomination, and Senator Arthur H. Vandenberg of Michigan, whose wishes were more in doubt. Vandenberg was not so well known then as he was to become after the war. As far as Massachusetts was concerned, I said, it made little difference which of the two was chosen. We took a vote and it went in Vandenberg's favor, eight to seven.

One of the group was sent to notify him. He searched for him everywhere without success and was informed finally that Vandenberg had retired. However, no amount of knocking on his door could evoke an answer. When our emissary returned with the word that he had been unable to rouse the Senator, interest in Vandenberg just seemed to evaporate. We got in touch with Knox, and his answer was *yes*.

An hour before the convention the next morning some of the Vandenberg people came to us and said that despite any statements which the Senator may have made to the contrary, he would accept the nomination. This was one more case of being too late in making a decision in a convention. Knox had been given the nod. Vandenberg sent a letter to the convention saying that he did not wish his name to be considered, and Knox was nominated unanimously on the first ballot.

A delegate cried

> Off the rocks
> With Landon and Knox

and we set out on the campaign, soon to be encouraged if not convinced by the *Literary Digest* poll. It was not our year, 1936. No Republican candidate would have had a chance against Roosevelt.

Four years later the outlook would be much more hopeful, and for me 1940 was also the beginning of a new role in Republican National Conventions, the role of permanent chairman, the man who wields the gavel, the boss—though not always the absolute boss.

10

THE CONVENTION that opened in Philadelphia on June 24, 1940, was one of the most momentous and, as events were to prove, one of the wildest in the history of the Republican Party.

Nazi troops were in Paris. Italy had entered the war against the Allies. The British Army was a shambles after Dunkerque. While Europe was falling apart under the blows of Germany, the United States was still struggling with the economic and social convulsions of the 1930s. The pressure of these events had cut deep fissures through our party. There were passionate differences of opinion as to whether Republicans should still try to repudiate the New Deal altogether or adjust their philosophy to some of the changes that had been forced upon us since 1933. Even deeper was the division of opinion about American interference in the course of events in Europe. In the turmoil that engulfed Philadelphia no one could foresee how these chasms were to be bridged, let alone closed.

Long before I reached the scene I found myself in the whirlpool of personal rivalries. Early in June, after I had been selected for permanent chairman, Sam Pryor and Sinclair Weeks called on me in Washington. They asked if I would decline the chairmanship and deliver the nominating speech for Wendell Willkie. They argued that he was the only Republican who had a chance of defeating Roosevelt. I could not go along with their proposal or with their argument.

"It wouldn't be fair to the National Committee for me to run out on the chairmanship on the eve of the convention," I told them. "And furthermore I don't think your man Willkie has a chance."

I knew Willkie only casually at this time. I had seen him around the Capitol at hearings affecting the electric utilities when he was president of the Commonwealth & Southern Corporation, and I had chatted with him at a political reception. But the thought that he might some day be the Republican nominee for President never really crossed my mind.

A few days after I had turned down Pryor and Weeks, Charles Halleck dropped by. He had been named as a delegate from Indiana. Since my name was being mentioned for the nomination and since I was his leader in the House, he offered to support me at Philadelphia. I assured him that I was not a candidate. Later he informed me that he had been invited to nominate Willkie, who not only was a fellow Hoosier but a fellow alumnus of the University of Indiana. He wanted to deliver the nominating speech for Willkie if I was not going to run.

"If I were you, Charlie, I'd do it," I advised him. "You're a young fellow looking for a place in the sun. It won't hurt you any. In fact it will give you a lot of prestige. Of course, your man isn't going to be nominated."

"What I first said to you about backing you goes," he replied.

"Oh, I'm not a candidate," I said and sent him off to prepare his speech for Willkie.

In this period a long-distance call came from Landon. He told me that Roosevelt had offered him the post of Secretary of War and that he was pondering the matter. I advised him not to accept. He was after all the titular head of the Republican Party, and I felt that it would be damaging to the party for him to enter Roosevelt's Cabinet at a time when we were coming up to a convention and a campaign. Furthermore I pointed out that he still had many years ahead of him, and that acceptance of such an appointment by a Democratic President now could jeopardize his whole future in the Republican Party.

In the end he did not accept, but three days before the convention Roosevelt threw the Republicans into confusion by nominating Stimson, who had been Secretary of War under

My mother cherished this photo of me as a school cadet in 1898.

The North Attleboro Police and Reporter's baseball team, 1904. You will find me in the front row, extreme left. I was a pretty fair shortstop; batted around .350. All my life baseball has been one of my great pleasures.

Associated Press

I make the rounds of my congressional district, sounding out my constituents. It's my regular summer job.

I enjoy having members of the press call upon me.

World Wide Photos

I'll always remember 1940 and Wendell Willkie. This was the first of n...five roles as permanent chairman of the Republican National Conventio... The convention turned into one of the wildest in the history of the part... Willkie would have been a good President.

Life photo by ROBERT W. KELLEY

Election night has never lost its excitement for me. My friends in North Attleboro join me in awaiting voting returns at the Evening Chronicle.

United Press International

President Roosevelt and I were good friends. Like myself, he was a practical politician, and we understood each other well. I often sat alone with him in his study in the White House, and much good-natured banter passed between us.

The House was home to me for thirty-five years. I am sworn in as Speaker in the Eightieth Congress, 1947, by Congressman Harold Knudsen of Minnesota.

This editorial cartoon by the late C. K. Berryman of the Washington Sunday Star *appeared during my first term as Speaker of the House, in 1947, after President Truman proposed that the Speaker be first in line of succession to the Presidency, should there be no President or Vice-president.*

In 1944, the first of my two appearances with Thomas E. Dewey before Republican national conventions. Four years later when Dewey campaigned through North Attleboro, my mother admonished him — with more wisdom than any of us realized at the time — "Don't take it so easy."

It gave me deep personal pleasure to pin a gold medal on former President Herbert Hoover at the 1956 convention for his service to the party. Over the years, whenever I turned to Hoover for advice, he gave me reassuring words and wise counsel.

Some members of my party resent my long and treasured friendship with Sam Rayburn, a Democrat from Texas. Mr. Sam and I often changed places in our game of musical chairs over the Speakership.

How fleeting is the interval that President Eisenhower had to accomplish his objectives. As in any great passage of human affairs, one looks back on this span of time with mixed emotions.

Life photo by HANK WALKER

En route to President Eisenhower's inauguration in 1953 with President Truman and Senator Styles Bridges of New Hampshire.

Associated Press

I hold General Douglas MacArthur's letter to me about our situation in Korea, 1951, that roused a storm in the Truman administration. I was appalled that I contributed to a chain of circumstances that deprived the United States of the services of its greatest general.

January 6, 1959. After twenty years as floor leader of the House, in which no vote had ever been cast against me for reelection, I am unexpectedly overthrown by Charles Halleck by a vote of 74-70. Halleck escorts me out of the caucus.

William Howard Taft and Secretary of State under Hoover, as Secretary of War and Knox as Secretary of the Navy.

This was a skillful move on Roosevelt's part and masterfully timed. It put us at a disadvantage in several respects, not the least important of which was that it aligned two eminent Republicans with war measures which so many of their fellows who were gathering in Philadelphia staunchly opposed. Some of these Republicans were ready to read Simpson and Knox out of the party, but I for one would have none of it. This would have turned disadvantage into disaster. The party was big enough, I said, to withstand the appointment of two of its leaders to the Cabinet of an opposition President under the circumstances. And since the stroke had been accomplished, I argued that our public position ought to be one of treating it as a compliment that Roosevelt should have had to turn to the Republican Party for his Secretary of War and Secretary of Navy.

I arrived in Philadelphia quite set in the opinion that Willkie, despite his barrage of publicity, was not a serious contender. He had practically no organization, not even a floor leader. Most of the other professionals shared my view. With the situation among the rival candidates in such a state of flux as it was, we had no idea whom the lightning would strike, but we felt that, barring a miracle, it would not be Willkie.

Certainly, my opinion was not modified by Halleck's nominating speech, which barely skirted disaster. To begin with the delegations for Dewey, Taft, and Vandenberg were in no mood to hear Willkie's name put into nomination, and Halleck, who was only thirty-nine, sharpened their tempers with a manner that was too brash. A blast of hostile reaction almost blew him off the platform. As the crescendo of boos rose from the floor I stepped forward to the rostrum and, with my arm on his shoulder, quieted the crowd in order to give him a fair hearing. "Get in there and finish it," I whispered, and somehow he did.

This was the least of a hundred crises I had to deal with at that convention. Every hour brought a new one. On the second night R. B. Creager, Taft's floor leader, who was head of the Texas delegation, came storming up to the platform. It was an open scandal that several hundred counterfeit tickets had been printed and given to a Willkie claque who filled the best seats in the gallery to the exclusion of holders of *bona fide* tickets. Creager wanted to be recognized to denounce the Willkie people for these tickets.

At this point I could not see how anything but more trouble could be accomplished by such an attack. We had no evidence in hand. No one knew for sure where the tickets had come from. We weren't even sure that we could distinguish the counterfeit tickets from the legitimate ones, so skillfully were the former printed.

"You won't be doing the party any good," I pleaded with Creager. "We are in a pretty weak position in the country as it is. Let's not make it worse. Sleep on it overnight, and if you still want to have your say, I'll recognize you tomorrow." He agreed. By morning he had dropped the idea.

The night before the balloting began I returned to my room in the Benjamin Franklin Hotel as soon as I could after adjournment and went to bed. I was nearly asleep when a knock came on the door. There was no one I wanted to talk to, and, determined to get some sleep, I let my visitor rap until he finally wearied and walked away. The next morning, thinking no more of it, I ran into Willkie.

"I came up to your room after adjournment to see you last night, Joe," he told me.

He did not say why, but I supposed that he had made a courtesy call to try to get on the good side of me. My only comment to him was, "You got there beyond my working hours, Wendell."

Dewey carried the first ballot but without enough votes to come close to the nomination. Taft ran second. Willkie was third. Willkie telegrams were now streaming into Convention

Hall by the thousands. I have never seen anything like this flood, which took me, for one, by surprise. I ordered a second ballot, but the outcome was the same. However, Dewey's strength had waned and Willkie's waxed. Not even the professionals could contrive to misread the lesson before us now. Neither Dewey, Taft, Vandenberg, nor any other candidate beside Willkie had caught fire. Thus the delegates, as they usually do in such circumstances, were starting to drift toward someone who looked as though he might really catch fire. And Willkie was becoming more inflammable by the moment. The galleries already were ablaze for him. In all my experience I have never seen a convention so tense. Certainly no other that I have presided over has been so hard to keep in hand.

"We want Willkie! We want Willkie! We want Willkie!"

It was maddening to try to communicate with delegations on the floor in this din.

"Mr. Chairman," I heard the head of the New Hampshire delegation shouting, "I call the attention of the chair to the fact that many people are in the aisles and buttonholing delegates who have no right to be on the floor of the convention."

I hammered the gavel until I must have looked more like a blacksmith than my father. "I regret to have to admonish those in the galleries to be quiet," I warned, "and to remind them that they are the guests of this convention and must conduct themselves accordingly."

"Guests, hell," one of them shouted back at me. "We *are* the convention."

After the second ballot Landon came up and talked to me as a personal friend about the course Kansas should pursue. I said that Kansas was a progressive state and that he ought to proceed in that light. I pointed out that Dewey was considered more progressive than Taft and that the Kansas delegation might get a better reaction at home, therefore, by supporting Dewey. Kansas had been casting a favorite-son vote for Senator Capper. But now on the third ballot it broke from him and gave eleven of his votes to Dewey. When the roll call was finished, Dewey still clung to a weak lead, but Willkie had moved into second place ahead of Taft.

Now *"We want Willkie"* was beating down on me in waves. With the start of the fourth ballot the disorder was so great that at times my gavel instead of ringing out commandingly merely blended in with other sounds like a kettledrum in a symphony orchestra. The aisles swarmed with politicians and reporters. States were waving their standards, each of which was surmounted with a gray elephant carrying an American flag in his curled-up trunk. Over the whole hall spread a haze of colors from the flags of the nations and the forty-eight states. The scene was a blend of noise and color, and the noise became almost overpowering when, on this fourth ballot, Willkie finally went into the lead with 306 votes to 254 for Taft and 250 for Dewey. A total of 501 was needed for the nomination.

Landon now consulted me again. The Willkie people had been working hard on him, and he was not unfriendly to their candidate. The Willkie camp knew that if Kansas, one of the great states of the Midwest, switched, it would have powerful psychological impact. I told Landon that Willkie appeared to be well on the way to victory and that Landon ought to do what was best for his state.

"The convention will be in order," I called. "No candidate having received a majority of votes of the convention and, therefore, no nomination of a candidate for the Presidency having been made, the secretary will call the roll of the states for the fifth ballot."

When Kansas was reached, it announced, "Mr. Chairman, Kansas casts her eighteen votes for Wendell Willkie." This set off the greatest tumult yet, and from now on we were to proceed in bedlam. With the announcement of each delegation's vote wild cheering swept the hall, and state by state the excitement and acrimony increased until I was desperate for some way of relieving the unbearable tension. At last a delegate from North Dakota offered me a chance.

"North Dakota," he intoned, "casts four votes for Senator Taft and four votes for Vendell Villkie."

"For who?" I demanded.

"For Vendell Villkie," he called.

"Spell it," I said. His reply was drowned in the loudest and most welcome laughter I have ever heard.

On the fifth ballot Willkie pulled into a long lead with a total of 429 votes, and the situation of the other candidates was desperate. The anti-Willkie forces now sought an overnight adjournment to give them a chance to select a compromise candidate around whom all of them could rally to defeat Willkie. In the last frantic effort from the Taft camp, Bricker came rushing up on the platform appealing to me to entertain a motion to adjourn.

"I can't do that," I said. "In announcing the vote at the end of the last ballot, I asked the convention to prepare for the sixth ballot. A motion to adjourn would be out of order."

The anti-Willkie people were in anguish. I told Bricker that if he still wished to move for adjournment after the sixth ballot, I would recognize him for that purpose. In the great milling of men on the platform, Landon got my ear. He believed that I was the one around whom an effective stop-Willkie drive could be organized. While he agreed with the propriety of my ruling, he inquired whether I realized where the nomination might go if I would permit an adjournment. I said I did.

"Unquestionably," Landon said, "you would be nominated. You are the talk of the convention because of the fair way in which you have handled it. There is no one else who could be considered."

"But the rules are clear," I said. "We have to go on. Anyway I don't know whether the nomination would do me any good, because under the circumstances I would be the choice of smoke-filled rooms. It would take me two months to get over that stigma. By that time the campaign would be lost."

"Nothing could have been fairer than [Martin's] rulings as permanent chairman," Gould Lincoln, the respected political columnist for the Washington *Evening Star,* wrote afterward. "He was not believed to be particularly enamored of the candidacy of Mr. Willkie, but his refusal to entertain a motion to recess the convention the night the nomination was made probably saved the bacon for Mr. Willkie."

The sixth ballot was the climax.

"Alabama."

"We want Willkie!"

"Alabama casts her thirteen votes as follows: For Taft seven; for Willkie six."

"We want Willkie!"

"Well, if you'll be quiet long enough," I shouted to the galleries, "maybe you'll get him."

When Michigan was reached, Governor Luren D. Dickinson got my attention. "Mr. Chairman," he called, "Mr. Lawrence wishes to go to the platform to announce Michigan's vote." The Willkie people were howling. Through five ballots Michigan had stayed with Vandenberg. Now Howard C. Lawrence, the Senator's floor manager, told the convention: "Senator Vandenberg has authorized me to release the Michigan delegation, and subject to that release the Michigan delegation has taken a poll. The chairman of the delegation has asked me to announce the result of that poll, as follows: For Hoover, one; Taft, two; Willkie, thirty-five." This was decisive.

Willkie votes were coming now in great chunks. After Pennsylvania had thrown its entire seventy-two votes to him for the first time, Bricker was on his feet again signaling me. I recognized him.

"Mr. Chairman," he said, "Ohio moves that the nomination of Wendell Willkie for President be made unanimous."

The roof came down on me, and I had a terrible time putting it back up again.

"The convention will be in order," I yelled. "The Chair is unable to recognize Governor Bricker of Ohio for that motion at this time. He will recognize Governor Bricker to change the vote of Ohio from 52 for Taft to 52 for Willkie, and following

the conclusion of the roll call the Chair will recognize Governor
Bricker to make the motion he has just suggested. The clerk
will resume the roll call."

It was downhill for Willkie all the rest of the way. The
nomination by a Republican National Convention of a figure
who had been a Democrat most of his life and had never held
public office has often been called a miracle. In retrospect, it
appears so logical under the circumstances that it is surprising
that more of us did not anticipate the outcome. Willkie had
marched into a vacuum, a powerfully supported man against
rivals with unseen weaknesses. None of the other contenders
had anything resembling the impetus that Willkie had behind
him. Vandenberg possessed no national following in those days.
Taft had been a Senator for a mere eighteen months. Dewey
was still only the young District Attorney of New York County
and was still slightly tinged with isolationism. Hoover would
have welcomed the nomination, but events did not shape the
course that way.

A new but solid national reputation had been built under
Willkie. He was glamorous. He was good-looking and an interesting speaker. He appealed to the independents. Much of
the business community was with him, and his cause was sung
by powerful publishers like Henry R. Luce, the Cowles
brothers, Roy Howard, and the Reids. Moreover the full extent
of Willkie's views on the war—opinions which before long
would repel many who had jumped on his band wagon in
Philadelphia—were not too widely understood by Republicans,
nor were they to be for nearly a year.

Only a few hours after he had been nominated Willkie, who
was also staying at the Benjamin Franklin, asked me to come
to his room to discuss the Vice-Presidential nomination. He
had made a commitment on the second place to Governor
Raymond E. Baldwin of Connecticut. Thus Connecticut was
the only state that gave Willkie its unanimous vote on every
ballot. However, immediately after Willkie was chosen, as I
understand it, many of his most powerful backers insisted

that, since he made his home in New York, he select a west-
erner for Vice-President to give the ticket greater national
strength. Among those mentioned was Senator McNary.

Sam Pryor, who was one of Willkie's managers, suggested
that he check the idea with me and that, if Willkie then finally
agreed to it, he ask me to approach McNary for him. When
I arrived in his room at sunrise, Willkie asked me about
McNary. The Senator struck me as an excellent choice.

"McNary would balance the ticket," I told Willkie. "While
you come from Indiana, you live in New York, and you're
identified with the East because of your connection with Commonwealth & Southern. McNary comes from the Far West.
You are known as a utilities man; McNary has sided with the
public power boys. You're supposed to represent big business
interests; McNary was the sponsor of the McNary–Haugen
farm bill. You aren't supposed to know much about the legislative process; McNary is a master of it. I think you'd make
a perfect team."

Willkie brought up certain personal reservations, but I satisfied him on these.

"Do you think he'd take it?" Willkie asked.

"I don't know," I said.

"Call him up," he urged.

McNary was in Washington at the time, and I said to him
on the telephone, "Charlie, we may have a job for you." When
I told him what it was, he exclaimed, "Hell, no, I wouldn't run
with Willkie." McNary had opposed Willkie's nomination from
the start. The two men were at odds not only on the public
power issue but on foreign policy as well.

"You have got to consider the Republican Party," I said.
"You are in a position to do the party a great service. Your
presence on the ticket would give it strength. We'd have a
better chance to win."

This is the appeal that politicians cannot reject, and in the
end he consented and was nominated with negligible opposition.
Willkie brought the momentous convention to a close with a

speech calling for a "great crusade," a term that has come into vogue with Republican candidates.

After the furor of 1940 my gavel arm got a good rest at the convention of 1944. The Republicans met in Chicago only three weeks after D-Day. The battle of Normandy subdued our conflicts at home. We took our cracks at New Deal "collectivism" and Roosevelt "court-packing," but they did not crackle the way they used to before the real guns were firing. The Republican platform reflected the transformation that war had wrought on our party. "We favor responsible participation by the United States in postwar cooperative organization among sovereign nations. . . ." Typical of the times, the typing of the platform was delayed by the manpower shortage. And when the Philippine Islands were reached on the roll call for the presidential nomination, John W. Haussermann, the "gold king" of Manila, said: "It is indeed with the deepest regret I have to announce that owing to the fact that the Japs are in control of the Philippines, the Republicans of those islands were unable to elect delegates to this convention."

In the years following the previous convention Governor Bricker of Ohio (he did not become a Senator until 1947) and Dewey, who had been elected governor of New York in 1942, emerged as the leading contenders for the 1944 nomination. Taft, having had his chance in 1940, stood aside to let his fellow Ohioan try his hand. By the time the convention met, however, Dewey was obviously so much the stronger that Bricker asked his followers to vote for the governor of New York. Although sharp differences of outlook existed between the two men, Dewey then accepted Bricker as his running mate for the sake of harmony. I supported Bricker strongly for the vice-presidential nomination. I felt that he deserved recognition for his rugged opposition to the Democrats. With his white hair he was a fine-looking man and had the appearance of a powerful candidate. Furthermore, historical association made it appealing to have an Ohioan on the Republican ticket.

About the only skullduggery in which I participated that year was teaming up with Vandenberg to block a nonsensical attempt by a few Wisconsin delegates to nominate General Douglas MacArthur for President. Thereupon, out of spite, one of them refused to make the nomination of Dewey unanimous.

Vandenberg, who was then a strong MacArthur booster, learned of their intention in advance. Knowing that I was very sympathetic to the general, he talked the matter over with me. We agreed that it would be poor judgment to put up MacArthur, who was fighting a war thousands of miles away. It would have been humiliating to him to have his name tossed into a convention that had made up its mind to nominate Dewey. Try as he would, however, Vandenberg could not dissuade Dr. John P. Koehler, of Wisconsin, from his decision to deliver a long nominating speech for MacArthur, so we had to resort to a little dipsy-doodle. When Koehler reached the stairs leading to the platform, Vandenberg was waiting on the first step to argue with him at some length. He engaged him just long enough for me to give Wisconsin the barest time I decently could on the roll call. By the time Koehler got past Vandenberg, Wyoming had been called, and I ruled him out of order.

Outraged, one of Wisconsin's MacArthur delegates, a dairy farmer from Beloit named Grant A. Ritter, refused to vote for Dewey. For all time, therefore, the record of that roll call will read: Dewey 1056; MacArthur 1.

Although Dewey made better speeches in the ensuing campaign than he was to make in his second try four years later, the 1944 campaign was drab. We never seemed to get going, and we never at any time looked as if we would win. We were simply unable to conquer Roosevelt in his role as a war leader.

In what was now becoming a long span of attendance at Republican National Conventions I already had witnessed the innovation of the loudspeaker, the motion picture, and the radio. Now in 1948, we moved into still another age, that of the televised convention, in which—frighteningly, to say the least—we were conducting our affairs in the living room of the U.S.A. The 1948 convention seemed to be set in a new age in other respects too. In the old days we used to pass from one convention to the next without hearing in the new convention a word that would have been unfamiliar four years previously. But what a different vocabulary was employed in Philadelphia in 1948—Yalta, Iron Curtain, atomic energy! When had a political convention ever listened to such esoteric language?

And, if my ears heard aright, there was another distinctive note in 1948, a strain of bitterness and deep acrimony that was radically different from some of the shenanigans of other years. The long tenure of the Democratic Party had poisoned the air we Republicans breathed. Fear of Communist penetration of the government was an ugly new phenomenon. Suspicion of the State Department was rife. We were disturbed and bewildered by the new power of the Soviet Union. President Truman's intense partisanship stung us. We were irritated by high taxes, the public debt, huge foreign aid expenditures, and rankled by the many issues that had led to political warfare between Truman and the Republican majority of the Eightieth Congress.

One great solace was our complete confidence. At every convention, Republican or Democratic, that I have ever attended or read about or listened to on a broadcast, someone has invariably said, "Mr. Chairman, we are assembled in this great city to nominate the next President of the United States." What was unique about Philadelphia in 1948 was that everyone from the permanent chairman to the man who fed hay to an elephant we had installed in the basement believed this with all his heart when he heard it, as hear it we did.

"Let us waste no time measuring the unfortunate man in the White House against our specifications," Mrs. Clare Boothe Luce of Connecticut told the convention. "Mr. Truman's time is short; his situation is hopeless. Frankly, he is a gone goose."

For the third time since 1940 I had come to the convention well advertised as a dark horse candidate for President, one to whom the delegates would be likely to turn in case of a deadlock. Expressed in terms of my own ambition, I have regarded the presidency about the same way that a man who joins the Fire Department regards the red car in front of the firehouse: it would be nice to be chief. Beyond that I have never been bitten by the presidential bug, nor have I ever plotted for the nomination. In 1948 I was the Speaker of the House of Representatives. That office was the greatest ambition of my life. I wanted nothing higher. Of course, I arrived at the convention not unaware that as Speaker I might, under certain circumstances, be considered for the nomination.

At Philadelphia my brother, Edward Everett Martin, whose name, it will be recalled, I had something to do with, was my right-hand man, as he has been at all conventions over which I have presided. Before the convention opened, H. J. Porter, the Republican National Committeeman from Texas, called on Ed and said that my friend H. Roy Cullen, the Houston oil millionaire, was determined to back me for the nomination and had bade Porter do whatever needed to be done to set my candidacy in motion. My brother stated my position—that I was not a candidate, but that I would accept the nomination in the event of a deadlock. He also explained that I did not believe that the convention would be deadlocked and that I would do nothing to cause a deadlock. Porter was insistent, however. He not only took an option on a ballroom to be used as a headquarters if I became a serious contender, but as a sort of interim headquarters he also rented the rooms of the Harvard Club in the Bellevue-Stratford Hotel and kept them so full of turkey sandwiches that one could hardly move about.

The crucial fight was between Taft and Dewey. Taft, a brilliant and by now famous Senator, had high hopes of being nominated. I knew that from my conversations with him. He felt that Dewey had had his chance in 1944 and that it was his own turn now. Dewey, on the other hand, was leading the pack again simply because of the blunder of Harold E. Stassen, who, having defeated him in several primaries, blew his advantage to pieces by engaging the New York governor in a nationally broadcast debate in the Oregon primary and bungling his role in that debate beyond belief. Almost heedless of the difficult legal problems involved, Stassen plunged into advocating the outlawing of the Communist Party. Dewey in a fine display of his skill in the law, demolished his opponent's case with a sweep that seemed to knock Stassen clear off the pedestal of his earlier victories.

Soon after I had settled in my suite at the Drake Hotel in Philadelphia, Representative John Vorys of Ohio called and asked if I would see Taft, which I was glad to do. The Senator entered, talking 200 words a minute even before he sat down. The stop-Dewey forces, he told me, had at least 600 votes, well over a majority. After these had blocked Dewey, as he foresaw it, the convention would turn to Taft. Although I did not say so, I doubted that the stop-Dewey votes totaled as much as 600 then, yet I believed—as I still do—that Dewey could have been stopped. The trouble was that the men who collectively could have stopped him—Taft, Warren, Stassen, Vandenberg, to name four—persisted, each in his own optimistic fashion, in seeking the nomination for himself.

Hence no anti-Dewey coalition was ever formed, although there was a moment in the convention immediately after the second ballot when this might have happened if the Dewey men had not been as smart as they were. One of the lessons I have learned over the years is that New York delegations to the conventions are smart.

On the first ballot Dewey got 434 votes, Taft 224, Stassen 157, Vandenberg 62, and so on. On the second ballot, with 547 needed for the nomination, Dewey had 515, Taft 274, Stassen 149, Vandenberg 62, and so forth.

Dewey was still thirty-two votes away, but he had gained. He had momentum. It was to his interest to move into a third roll call without delay, and the Dewey people wanted to go on, even though the dinner hour was approaching. The anti-Dewey forces wanted a recess. Many felt that if Taft and Stassen could get together in the interval, they could turn the tide. Accordingly, a motion was made to recess until 7:30 P.M. I put it to a voice vote. The ayes seemed to have it, but it was very close. New York could have tried to force a roll call on the question. Instead William G. Bleakley, the head of the delegation, rose and said that New York had no objection to a recess.

Of course the New Yorkers did not want a recess, but they were too astute to put the issue to a test, because if they lost, as it appeared that they would, it would have been a tactical defeat for Dewey at a critical moment. The psychological effect could have been disastrous.

Dewey thereby avoided the kind of pitfall that Taft was to tumble into four years later in Chicago when he engaged in a contest with Eisenhower for delegates from Louisiana, Texas, and Georgia. Taft was defeated on this issue in the opening skirmishes of the convention, and he never recovered from the blow. If, like Dewey, he had avoided the fight, he not only would have spared himself the melodramatic defeat but he would have denied the Eisenhower forces the "fair play" issue upon which they capitalized so effectively in the convention.

The anti-Dewey forces got their recess, therefore, but they could not turn the tide. When the convention resumed in the evening and "The Battle Hymn of the Republic" had been sung, Bricker asked for the floor, and I recognized him.

"I have a statement," he said, "which I have been authorized to present to this convention on behalf of Senator Taft. These are his words as he dictated them to me: 'A careful analysis of the situation shows that a majority of the delegates will support Governor Dewey on the third ballot. I therefore release my delegates and ask them to vote for Governor Dewey with all of their force and enthusiasm. . . .'" One after another the other contenders followed suit. The vote for Dewey was unanimous.

Leaving the hall that evening I ran into Representative Forest A. Harness, of Indiana, who greeted me with, "Isn't it great for Charlie!" "Charlie who?" I asked. "Halleck," he said. "Why, what's doing with him?" I inquired. "He's getting the vice-presidential nomination," Harness gloated. "Is that so?" I commented. "Yes, it's been promised to him," Harness assured me. "I doubt that it will materialize," I said. I was certain that neither in his forward manner nor in his Midwestern outlook was Halleck a man who would appeal to Dewey as a running mate.

"If they don't give it to him," Harness threatened, "there's going to be hell to pay in Indiana."

"I'm afraid, Forest, there's going to be hell to pay in Indiana," I said.

Later Herbert Brownell, who was Dewey's manager, came to me and told me that the Dewey people had held a meeting and had finally narrowed the choice for Vice-President to three names. They were written on a piece of paper, which he showed me: Senator Bricker, Governor Dwight H. Green of Illinois, and Governor Earl Warren of California.

"What do you think?" Brownell asked.

"In my judgment Warren would be your best bet," I replied. "Dewey and Bricker ran together in Forty-four, and you would want at least one new face on the ticket this year. With Green you would run into a lot of trouble with Colonel McCormick—he'd kick up a fuss for sure. [The publisher of the Chicago *Tribune* and the Governor were political enemies.] Besides, Warren should bring you California."

One of my closest associates had attended the meeting at which the list was drawn, and the story he told me about it after my talk with Brownell was this:

When the names of the prospective vice-presidential candidates were being raised, someone said, "Well, how about

Charlie?" One of Dewey's people, it appears, did promise him
the vice-presidential nomination in return for Indiana's support
of Dewey for the presidential nomination. Vandenberg rose up
and demanded, "Charlie who?" "Charlie Halleck." "Oh, my
God!" Vandenberg fairly roared. That was the end of Halleck
in 1948. Later I heard that he went around asking, "Did Joe
Martin knock me off?"

In June 1952, a month before our next convention opened in
Chicago, I called on General MacArthur, a dedicated Republican, at his suite in the Waldorf Towers in New York and
discussed the political situation with him. MacArthur, who had
been relieved of his command in the Far East fifteen months
earlier by President Truman, was now my personal choice for
President. The room he used as his office was furnished with
pieces from the Orient. The two of us sat on bamboo chairs.
The general and I had been friends for many years, and in
recent months we had been drawn together by our mutual opposition to Truman.

"You know, you could win this election," I told MacArthur.

I believed that, and I believed that he would make a good
President. He is solid. He is a great patriot. He knows the
world. One of the most engrossing hours I had ever spent in
my life was in that very same suite some time before when I
listened to MacArthur discuss the economy of the Far East,
country by country. He understands foreign affairs, and, of
course, his grasp of military problems is immense.

In that spring of 1952 H. L. Hunt, another of the Texas oil
men, urged me to head up a movement for MacArthur. I did
not feel that I could do it for a variety of reasons, not the least
of which was that I liked Taft and would not have wished personally to lead a campaign against him. These considerations,
however, did not deter me from urging MacArthur to seek the
nomination.

"You could win it very easily," I said, pressing my arguments with the general. "I think you ought to do it for the party."

MacArthur thanked me. I got the impression that he was available if the convention should turn to him, but he would make no move to get the nomination for himself. He was distinctly not for Eisenhower, who had served under him in the Philippines before World War II. His choice was Taft. He told me that Taft had earned the nomination and that he would not want to do anything that might rob him of it.

"I really think the Republican Party owes it to Taft," he told me. "He should be nominated."

Taft was more than MacArthur's choice. He was the true sentimental favorite of the Republican delegates who gathered in Chicago. That convention was not what I would call consumed with a desire to nominate Eisenhower. Indeed, if his rivals could have got together beforehand and agreed upon one man, like MacArthur, it would not have taken a great deal to have tipped the nomination away from him.

In his own contest with Eisenhower, Taft had an incurable and all-too-well-known weakness. As in 1948, most of the delegates were afraid that, if nominated, Taft could not win the election. My own opinion is that Taft, if nominated, could have won in 1948, and he could have won in 1952. But delegates are like the rest of the American people: they like to have someone else do their thinking for them.

The newspapers, magazines, and public-opinion polls were forever thrumming the tune that Taft couldn't win. This became an easy substitute for hard thought and analysis on the part of a great many delegates. Together with the fact that in public Taft lacked some of the glamor of his rivals this produced a psychology, however irrational, that gripped the convention. I have little doubt, on the other hand, that if Taft had been willing to submerge his own ambition and had thrown his full weight behind MacArthur in advance of the convention, the Republicans would have swung to MacArthur in 1952.

After Eisenhower, triumphant in his quest for the nomination, began stumping the country against Adlai Stevenson, I suggested to him when he came through Massachusetts that he do something to bring MacArthur into the campaign. I was to introduce Eisenhower at an outdoor rally in Fall River. As we sat together on the platform on a cold afternoon, I said to him, "You ought to get MacArthur into the picture. A lot of people believe in him." I got no response.

Taft's third and last defeat, at the 1952 convention, shattered the hope of his life. I recall meeting him shortly beforehand at National Airport in Washington. As he was about to board a plane, he cheerfully told me that he was going to make a speech somewhere or other that he was sure would nail down a significant number of delegates. He had often talked to me in this vein, but now he seemed convinced that the nomination was within his grasp. I knew then, or came to know soon afterward, that he would have accepted MacArthur or me as a running mate. However, I definitely was not a candidate, and as for MacArthur, who was going to ask him to take second place? If, on the other hand, Taft had been nominated and if MacArthur had felt that his presence on the ticket would have improved the chances of victory, he might well have accepted the nomination for Vice-President.

Taft would have made a fearless and an able President. No Republican had more cause than he to expect the nomination. None was better qualified for it. When he lost on the first ballot, he took his defeat hard, but he took it like a gentleman. Although he was assailed by deep doubts about the Eisenhower administration, he tried until the day of his death to help the man who had defeated him in Chicago succeed in Washington.

Unquestionably, there were some delegates who had voted for Eisenhower in Chicago while still uncertain about the authenticity of his Republicanism. Any doubts that I may have entertained had been resolved many years before when he was still in uniform. The time was, I suppose, soon after World War II. The place was Sam Rayburn's office in the Capitol.

General Eisenhower was there in the presence of a number of members of the House, of whom I was the only Republican. For some reason or other someone referred to him as "Eisenhower of Texas." That is where he was born. The general corrected the speaker. "Eisenhower of Kansas," he said. This was all I needed to convince me that he was a Republican. If he were a Democrat, he would, in a gathering of that political complexion, have let "Eisenhower of Texas" stand. There are rather more Democrats in Texas than there are in Kansas.

In San Francisco's Cow Palace the Republican convention of 1956 was opened with inquiries from the platform, "Is everybody happy?" and "Who likes Ike?" The delegates gave their fullest possible affirmation in both instances and proceeded automatically to renominate the ticket of 1952. However, the two names that offered me as permanent chairman the most trouble were not Eisenhower and Nixon, but Harold Stassen and Joe Smith.

Stassen's attempt before the convention to dump Nixon as the vice-presidential nominee and substitute Christian A. Herter, then governor of Massachusetts, caused a brief sensation when it was announced but was a joke by the time the delegates began assembling in San Francisco. Still, since Stassen persisted to the end, it was a vexing business to dispose of without embarrassment and ridicule to the party. Herter, who had been entirely innocent of Stassen's act, wrote me three days before the convention, asking that his name be withdrawn from any consideration whatever. When the President flew to San Francisco from Washington after the convention had opened, he asked me if I would meet him the following morning at his suite in the St. Francis Hotel. When I arrived, Sherman Adams, the Assistant to the President, and Senator William F. Knowland of California met me outside the President's door.

"I have Harold Stassen in my office now," Adams said, "and he is willing to quit, but the trick is to find the best formula."

When I went in to see the President, I had in mind suggesting to him that Stassen make a simple statement either to the press or to the convention that he no longer opposed the re-nomination of Nixon. Before I had a chance to mention it, the President told me that Stassen now wished to deliver a speech seconding Nixon's nomination.

If this crowning absurdity was what Stassen wanted, I had no objection. There was the slight complication that Nixon had already arranged for the maximum number of seconding speeches that the rules would permit, but in the interest of party harmony I was glad to overlook an extra one. Also when Stassen came marching up to the platform at the Cow Palace later on the rule was that seconding speeches were to be limited to two minutes each. It took him that long just to warm up. As he went rambling on, I should, strictly speaking, have looked to my gavel. I decided, however, that in a situation like this the easiest way was the best way. On the assumption that al-most any small infraction was justified that would end this painful farce I let him continue uninterrupted until, after some twelve minutes, he finished.

On the roll call of the states for nominating speeches for Vice-President rumors reached me on the platform that Ne-braska intended to nominate her own candidate for Vice-Presi-dent. Presently, a messenger brought up a handwritten note jotted on the back of an envelope:

Joe: A misguided and recalcitrant Nebr. delegate (Terry Car-penter) insists on getting recognition, if he can, and nominate someone besides Nixon for Vice-President and then asking consent to with-draw the name. I'm afraid he means me. In any event, I've talked it over with the chairman of the delegation, and we hope you will recog-nize *no* one in Nebraska during nomination of V.P. candidate.

Fred A. Seaton

Seaton, the Secretary of Interior, was a former Senator from Nebraska. Carpenter was a man I had known well in Washing-ton early in the New Deal when he was a Democratic Congress-man. At that time he talked to me about switching parties in quest of broader political opportunities in Nebraska. Of course, I encouraged him—we Republicans needed all the converts we could get in those days. In time Carpenter became a Republican, made a pile of money and was now a delegate to the 1956 convention.

Leonard W. Hall, the Republican National Chairman, told me in great dismay that he had heard that Carpenter, in his nominating speech, was going to say some alarming things about the President's health. Supposedly, this was to be the basis of his case for proposing a Vice-President other than Nixon. Not only would it have been a distortion, as subsequent history has proved so dramatically, to proclaim that the President was in poor health, but it would have been wretched politics on our part to allow anyone fifteen minutes of national television time to make such a statement from the platform of the Republican National Convention. With the Seaton letter as justification I was determined that this was not going to happen.

When Nebraska was reached, the chairman of the delegation, Mrs. George P. Abel, informed me that Carpenter desired to have the floor. I am not sure that I had the right to do so, but I inquired, "Who does he desire to nominate?" Mrs. Abel did not know.

"I would say for the benefit of the Nebraska delegation," I told her, "the reason I am making this inquiry is that I have a letter from a distinguished son of Nebraska in which he states he does not want his name to be presented. That being the case I could not receive the nomination of that individual, and I make an inquiry for information."

This robbed Carpenter of his candidate, and he had to think fast.

"Mr. Chairman," he said, "we are going to nominate Joe Smith."

"Joe who?" I demanded.

"Joe Smith," Carpenter replied, as the crowd roared in the merriest moment of an otherwise dull convention.

"Nebraska reserves the right to nominate Joe Smith, whoever he is," I said, again taking some liberty with the rules perhaps to prevent Carpenter from switching to someone else when we returned to him. However, Carpenter never sought the floor again, and Joe Smith was never nominated. Nevertheless reporters and television cameramen, starving on the thin fare of a cut-and-dried convention, pounced upon this episode with an eagerness that produced bedlam around the Nebraska delegation. No amount of gaveling, it seemed, could restore order, and in exasperation I finally shouted, "Take your Joe Smith and get outa here." I didn't realize that I had spoken the immortal line of the 1956 convention.

The Democrats tried to make an issue of this affair, playing it up as a case of Republican disregard of the little fellow. "Joe Smith for Stevenson" signs began appearing around the country along with "Joe Smith" buttons. But it was all too silly to have any effect. For weeks, however, I was deluged with letters and telegrams from Joseph Smiths, some of whom, like a judge in Connecticut, I knew, but most of whom I did not. One of these Joe Smiths was a policeman in Fall River. All he wanted was to have his picture taken with me, and I obliged him.

I have listened to all kinds of criticism of the American political convention, its tumult, its hippodromery, its intrigue, its concentration on men instead of principles. In the end, however, I return to James Bryce's observation in *The American Commonwealth* that the nominating convention "is so exactly conformable to the political habits of the people that it is not likely soon to disappear." I always ask, "What system would be better?" and I have yet to hear a convincing answer.

It has been my own observation that when a party believes it has a chance to win, the delegates invariably will vote for the man who will make the best candidate—not necessarily the best President perhaps, but the best candidate.

When the delegates sense that the party is destined to lose in November, this rule does not necessarily apply. Then they are likely to nominate the man who is best suited to holding the organization together for the ensuing four years. That is what the Republicans did when they renominated Taft in 1912. The Democrats did the same when they renominated Truman in 1948. He surprised his own party as much as he surprised the Republicans.

11

THE ONE CERTAIN CONCLUSION that can be drawn about Harry Truman is that he was, and remains, a surprising man, smarter by far than most people realized when he entered the White House on April 12, 1945. The years of his presidency were a period of dizzying surprises. They were crammed with drama and suspense, wisdom and folly, greatness and smallness, comedy and tragedy. The Truman era was an incredible kaleidoscope, alternately dazzling, bewildering, and distressing. It was my lot to live without rest among its flashes and shadows, for Truman's career and mine reached their pinnacle in the same period. In the nearly eight years that he was President, I was Speaker of the House for two years and, by now, the veteran Republican floor leader for six more.

Personally, Truman and I were then and long have been friends. Politically, because of the leading roles we played in our opposing parties, we often carried on like cobra and mongoose.

The tremors of the Truman years resulted mainly from the upheavals of World War II. No political system could have remained insulated against such shocks. Not even the New Deal produced moments of greater division and dispute. The unstable period between 1945 and 1953 was the time of the Hiss case, the meat shortage, the Brannan plan, the loyalty program, the rise of Senator Joseph R. McCarthy, the Truman Doctrine, the Eightieth Congress, the Marshall Plan, the Taft-Hartley law, the peacetime draft, the Communist triumph in Asia, the great population expansion, Dixiecrats, 5 per centers, nuclear bombs, deep freezers, mink coats, and the Korean war.

176

Many of my differences with President Truman were simply a revival of my fights with Roosevelt. Thus as Speaker of the Eightieth Congress in 1947–48, I led the Republicans in what looks in retrospect like the last stand against heavy federal spending, high taxes, centralization, and extravagance. That was a continuation of the old battle of the Thirties. On other occasions, however, our conflict moved to new grounds. Such was the case when, during the Korean war, I engaged in an exchange of letters with General MacArthur that led to Truman's rash act of removing MacArthur from his command in the Far East.

I first met Truman, then a freshman Senator, before the war on a train bound for Washington from New England. He had been visiting Senator Maloney, and I encountered the two of them when they came aboard at New Haven. By this time I was an established leader of the Republican Party, whereas Truman by contrast was practically unknown outside Missouri and the confines of the Senate. He was very modest and unassuming, and as we chatted, I could as easily have imagined him sitting on the moon as occupying the White House. After that I used to see him around the Capitol and at parties. I never was more surprised than when he was nominated for Vice-President. For some time it had been plain that Roosevelt's health was failing. Serious conflicts rarely develop over the vice-presidential nomination, and when such a fight broke out at the Democratic National Convention in 1944, it was a sign to me that the Democrats were assuming that the next Vice-President, if their ticket was elected, would become President. In such circumstances I took it for granted that the vice-presidential nomination would go to someone like James F. Byrnes. Hence I was scarcely prepared for the news of the nomination of the man from Independence.

I was in Washington the day Roosevelt died, and late that afternoon I was summoned to the White House to be present when Truman took the oath of office. As I watched him with his hand upraised, I wondered what his succession to the presidency would mean to the destiny of the country. He was so different from Roosevelt that it was obvious great changes were in store. At the outset Truman spoke in accents conservative enough to hearten us Republicans. In fact, amusing as this soon would seem, we thought that he might be the answer to our prayers. I believed he erred in ordering the atomic bomb dropped on Japan because surrender appeared near in any case. Following V-J Day, he demobilized our military forces more rapidly than has been judged wise after the act, though I do not see how as a practical matter he could have done otherwise in the face of the glacial pressure from the American people at home and the troops abroad. On the whole, however, his first months in office were reassuring.

Nevertheless we were soon to learn that Harry Truman was not Herbert Hoover. On September 6, 1945, barely five months after becoming President, he sent up a special message outlining in twenty-one points his Fair Deal program. A long decade, more or less, had passed since our struggles against the alphabet agencies, government handouts, and socialistic experiments. A global war had been fought at frightful expense. At last the time seemed propitious in spite of the disruption on all sides for a gradual advance toward sound, conservative, nonmeddling government. But here we were being urged back on the same dreary old circuit of paternalism, controls, spending, high taxes, and vague objectives. The acts had other names. The characters had fresh faces, some of them. "The scenery is new," I commented after hearing the message, "There is a little better decoration. Mr. Truman does dish it out a little easier. But it's just a plain case of out-New Dealing the New Deal."

As the ensuing months and years of rasping controversy were to prove, however, the Fair Deal was not the juggernaut the New Deal had been. We could not stop the New Deal. When we tried it ran over us. The Fair Deal, by which I mean Truman's domestic reforms as distinct from his estimable foreign program, we stopped in its tracks. The opposition was more formidable than anything we had been able to muster against the New Deal. The Republican leadership in the House was strong and experienced. In the Senate, Bob Taft was in his prime, a deadly critic of Truman's policies. Southern Democrats were again stout allies. And once again the Republicans were fired up in the illusion that after four successive defeats we would recapture the White House at last in 1948.

Any doubts that any Republican was foolish enough to harbor on this point were happily washed away in the Congressional elections of 1946. Exasperated with government controls and the shortage of meat, the voters marched to the polls that November to answer the question we Republicans had been asking them all fall, "Had enough?" In replying with a resounding "Yes," the people put the Republican Party back in control of both houses of Congress for the first time since the early part of the Hoover administration.

This was the greatest Republican victory in eighteen years. It was the revival of the Republican Party, the ultimate proof that the party had survived the ordeal of the Thirties. While we were to suffer other setbacks, of course, the elections of 1946 restored the foundations on which the party stands today.

To me the gain of fifty-five seats that assured us control of the House had a special meaning. I was receiving the returns in the *Evening Chronicle* office in North Attleboro when a call came during the night from Leonard Hall, who was then chairman of the National Republican Congressional Committee.

"Well, Joe," he said, "it's going to be 'Mr. Speaker' from now on."

My supporters from the nearby town of Plainville wanted to bring a band over in the middle of the night to serenade me, but I would not let them. At 3 A.M. William C. Cole of Missouri called to say that he had been elected to Congress. The Republicans had not expected to take his district, and in his elation he insisted on introducing me over the telephone to fifty-seven of his friends, one by one. By the time the introductions were over I was so tired and the hour was so late that I had little time to savor the happy experience of a dream realized after many long years of waiting.

I assumed the duties of Speaker of the House of Representatives on January 3, 1947, receiving the gavel from Sam Rayburn who had been elected Speaker in 1940 after the death of William Bankhead.

Next to the President, the Speaker is the most powerful elective official in the United States. In some respects he is less powerful than he was years ago, but in others he is more so.

His power over committees, for example, is less than it was. In the 1890s Speaker Thomas B. Reed, a Republican from Maine, usurped the authority of the Rules Committee by making himself a member and taking control of it. He thus installed himself in a position from which he could dictate which legislation would reach the floor and which would not. This comes close to being the ultimate power in a legislative body. From the autocracy of Reed the House passed to the despotism of Speaker Joseph G. (Uncle Joe) Cannon, a Republican from Illinois, who adopted tactics similar to Reed's but prosecuted them with tyrannical force. Cannon had quit Congress before I arrived, but I had formed a speaking acquaintance with him earlier at various party gatherings. The last time I saw him was at the Republican National Convention in Cleveland in 1924 when he gave me a "How-de-do" as he passed with a long cigar in his mouth. He was a tall, bearded, grizzled man, typical of the tough old politicians of his generation. His appearance matched his dictatorial manner. In his early days as Speaker he once refused a dinner invitation from President Theodore Roosevelt when he learned that he would be accorded a rank lower than third at the table. This incident led to the establishment by Roosevelt of the Speaker's dinner, which has become a fixture on the White House social calendar. In my time I was honored by both Truman and Eisenhower at this state dinner.

In 1910 the House revolted against Cannon's tyranny and

stripped the Speakership of most of its powers. The rebellious members took particular care to enlarge and liberate the Rules Committee. The Speaker lost his absolute power to appoint and remove members of this and other standing committees. The seniority system was strengthened, and the committee on committees in each party took over the function of selecting new members for standing committees.

During the half-century since that revolt against Cannon's rule Speakers have succeeded in rebuilding a great deal of the power that "Uncle Joe" lost. While the committee on committees may formally select members for committees, for example, the Speaker does in fact exercise a strong influence over these choices from among the ranks of his own party. Thus members must look to him for a chance of advancement. In the four years that I served as Speaker no Republican went on an important committee without my approval. In the case of select committees created for certain limited but important tasks the Speaker does appoint the members from his own party. The Speaker is in a position to expedite or delay legislation and to encourage or shut off debate. Another element that goes to make up his authority is his power of recognition. Merely by ignoring a member he can deprive him of the floor. I believe, however, that many tend to exaggerate this power. In order to maintain his effectiveness a Speaker has to be fair. He is no longer a Reed or a Cannon. His rulings can be overturned by the House.

The thing that makes the Speaker's influence greater in a way than it used to be is the much broader role the House plays in the government than it did in Cannon's day. Until World War II, for example, the House had scant voice in foreign affairs, as contrasted with the Senate, which has the constitutional responsibility for ratifying treaties. In the postwar world, however, United States foreign policy has rested on programs which, like Greek–Turkish aid, the Marshall Plan, and Mutual Security, require large sums of money. Since the Constitution provides that all appropriations must originate in the House, the House has come to have a large influence over the scope and nature of these instrumentalities of foreign policy. As the role of the House has grown, the Speaker's influence has increased.

For one who has as little taste for public speaking as I have always had the title of Speaker was a trifle incongruous. But the Speaker does a good deal more than speak. Presiding over the House is his chief function, but only one of a great many duties. He is, for example, the manager of a very sizable estate including two office buildings and a power plant. The police force and the page boys in the House are under his jurisdiction. No tree can be cut down on the House side of the Capitol grounds without his consent. He determines what hours the House restaurant shall open and close. He has supervision over a Capitol bank with assets of three or four million dollars. He is responsible for the management of the press galleries and rules on matters like the televising of House committee hearings. On this subject Speaker Rayburn and I have differed occasionally. He has banned the televising of all House proceedings except the joint sessions addressed by the President. I left it to the discretion of the respective committees to decide whether their hearings should be televised, believing that they would be in a better position to judge each case on its merits than I. The sprawling household that the Speaker keeps includes four barbershops and a beauty parlor. When I was elected to the office, I called in a colleague and said, "I think I'll let you run the beauty parlor. You are more experienced with the women than I am."

An effective Speaker needs to hold the good will of members of the Rules Committee, which controls the flow of legislation to the floor. I never had any trouble on this score, partly perhaps because I had been a member of that committee since before most of the members then sitting ever came to Congress.

In addition to all his other duties the Speaker remains the leader of his party in the House. The details of leadership are handled by the chosen floor leader, who in my two terms as

Speaker was Halleck, but the Speaker himself is the grand strategist and guiding spirit. Each Speaker, of course, exercises his leadership according to his own character and the prevailing political situation. For my own part I was never dictatorial. I worked by persuasion and drew heavily on long-established personal friendships. I found that I could best keep my members with me by tact and discretion. Unless it was absolutely necessary I never asked a man to side with me if his vote would hurt him in his district. Whenever I could spare a man this kind of embarrassment I did so and saved him for another time when I might need him more urgently. In fact I often counseled members against taking positions on legislation that could cost them the next election.

One instance I particularly remember occurred during consideration of the Taft–Hartley bill. Among the Republicans in the House was Representative Louis E. Graham, who came from a district in Pennsylvania where labor was strong. We did not need Graham's vote to put the bill through, and I sauntered over to his desk to tell him so.

"I am going to stay with you," he assured me.

"We've got plenty of votes," I replied. "If I were you, I'd think it over. You've got a bad district. If you decide to go the other way, I'm not going to hold it against you."

When the roll was called Graham loyally voted for the Taft–Hartley bill. On election day he retained his seat, though he was to lose it later on.

While I was not iron-handed with members, I nevertheless expected the Republicans to keep me informed about their moves in the House, and I sometimes showed my annoyance when they failed to do so. Without my knowledge, for example, one of our men rose one day and delivered a long, controversial, rambling speech on foreign affairs. When it was over he came to me with light in his eyes.

"How did I go, Joe?" he asked.

"You didn't go anywhere," I replied.

The Speaker is the arbiter of an infinite variety of disputes on the floor of the House. A typical case that comes to mind was a quarrel one day in 1948 between Representative Emanuel Celler, a Democrat from New York, and Representative John E. Rankin, a Democrat from Mississippi. Rankin had insinuated that the new settlers of Palestine were Communists.

"That is a damnable statement to make," Celler thundered.

"Mr. Speaker," Rankin shouted, "I demand that those words be taken down."

"The gentlemen will suspend," I ordered. "The gentleman from New York will take his seat. The clerk will report the words objected to."

After the clerk had finished, I said to Rankin, "The gentleman from Mississippi objects to the word 'damnable,' is that it?"

"Yes," Rankin answered. "As used, it is a violation of the rules of the House and of all rules of common decency."

"Mr. Speaker, may I be heard?" Celler demanded.

"This is not debatable," I said. "The Chair will pass on the question. The Chair is not too conversant with the word 'damnable' but does not find that it is banned in the rules of parliamentary procedure. The Chair thinks it is a rather harsh word. The Chair hopes that the members will not take this as a precedent for using the word on too many occasions."

I had not been Speaker long when Mary Randolph, who had been social secretary to Mrs. Coolidge in the White House, approached me in great concern over a problem bearing on the dignity of my office. In the traditional order of social precedence, it seems, the Vice-President came after the President, the Speaker after the Vice-President, and the Chief Justice after the Speaker. However, Miss Randolph said, when William Howard Taft was Chief Justice, this well-established order was thrown out of kilter because Taft was also a former President. Since a former President enjoys social precedence over the Speaker, the Chief Justice came to take precedence, in his role as former President, over the Speaker. Even though Chief Justice Taft had been dead for some years in 1947, the new order created by his special situation still prevailed. Thus Chief Justice Fred M. Vinson, though he had never been President, enjoyed social precedence over the Speaker.

Miss Randolph wanted me to insist upon a restoration of the traditional order.

The more I thought about it the less I was inclined to do so. For one thing Fred Vinson was a good friend of mine, and I shrank from anything that might conceivably lead to a petty misunderstanding between us.

Of much greater weight with me, however, was the recollection that the last time the Republicans had been in power a catastrophic social war had broken out between Dolly Gann, the sister of Vice-President Curtis, who was a bachelor, and Mrs. Alice Roosevelt Longworth, the wife of the Speaker. This conflict over which of the two women had precedence kept Washington in turmoil for years. Now that I was Speaker I did not want to start some new uproar. Even though Rayburn encouraged me to try to reestablish the old order, I did not wish to risk making it appear that every time a Republican obtained one of the high offices in Washington, an unholy war over social precedence followed.

In 1947, early in my first term as Speaker, a new dimension was added to the office. President Truman proposed that the Speaker be designated by law as first in line of succession to the Presidency in the event of the removal, resignation, death, or inability of both the President and the Vice-President.

The original legislation on this question in 1792 provided that in such circumstances the first in line would be the President pro tempore of the Senate. The next after him would be the Speaker. This law remained in effect for ninety-four years until 1886 when, in the first administration of Grover Cleveland, Congress substituted a new system, designating the Secretary of State as first in line after the Vice-President. Following the Secretary of State, in the event he was unavailable, the line of succession followed, in descending order of seniority, through the Cabinet. After the Secretary of State came the Secretary of the Treasury; after him the Secretary of War, and so on.

President Truman, who in his first term had no Vice-President, having himself succeeded from that office to the White House, proposed to revert to a variation of the 1792 law. He recommended that the first in line of succession, if there was no Vice-President, should be the Speaker and after him the President pro tempore of the Senate, an office occupied in 1947 by Vandenberg. In his memoirs Truman has explained:

"Inasmuch as the President and Vice-President are the only officers of the government elected by all the voters of the United States, I felt that the Speaker of the House of Representatives most nearly represents selection by the people because as a member of the House, he is elected to the Congress by the voters of his district and, as Speaker, he is chosen by a majority of the Representatives from all the states."

In a letter to the Congress in 1947 Truman also made this point:

"A completely new House is elected every two years and always at the same time as the President and Vice-President. Usually, it is in agreement politically with the Chief Executive. Only one-third of the Senate, however, is elected with the President and Vice-President. The Senate might, therefore, have a majority hostile to the policies of the President and might conceivably fill the Presidential office with one not in sympathy with the will of the majority of the people."

When the matter came up in the House, I thought it proper, because of the peculiar applicability of the legislation to me, to leave the chamber. I turned the chair over to Halleck. The bill, already approved by the Senate with the strong support of Vandenberg, was passed 365 to 11. When reporters descended on me, I told them I sincerely hoped that Harry Truman would live out his term.

"I have no wish to be President," I said.

From July 18, 1947, until January 20, 1949, when Alben W. Barkley of Kentucky took the oath of office of Vice-President in Truman's second administration I was first in line of succession to the Presidency. The situation had many interesting facets.

For one thing I always have felt that Truman showed a commendable lack of partisanship in recommending that a Republican Speaker be put in line as successor to a Democratic President. Yet, curiously, Truman never mentioned one word about this whole matter to me before sending up the bill or after it had passed. Even though he himself had been compelled to take over from Roosevelt without preparation, Truman did not make the slightest attempt to keep me informed about the sensitive inner policies of the government in case I might suddenly become President. The problem was radically different in my case, of course, because instead of being a member of the administration, I was the leader of the opposition.

After the bill was passed the Secret Service without my consent provided a personal guard for me. I made them call it off. In that same summer of 1947 Truman, while on a visit to South America, came dangerously close to plunging down a mountainside in an automobile. The news was a sobering reminder of how near I was living day and night to the edge of great responsibility. While I never gave systematic thought to what I would have done or whom I would have appointed to my cabinet if it had fallen to my lot suddenly to be President, the idea lurked in my mind that I might ask Herbert Hoover to return to Washington as Secretary of State. His great experience both as cabinet officer and President would have been almost indispensable to me.

While I am not aware that my relatives and I thought of it consciously, the realization that a dramatic change of fate might strike me without warning at any moment must have lain just below the surface of our minds. I say this because of an incident that occurred in July 1948, during the Democratic National Convention in Philadelphia. Truman, it will be recalled, delivered a fiery acceptance speech in the middle of the night following his nomination for a second term. As a climax

he announced that he was calling Congress into special session
on "Turnip Day," July 26, to challenge the Republicans to
deliver on their new campaign pledges.

This devilishly astute piece of politics went unheard by me
because I was at home in North Attleboro, and we had all
retired before Truman started to speak. Sometime around
3 A.M. we were startled by the telephone. When my sister,
Mrs. Jeanette Kelley, picked it up she heard the excited voice
of a reporter in Philadelphia demanding to speak with me to
ask me, of course, for my reaction.

"What do you want him for at this hour?" she inquired,
unsuspecting.

"Haven't you heard about *the President?*" he gasped.

My sister nearly swooned. I suppose she had a vision of my
taking the oath of office right there in the living room, like
Calvin Coolidge.

One of the unexpected consequences of my becoming first in line
of succession was that, being a bachelor, I was deluged with
offers of marriage by women who sensed that this was a possible way to become First Lady.

After I had first been elected to Congress in 1924 I dropped
by the Red Cross in North Attleboro, where I was surrounded
by twenty-five women. Since I was going to Washington, they
said, I would have to have a wife. When I asked them if they
had any candidates, they came forward with the names of two
charming women in town, whereupon I made the group a proposition which I knew would be a safe one for me.

"Fair enough, girls," I said, "if you can unanimously agree
on one or the other, I'll marry her."

I doubt that they have achieved unanimity yet. When the
White House lay just a heartbeat away from me, as the saying
goes, the proposals became more insistent. One woman wrote
from Finland giving her weight and height, dimensions of
waist and bust, and boasting that she could speak seven lan-

guages. When I showed the letter to Representative Leslie C. Arends of Illinois, he advised me to decline.

"For a woman one language is enough," he admonished.

The letter that outdid all the rest came from a woman spiritualist in Clarksburg, West Virginia, in the spring of 1948, some four years after Willkie's death. She wrote:

My dear Mr. Speaker:

I was talking to Wendell Willkie last night and he asked me to deliver this message to you:

"Tell Joe Martin he can be President and he should be President, but he must get married before the Republican convention next June."

P.S. I am single.

I didn't get married, but then I did not become President either.

Contemporary historians may not know it, but on his final day in office Truman practically invoked the new law of succession. He, President-elect Eisenhower, Senator Styles Bridges (then President pro tem of the Senate), and I rode from the White House to the Capitol together on January 20, 1953, for the inauguration of the new President. I had again been elected Speaker of the Eighty-third Congress. While the rest of us assembled on the inaugural stands, Eisenhower became delayed inside the Capitol beyond the hour of noon when the terms of Truman and Barkley expired by law. After glancing at his watch, Truman turned to me and said, "Well, you're President now, Joe." Shortly, however, Eisenhower and Nixon appeared and saved the situation.

12

WHEN I FIRST became Speaker, in January 1947, early in the Eightieth Congress, the Republicans had been through twelve years of Franklin Roosevelt and nearly two years of Harry Truman. Now that we were at last in control of both houses we were determined that Congress should be a much stronger, more independent force than it had been since 1933.

"Our American concept of government," I told the House in my first address as Speaker, "rests upon the idea of a dominant Congress. Congress is the people's special instrument of control over their government. . . . This nation can remain free only through a strong, vigorous Congress . . . which will protect the liberties of the people and not delegate its fundamental powers either to the executive or to arrogant bureaucrats."

These words fairly captured, I believe, the attitude of the majority of the Eightieth Congress. It was a strong, independent Congress. In Truman it was pitted against a strong, impulsive President. The result, naturally, was almost continual conflict, much of it going to fundamental differences between the Democratic and the Republican parties.

Truman proposed the Brannan farm plan. He proposed compulsory national health insurance. He proposed an extensive public housing program. These and other similar measures were the heart of his Fair Deal program, yet not one of them was enacted by Congress.

As often as Truman threw these at us we hurled them back at him. Moreover, in spite of his veto we passed the Taft–

190

Hartley act. Over his vetoes we reduced taxes by $4,800,000,-000 and removed 7,400,000 persons of low income from the tax rolls. We proposed to the states—and they promptly ratified —the Twenty-second Amendment, limiting the tenure of Presidents to two terms. We created the Commission on the Organization of the Executive Branch of the Government, which, as a result of a *coup* of mine, soon became known as the Hoover Commission.

The law authorized the President, the President pro tem of the Senate, and the Speaker each to appoint four members; the twelve would then choose a chairman from among themselves. I thought at once of Hoover, knowing that if a former President became a member, he would almost automatically be elected chairman. I reached him by telephone in Idaho where he was on a fishing trip. "I've got a job for you, Chief," I said. When I explained what it was, he was reluctant at first.

"This can be the biggest thing that has happened in a generation if it works out the way I think it will work out," I pleaded.

He agreed to consider it and in the end accepted and was, of course, named chairman. The strategy I had in mind was for the commission to complete its recommendations by the end of 1948. Then we would make these the first order of business in the Eighty-first Congress in January 1949, and enact the whole Hoover plan into law. As it turned out, the flaw in this strategy was that the Republicans lost control of Congress in the Truman–Dewey election, and in 1949 it was the Democrats and not we who called the tune. Even so, many useful reforms recommended by the commission were eventually put into effect.

I exerted all the influence I could to get the Twenty-second Amendment through the House. In earlier Congresses I had sponsored the resolution myself. In fact the first time I introduced it was in January 1945, before Roosevelt's death, to carry out a plank of the Republican platform of 1944. In the Eightieth Congress, since I was Speaker, I had the resolution introduced by the chairman of the Judiciary Committee, Representative Earl C. Michener of Michigan. Like almost all Republicans, I had resented Roosevelt's election to four terms as a violation of a wise tradition established by George Washington. The amendment, however, was not intended merely as a swipe at Roosevelt or at his memory. As one Democrat warned me, the amendment, since it exempted Truman, would probably apply first to a Republican President, which has proved to be the case. But this was beside the point. I did not wish to see a third-term Republican President any more than a third-term Democratic President—or not much more, anyhow. I believed that the United States has enough men and brains to yield a good President every four or eight years without having to take the risk of keeping one man in office until his power outruns the purposes of the framers of the Constitution. Furthermore I felt that the amendment was a good issue for the Republicans, and I exerted all the influence I had in the various states to get it ratified, which it was in remarkably quick time.

I was never persuaded by the argument that the amendment would weaken a President in his second term by making him a lame duck. I did not accept the theory that a President would be handicapped simply because he would be denied the option of masking his intentions as to a third term. The only case we have by which to test these questions is that of President Eisenhower. Despite the two-term limitation, he has been more powerful in his second term than in his first. And while he himself has certain philosophical reservations about the amendment, he has said that he has never been aware that it has weakened his authority.

The great achievements of the Eightieth Congress were in the field of foreign affairs, notably the enactment of the Greek–Turkish aid program and the Marshall Plan, both of which were designed to check the flood of Communism into Western Europe.

For Republicans, as for everyone else, the world of 1947–48 was a far different place from what it had been in the days when we were challenging Roosevelt's interventionism. This issue was now dead. Whether one liked it or not, events of the previous decade had made the United States the leader of the non-Communist nations. The country could not, if it wished, isolate itself from a world suddenly drawn close together. We had to carry the burden of leadership, costly as it was. There was no other practical choice.

I voted for Truman's foreign programs even though, to the distress of certain liberal columnists, I effectively supported the Appropriations Committee's cut of $1,500,000,000 in Marshall Plan funds in 1948. The total of nearly $6,000,000,000 that we did approve seemed ample to me.

For a great many Republicans the incentive to help the Allies was keener in the 1940s than it had been in the 1930s because, among other things, of the rise of the Soviet Union and the spread of Communism. To us the Communist menace looked more alarming than had the Hitler menace, dangerous though the latter was. In addition to military power, there was the threat of subversion in Communism that had not been present in Hitlerism, and Republicans were quick to sense that in militant, imperialistic Communism the United States faced a deadly enemy. Also the problem of dealing with Russia was less complicated politically than the problem of dealing with Germany had been because, whereas there were few voters of Red Russian descent in the United States, there were at the time of the pre-Pearl Harbor debates something like 15,000,000 voters of German descent. Then there was another very subtle factor after the war. This was that by taking the liberal, the progressive, one might even say (in view of Republican traditions) the radical line in foreign policy, we were in a stronger position to champion conservativism at home. Somehow it provided for us a political equilibrium that probably could not have existed if we had pursued the conservative course in both fields.

Some interesting footnotes to subsequent history may be found in certain committee appointments in the Eightieth Congress. For example, in accordance with a proposal by Representative Christian A. Herter, a Republican from Massachusetts, who is now the Secretary of State, a select committee was created to visit Europe and survey postwar needs. In the normal course, I appointed Herter chairman. As one of the Republican members I named at Herter's suggestion a thirty-four-year-old Californian of the Congressional "Class of '46," one Richard M. Nixon. This was one of the assignments that started Nixon on his rise in Congress.

Infinitely more important to him, however, was his appointment to the Un-American Activities Committee. It was not my function to make this appointment, but it was with my explicit approval that Nixon went on this committee. While Nixon may not make so much of it today, the Un-American Activities Committee was considered a choice assignment in 1947. There was keen competition for it. No one went on a committee of that kind who did not wish very much to become a member. It was a "headline committee," so to speak. We wanted to appoint a lawyer. Some people from the Coast came to us with a high recommendation of Nixon's legal talents. In the end we decided he would be a good man for it. It was his work on the committee, particularly his role in pressing the investigation of Alger Hiss, that catapulted him into the vice-presidential nomination in 1952.

The Marshall Plan, Greek–Turkish aid, the Taft–Hartley Act, tax reduction, the first balanced budget in seventeen years, unification of the armed forces under the newly established Department of Defense, the Twenty-second Amendment, the presidential succession bill, the Hoover Commission, expansion of the Voice of America—these and many other substantial measures made the Eightieth a particularly constructive and progressive Congress.

The last thing in the world one would have expected was that such a record could have been twisted into a weapon that was to help send the Republican Party to disastrous defeat in November 1948. Here we had written a record on which the Republicans could have run proudly—and won! Yet, incomprehensible though it still seems, Truman was permitted not only to distort this record but to turn the very term *Eightieth Congress* into a household word of opprobrium. Truman snatched the issue that we should have been using, and it was one of the greatest blunders in the history of the Republican Party that he should have been allowed to get away with it.

No one can say that we were not given fair warning. In June 1948, before the conventions and before adjournment of Congress, the President took off on a coast-to-coast whistle-stop tour, lambasting the Eightieth at every crossroads. He peppered us with such epithets as "the good-for-nothing, Taft–Hartley Eightieth Congress," "the do-nothing Eightieth Congress," and "the worst Congress since Thaddeus Stevens." He denounced the Republican leaders as "mossbacks" (which his official stenographer once took down as "moth bags") and as tools of special interests.

By the time the Republican National Convention met in Philadelphia and nominated Dewey and Warren I was becoming concerned about these attacks. As the permanent chairman I told the convention that "the accomplishments of the Eightieth Congress have been substantial and we can be justly proud of them." I urged that the record of the Congress be made a Republican issue in the campaign.

As the summer wore on Truman kept up his attacks. I was increasingly irritated by his wild charges that "Wall Street gluttons of privilege" had manipulated the Republican Congress and that the Republicans, as he told a farm audience in Iowa, "have stuck a pitchfork in your backs."

Dewey was in Albany preparing for his campaign. I telephoned him from North Attleboro and told him, as I recall, that the best defense was a good offense. I cautioned him that he would be making a mistake if he did not begin to talk about the constructive aspects of the Eightieth Congress and not let Truman get away, unanswered, with his constant criticism of our record.

Before Labor Day I lunched with Dewey at the Executive

Mansion in Albany and discussed the Eightieth Congress with him. While we had taken certain actions that he did not approve, the impression I got from our talk was that he considered the whole record a good one. Yet during the campaign he remained generally aloof from this issue, believing he had the election won without it, while Truman, smart political operator that he was, tore into the record all the harder when he saw that it was not being defended.

I also believed we were going to win in 1948, and, like Dewey and nearly everyone else except perhaps Truman, I viewed the polls as the handwriting on the wall. Yet as the campaign wore on, certain doubts were planted in my mind that should have assumed greater proportions than they did. I can't recall the exact conversations, but as I traveled across the country, I was forever hearing from our state leaders such comments as, "Dewey will carry Illinois, but Stevenson will be elected governor," and "Oh, Dewey is going to take Ohio, but we are going to lose this, this, and this House seat," and "Dewey's a cinch to take Iowa but Gillette will be elected to the Senate." I remember thinking how curious it was that we were going to lose so much and still win the presidency. Something was in the air that fall that kept us from following evidence through to the logical conclusion.

On his final swing through New England I rode with Dewey on his train into North Attleboro. Brimming with confidence, he cited the polls to me as an omen of victory. That was the trip on which my mother urged him, when he visited our house, to fight harder. It also was the trip on which I was keenly embarrassed by a seemingly personal poke at Dewey that came about utterly by chance, although the Democrats, naturally, blew it up as an attack by the Speaker of the House of Representatives on his party's presidential nominee.

That afternoon the *Evening Chronicle*, of which I was still editor and publisher, as I am today, appeared on the streets (and copies were put aboard the Dewey train) with an editorial saying:

Dewey's speeches are designed for tonal effect. His addresses are filled with maxims old and new, such as, "We need a rudder to our ship of state and a firm hand on the tiller." Sounds good and brings the applause. But promises nothing. "Our country is at the crossroads of its history" is another Dewey phrase, old and a bit trite. Dewey also still uses "profound" and "profoundly," although he wore both phrases threadbare in 1944. . . .

Whether or not Dewey ever saw the editorial, which also contained criticism of Truman, I do not know, but that had little bearing on what followed. As I have since learned, Jack Redding, publicity director for the Democratic National Committee, persuaded Democratic National Chairman J. Howard McGrath to treat this as a deliberate attack by me on Dewey, even though Redding himself, as he has recalled, did not believe that this was the case. He and McGrath took the portion of the editorial criticizing Dewey and telegraphed it across the country to Democratic state and city organizations, urging them, as Redding has written, "to 'get it around' to every precinct captain, to print it as a flyer for distribution before the polls opened on Tuesday."

Behind all this fuss was a very simple explanation. Having a small staff, the *Evening Chronicle* bought "boilerplate" editorials prepared by a syndicate. The day of Dewey's visit the editorial in question happened to be on top of the pile and a man in the composing room slapped it into the paper. Ironically, he was one of the most ardent Dewey supporters in North Attleboro. As for myself, I never read the editorial until it was well on its way to fame.

Dewey would have made a strong President. His defeat was more than a calamity for the Republican Party, which, in losing its fifth consecutive presidential election, seemed dangerously close to losing its own existence. It was a calamity also for the political stability of the United States. The Democratic dominance was abnormal. Our political system was out of joint. The rhythm of parties alternating in power, which had made for an equitable balance in the past, was shattered. Instead of two healthy parties, we had one party bloated with a too-long tenure and another party reduced to dark frustration. In this unwholesome state some Republicans turned to extremism because, as the Dewey defeat seemed to prove, the course of moderation had failed us once again.

The nation sank into division and bitterness that it need not have known, nor would have, under anything like normal circumstances. If Dewey had been elected in 1948, we never would have experienced the McCarthy era because Republican energies would have been working in a different direction, discharging the responsibilities of administering the government. The deepening quarrels and disagreements that followed Truman's inauguration for a second term in 1949 distracted the country from its true greatness and left us ill prepared in spirit for the terrible ordeal that would soon befall us in Korea.

No misfortune since the Civil War troubled the American people more deeply than the bottomless war in Korea. Through an odd turn of circumstances I was caught in the middle of the most explosive of all the political incidents attendant upon that unhappy war, the dismissal of Douglas MacArthur.

13

THE STORY OF my unsuspecting role in the drama of
General MacArthur's banishment on April 11, 1951, really
began two months earlier with a speech I delivered at a Lincoln
Day Republican dinner in Brooklyn on the Far Eastern situation. However, my acquaintance with MacArthur went back
many years to the early Thirties when he was the Chief of Staff
of the Army and I was a little-known Congressman. Neither of
us has been able to remember the exact circumstances of our
first meeting. We both recollect vaguely that it was at an informal party somewhere in Washington, at which Fiorello
La Guardia prepared the dinner. Even though I cannot recall
the details, I am still amused at the thought of the impetuous
son of an Army trumpet player whipping up spaghetti and
meatballs for Douglas MacArthur.

From time to time thereafter the General and I met in Washington; occasionally we used to ride home together from parties.
We became warm, though not intimate, friends. After he left
for the Philippines in 1935 our paths diverged, and by the time
of his command in Korea many years had elapsed since we had
seen one another.

Needless to say, MacArthur's exploits during World War II
and the Korean conflict were followed with great enthusiasm
not only by myself along with millions of Americans, but by all
of us Republicans in Congress, who had a particularly friendly
interest in the General. We knew from long association that he
was a Republican. We recognized in him one who spoke our
language and cherished our ideals. His triumphs evoked an

199

especially warm and comradely sentiment in us because he was the most distinctively Republican of all the commanders of our armed forces. Naturally, we were sensitive to any policies that gave him less than he needed for swift victory. Thus many of us felt during World War II that an excess of men and matériel was being sent to the European theater at the expense of the Pacific. Certainly, I wished the European theater to be supplied with all that was required for an early victory over Hitler, but I believed that in view of the situation in the Pacific, this largesse was overdone. Some of it could without hindrance to the prosecution of the war in Europe have been diverted to MacArthur to have enabled him to defeat Japan before the Russians entered the Pacific war at their own convenience and for their own selfish purposes.

Republicans resented any signs that MacArthur's theater was being slighted. Indeed there were even trickles of apprehension among us that the Roosevelt administration was skimping a bit on MacArthur out of fear he might become a Republican candidate for President when victory had been won. During and after World War II and throughout the Korean war, cleavages frequently developed between Republicans and Democrats over whether Europe or Asia was of primary concern to American security. Democrats emphasized the importance of Europe. Republicans, while granting that Europe was vitally important, were more insistent than the Democrats about the problem of Asia.

This was in line with the party's traditions. The United States became a Far Eastern power through the acquisition of the Philippines in the Spanish-American war, fought under the McKinley administration. As a result of this and the subsequent diplomacy of Henry L. Stimson, concern over Asia has been a Republican legacy. But our attitude was influenced also to some degree by Republican sympathy for MacArthur. In Congress Republicans harbored deep fears about the rise of Communism in Asia. We felt that in eastern Europe, for example, religious conviction and improving standards of living would impede Communist domination. By contrast, Asia, with its infinite poverty, looked alarmingly susceptible to Communism.

This, briefly, was the background of Republican philosophy, against which the party faced the appalling conflict in Korea. At the outset Republicans supported Truman's decision to oppose Communist aggression, however much they may have questioned his methods and the policies of his administration that preceded the war. As the fighting grew harsher through the second half of 1950, however, we became increasingly and intensely critical of the way in which it was being conducted. Along with other members of my party in Congress I was indignant that, beside the South Koreans themselves, United States forces were carrying practically the whole burden of fighting a United Nations war. I shared the resentment that permeated our side of the aisle over evidence that the British were standing in the way of employment of troops of other nations, notably those of Chiang Kai-shek on Formosa.

At a conference in the White House on December 13, 1950, attended by the President, his advisers, and Congressional leaders of both parties, I put the question to Truman. What were we doing to get troops from India, Japan, and Formosa? Truman turned the question over to Secretary of Defense George C. Marshall, who replied, in effect, that it was impractical. There was no chance of getting much help from India, he observed. As for Japan, he said that the Soviet–Chinese mutual assistance pact was specifically drawn against the possibility that Japan might attack Russia or China. Thus, in Marshall's opinion, the employment of Japanese troops against China might well bring Russia into the war on China's side. I did not think that this would happen because I was convinced then, as I am now, that war is not in Russia's interest.

While I do not recall that Marshall addressed himself to the part of my question dealing with use of Chiang's Chinese Nationalist troops, the Truman administration's position on this was clear, even though it was not convincing. The President opposed sending Chiang's troops against Chinese Communists out of fear that any encroachment on Red Chinese territory might start a third world war.

To Truman's great displeasure, MacArthur already had made it known publicly in a message to the Veterans of Foreign Wars that he did not sympathize with this policy.

By the time of the December conference another serious disagreement had developed between the Truman administration and MacArthur. After the Chinese Reds had entered the war in October, MacArthur ordered American planes to bomb the routes and installations across the Yalu River, whence their troops and supplies were coming. However, the administration's policy against assault on Chinese mainland territory, reinforced as it was by a commitment to the British not to attack the Manchurian side of the Yalu without consulting them, resulted in MacArthur's order being countermanded from Washington before the bombers took off. Subsequently, he was allowed to bomb the bridges over the river, but he was denied authority to bomb Manchurian bases or to engage in hot pursuit of enemy planes fleeing from Korea into Manchuria.

In both this controversy and the debate over the use of Formosan troops I sided with MacArthur as did other leading Republicans in Congress. In fact this concurrence with MacArthur's views became a coordinated Republican policy, supported alike by the party's leadership in the House and by such Senate leaders as Taft, Bridges, and Knowland. We believed that Secretary Acheson was largely to blame for the administration's course, and as an expression of this attitude I introduced in the House Republican Conference a resolution calling on the President to replace him as Secretary of State because he had "lost the confidence of Congress and the American people." This was no personal vindictiveness on my part. Acheson was simply in the line of fire, as I had been in Roosevelt's line of fire when he delivered his "Martin, Barton and Fish" speeches.

When I accepted an invitation to the dinner of the Kings County Republican Committee at the Towers Hotel in Brooklyn on February 12, 1951, I decided to deliver a speech expounding Republican policy on the Far East.

I noted in my talk that Chiang had an army of 800,000 men on Formosa. The administration, I complained, was continuing to concentrate on Europe despite the Korean war. Why, I demanded, did we not bring Chiang's troops to the support of Americans in Korea?

"What," I asked, "could be sounder logic . . . than to allow the anticommunist forces of the Generalissimo on Formosa to participate in the war against the Chinese Reds? Why not let them open a second front in Asia? . . . What kind of logic is it that lets our soldiers die in Korea when, by shipping the proper supplies to the Generalissimo, a second front could be opened in China without a single GI being forced to place a foot on the soil of the Chinese mainland? . . . What are we in Korea for—to win or to lose? . . . If we are not in Korea to win, then this administration should be indicted for the murder of thousands of American boys."

This was on February 12. The speech produced fresh Democratic attacks on the Republican position. As these continued, I finally decided after a month to do something about the situation. I made up my mind that I would get the facts from the horse's mouth. While the controversy waxed at home in a state that often bordered on ignorance about the true state of affairs in the Far East, MacArthur was on the scene and knew what was happening. I felt that the Republicans were entitled to the truth if we were effectively to defend our side of the argument. Since MacArthur was an old friend of mine, I was confident that he would give me an expert opinion on which I could rely in pressing our case. Therefore I dictated the following letter in my office at the Capitol:

March 8, 1951

PERSONAL

My dear General:

In the current discussions on foreign policy and overall strategy many of us have been distressed that although the European

aspects have been heavily emphasized we have been without the
views of yourself as Commander-in-Chief of the Far Eastern
Command.

I think it is imperative to the security of our nation and for
the safety of the world that policies of the United States embrace
the broadest possible strategy and that in our earnest desire to
protect Europe we not weaken our position in Asia.

Enclosed is a copy of an address I delivered in Brooklyn, N.Y.
February 12, stressing this vital point and suggesting that the
forces of Generalissimo Chiang-Kai-shek on Formosa might be
employed in the opening of a second Asiatic front to relieve the
pressure on our forces in Korea.

I have since repeated the essence of this thesis in other
speeches and intend to do so again on March 21 when I will be
on a radio hookup.

I would deem it a great help if I could have your views on this
point, either on a confidential basis or otherwise. Your admirers
are legion and the respect you command is enormous. May success be yours in the gigantic undertaking which you direct.

> Sincerely yours,
> *Joseph W. Martin jr.*

Two weeks later I was on a short visit to North Attleboro
when my Washington office called to notify me that I had
received the following letter:

GENERAL HEADQUARTERS
SUPREME COMMANDER FOR THE ALLIED POWERS
Office of the Supreme Commander

> Tokyo, Japan.
> 20 March 1951.

Dear Congressman Martin:

I am most grateful for your note of the 8th forwarding me a
copy of your address of February 12th. The latter I have read
with much interest, and find that with the passage of years you
have certainly lost none of your old time punch.

My views and recommendations with respect to the situation
created by Red China's entry into the war against us in Korea

have been submitted to Washington in most complete detail. Generally these views are well known and clearly understood, as they follow the conventional pattern of meeting force with maximum counterforce as we have never failed to do in the past. Your view with respect to the utilization of the Chinese forces on Formosa is in conflict with neither logic nor this tradition.

It seems strangely difficult for some to realize that here in Asia is where the Communist conspirators have elected to make their play for global conquest, and that we have joined the issue thus raised on the battlefield; that here we fight Europe's war with arms while the diplomats there still fight it with words; that if we lose the war to Communism in Asia the fall of Europe is inevitable, win it and Europe most probably would avoid war and yet preserve freedom. As you point out, we must win. There is no substitute for victory.

With renewed thanks and expressions of most cordial regard, I am,

> Faithfully yours,
> *Douglas MacArthur*

That this letter would, if published, bring an outcry from the Truman administration and its sympathizers I had little doubt. It was a direct contradiction of Truman's policy against employment of Chiang's troops. It deplored in the bluntest terms the unwillingness of the administration to marshal all available force against the Communist aggressors. It was bitingly critical of the attitude of our allies in Europe. Certainly, everything about it would give provocation to the President. Still, at no time did I ever dream what a world-shaking explosion was latent in its plain prose.

On the other hand, possession of the letter troubled me. When it arrived I did not know at first what to do with it. Except for immediate members of my staff, like my administrative assistant, James N. Milne, and for Robert Humphreys, the public relations director for the National Republican Campaign Committee, no one in Washington realized that I had it. For a spell there was no particular development that would have occasioned my making it public. Furthermore I did not

know whether, as far as MacArthur was concerned, I was
privileged to do so. In writing him, I had requested his views
"either on a confidential basis or otherwise," and there was no
notation on his reply to indicate how it was classified.

At that period of my life I used to take walks at night, particularly if something was weighing on my mind. When I was
worried, I could think better while walking. It was not unusual
for me to tramp the streets for a mile or so before retiring,
and when I had the MacArthur letter on my hands, I know
I covered a few extra blocks each night for good measure.

With every week that passed the administration's course in
Korea seemed more ruinous. I had forebodings that as a way
out we would agree to recognize Red China. I feared that
Truman and Acheson would yield to pressures to compromise
on admitting the Chinese Communists to the United Nations
and perhaps surrender Formosa and Korea before they were
through, thereby delivering Japan to the Communist orbit.
Even if these diplomatic debacles did not materialize, I was
afraid that the military situation was deteriorating to a point
where the Communists might defeat us on the battlefield in
Korea. I came increasingly to feel that some arresting hue and
cry was needed to bring the President and the Secretary of
State to their senses, and the more I pondered this need the
more the MacArthur letter took shape in my mind as a tocsin.

Suddenly, on April 4 a situation came about in Congress
that swept aside all my earlier hesitations about it. In the
Senate the chairman of the Foreign Relations Committee, Tom
Connally, declared that "the course of world events is uncertain
but it is my view that there will be no world war this year.
The Russians will not defy the free nations of the world."
Coming from one as well informed by the administration as
Connally presumably was, I would have supposed that this was
a judgment that sensible men could respect at least. But on
the very same day that Connally was reassuring the Senate,
Speaker Rayburn, one of the great figures in the administration
party, took the floor of the House and warned, "I think that

we stand in the face of terrible danger and maybe the beginning of World War III." Gravely, the Speaker gave it as his "firm belief that we are in greater danger of an expanded war today than we have been at any time since the close of the world war in 1945."

This confusion was intolerable. Who and what were the American people to believe in this moment of danger? If ever there was a time when a voice of authority needed to be heard it was now. I reasoned that if MacArthur had not wished his letter to be released under any circumstances, he would have marked it confidential. Since he had not done so, I decided that I would make it public on my own discretion the next day. On April 5, therefore, I rose in the House and delivered a short speech on the Far Eastern crisis, in the course of which I read the General's letter.

I anticipated that it would cause a jolt, and it did, here and abroad. On the other hand, I did not expect that it would blow up into a crisis, and it did not—at first. For a few days in fact the result was a stir rather than a storm. Over the White House, however, there settled an unnatural calm. The wind died down. The surface was placid. Five days dragged by, but nothing happened. When I retired on the night of April 10 the stillness outside the President's office was glacial. In a few hours it was shattered, and for me the first crash of the storm sounded in the ring of the telephone beside my bed at one-thirty in the morning. A woman whom I did not know was calling me, long-distance, from I know not where—it may have been Connecticut or it may have been Oregon—and as I was trying to wake up, I heard her saying, "Isn't it terrible news about General Mac-Arthur?"

"What about General MacArthur?" I exclaimed.

"All five members of my family are Democrats," she continued, excitedly, ignoring my question, "but from now on we're going to vote Republican. I wanted you to know."

"What *about* MacArthur?" I demanded.

"Truman's fired him," she said. "I heard it on the radio."

I was astounded and appalled. I was astounded at Truman's recklessness because I knew that he was an astute enough politician to foresee the results, and I could not believe that he would be so foolish as to invite them. I was appalled that I should have contributed to a chain of circumstances that had deprived the United States of the services of its greatest general.

After breakfast that morning I telephoned MacArthur's headquarters in Tokyo. Put in touch with his aide, General Courtney Whitney, I inquired whether, if invited, MacArthur would come to Washington to address a joint session of Congress. I have the impression MacArthur must have been in the same room with his aide, because almost immediately Whitney assured me that he would.

At 9:30 A.M. I met in my office with a group of Republicans that included Taft, Knowland, Bridges, Halleck, Leonard Hall, Representative Dewey Short of Missouri—ranking minority member of the House Armed Services Committee—and Bob Humphreys. The room was filled with indignation. Men vied with one another in characterizing the stupidity of Truman's action. I told them of MacArthur's willingness to address a joint session, and it was quickly agreed that we should approach Rayburn about inviting him.

Taft spoke rapidly for nearly ten minutes. One of the ideas he tossed off like sparks from a wheel was that Truman should be impeached. Humphreys said that in connection with the case of a certain judge he had had a study made of the process of impeachment. It was an extremely complicated business, he observed.

"Do you know who the greatest authority on impeachment is?" he asked Taft.

"Who?" the senator inquired.

"Your father," Humphreys said.

The study Humphreys mentioned was sent for, but nothing more came of the matter. I did not warm up to the idea of impeachment because I felt that, however unwise he may have been, Truman had acted within his constitutional rights as Commander in Chief.

My secretary stuck her head in and told Dewey Short he was wanted on the telephone.

"Tokyo is calling," she added.

We gasped and waited with unbearable curiosity for Short's return. It was the only anticlimax of that dramatic week. The call concerned some business of one of his constituents who was a serviceman in the Far East.

At 10:10 A.M. a call came for Taft, and he took it at my desk.

"Very well," he said, "we'll come over right away."

Hanging up, he told me that he and Bridges and Knowland must drop out for a few minutes because John Foster Dulles had asked to see the Senators at once in Taft's office. Dulles at that time was a Republican adviser to Acheson. After thirty minutes the Senators returned. They reported that Dulles had notified them that he was going to resign from the State Department in protest against the President's dismissal of MacArthur, but that they had persuaded him he could be more useful to the Republican Party by remaining, which he finally consented to do.

Before we broke up we all agreed that Congress should undertake an investigation into the military and foreign policies of the country. Incorporated in a statement later issued to the press, this was the genesis of the celebrated MacArthur hearings that were held after the general's return.

Following our meeting I approached Speaker Rayburn about an invitation to MacArthur to address Congress. He did not jump up and down with enthusiasm, but I had precedent on my side because of the joint sessions that had been called to hear Eisenhower and other returning generals of those years. Accordingly, MacArthur was invited.

Already I had visions of him as the Republican nominee in 1952. This deposed hero, I thought, might truly be the answer to our prayers. When Whitney, who preceded MacArthur home, came to see me, I bared my thoughts to him and he embraced them without reservation.

"If he wants to be President," I told Whitney, "many avenues will open up. First he'll get a tremendous reception when he arrives in San Francisco from Tokyo. Then he'll have the televised joint session. After that go and march up Fifth Avenue in New York, then on to Chicago and finally a great reception in Wisconsin, which he calls home. You'll be on your way to the presidential nomination."

Whitney was pleased, but, of course, it was not to work out that way. The reasons were many. MacArthur had no political organization. He had no money, although it could have been raised. With the convention little more than a year off, the time was already growing late. Finally, as I mentioned earlier, MacArthur felt that it would not be right for him to buck Taft.

As MacArthur headed for Washington I had some qualms about his feeling toward me because of my publication of his letter. These proved groundless because he was never anything but completely affable and friendly. Still, I did not mention our correspondence and neither did he. It remains to this day a subject we have never discussed. After his immensely moving speech to the joint session, I gave a luncheon for him in the Capitol. The air was full of tension. The Democratic leaders present could not be altogether sure that they were not sitting down with the next President of the United States. My brother Ed had helped me arrange the affair, and when Vice-President Barkley discovered that I was to sit between him and MacArthur he asked Ed whether this was protocol. "It's Joe Martin's protocol," Ed replied.

Afterward I took MacArthur to Constitution Hall to address the Daughters of the American Revolution. When, finally, I was leaving him for the day to return to the uproar he had left on Capitol Hill, he shook my hand and said, "Good-bye, Joe, don't let them put anything over." After the passage of many years the friendship that had begun over Fiorello La Guardia's spaghetti was resumed. Eight years later, shortly after I was overthrown by Halleck as House leader, MacArthur happened to be talking with Representative J. Edgar Chenoweth, a Republican from Colorado. "Tell Joe," he said, "to keep his chin up, to keep in there fighting and give that gang hell."

14

MacArthur's speech, climaxing the greatest epic of its kind in American history, at least since President Lincoln relieved General George B. McClellan of his command of the Army of the Potomac, was the most emotional moment I have witnessed in thirty-five years in Congress. It was a drama that forced gasps from men and women who were long hardened to the excitements of public life. When MacArthur told us that, "like the old soldier of that ballad," he was just going to fade away, there wasn't, someone remarked, a dry eye on the Republican side nor a dry seat on the Democratic. The theatrical effect was superb.

Theatrics are part of the Congressional way of life. We have our daily comedies and tragedies, our farces, pantomimes, and romances. Ours is a stage that is forever crowded with villains, heroes, clowns, saints, prophets, saviors, and con men of one kind and another. By no means all of these, I hasten to add, are members of Congress. We enjoy the services of many auxiliaries. I can see some of them distinctly in my memory: The woman dressed in pure white, who suddenly appeared in the center aisle and walked majestically to the well of the House, hoping to deliver a message. Another mysterious woman dressed in pure black, who slipped past a doorkeeper and took her seat on the Democratic side in such dignity that no one at first could be sure whether she was a member of Congress or not, even though she had not been seen there before. The three men and a woman who spread blood and panic on the floor of the House with blazing pistols.

212

Physical violence is no longer, if it ever was, a common occurrence in the House, yet in my time I either have witnessed or have been close to a good many outbursts of it. In my earliest years in Congress, for example, I just missed a hearing at which Representative Thomas L. Blanton, a Democrat from Texas, hurled an inkwell at Representative Ogden L. Mills, a Republican from New York, A.B. Harvard '04, LL.B. Harvard Law School '07, and Secretary of the Treasury 1932–33. Mills, a member of the House from 1921 to 1927, was an articulate and aggressive debater, whose challenging manner led to his having to duck more than inkwells. He also had to duck fists on occasion. In my second year in the House, 1926, he and Representative Rankin became embroiled in an angry dispute during impeachment proceedings against a federal judge in Illinois.

Mills had marched over to the Democratic side and accused Rankin of trying to delay the proceedings. Now long retired from Congress, Rankin was a fireball, a slight, nervous man with an incandescent temper, who was an improbable combination of Mississippi extremist and serious Shakespearean scholar.

"Get over on your own side of the House," he shouted at Mills. "You have no right here. You can't insult me in that manner."

Fists clenched, he approached Mills, swinging. Above the buzz of excited voices he could be heard calling the future Secretary of the Treasury "a dirty, contemptible scoundrel." Before the two could come to blows, however, they were seized by colleagues on both sides, though for my own part I respectfully remained on the sidelines because as a second-year man I felt that I could not interfere in quarrels involving so much seniority.

Mills was the victim, or should I say beneficiary, of other near-misses. One day when he was speaking, the gavel rang out, but he went right on. Representative Martin B. Madden, a Republican from Illinois, who was in the chair at the time, brought the gavel down again, this time with a crash that tore off the head and sent it whizzing past Mills's ear. It was difficult to say whether Mills or Madden was the more startled, but from that day to this the heads of gavels used in the House are firmly fixed to the handles with pins. A year or so later Madden collapsed and died in the House Appropriations Committee room, one of several members who have been fatally stricken in the Capitol, some of them on the floor of the House, during my days in Congress.

Afterward Rankin himself escaped with a near-miss. In the course of a spat over some question now long forgotten, he struck one of his fellow Democrats, Representative Frank E. Hook, of Ironwood, Michigan. Twice Rankin's size, Hook was a former World War I sergeant, a former miner and, as I recall, a former wrestler. "Rankin is going to get killed!" someone exclaimed. However, the House of Representatives is, despite its faults, a very efficient body, and as usually happens in such cases, the two men were separated by their friends before more harm was done.

One afternoon in 1932 I happened to enter the House by the center door as members were filing down the aisle to be counted in a teller vote. I had not gone ten feet when one of the pageboys pointed to the gallery and started shouting, "He's got a gun! He's got a gun!"

We were still in the Capone era, and at the word gun all the Congressmen from the Chicago area hit the floor as one man. With members lunging for doors and scrambling under desks the chamber was filled with wild commotion. Representative Edward W. Goss of Connecticut, an athlete in his youth, whizzed by me, shouting, "Make room for a fellow to run who knows how to run." Representative Thomas S. McMillan of South Carolina, who was in the chair at the moment, started from the Speaker's desk, but Lewis Deschler, the parliamentarian, a practical man as he would have to be in such a post, held on to him.

"You can't leave," Deschler said, "you're presiding."

The cause of the furor was a young department-store clerk

from Allentown, Pennsylvania, who was standing at the rail of the gallery swinging an enormous revolver in a wide arc and saying, "I want twenty minutes to address the House."

With the muzzle moving in a circle I reasoned that if I stood where I was, I might be hit once, but that if I ran, I might be hit by two or more bullets. Hence I planted myself firmly in the aisle and put my faith in the law of averages.

La Guardia had made it out of the chamber and was dashing upstairs to the gallery. Meanwhile Representative Melvin J. Maas, of Minnesota, a fighting marine in both world wars, threaded his way across the floor to the point nearest the deranged gunman, whose name was Marlin R. M. Kemmerer.

"Will you give me twenty minutes to make a speech?" Kemmerer asked Maas.

"Sure, sure," Maas replied, "you can make a speech, but it's against the rules to speak with a gun in your hand. Come on, buddy, give me your gun and you can make your speech."

Instead Kemmerer cocked the revolver and pointed it straight at Maas's head. Afterward the papers reported that Maas had disarmed the fellow with a smile, but Maas confessed to his friends that it was no smile but rather a silly grin caused by a paralysis of fear. Still he had the courage to continue asking for the revolver. Suddenly after terrible suspense Kemmerer leaned over and dropped the weapon. Maas caught it, cocked and loaded. By this time La Guardia was poised in the gallery behind Kemmerer and with the help of a policeman and a spectator overcame the man. Deservedly, Maas was awarded the Carnegie Silver Medal for bravery.

From time to time most members of Congress are approached by unfortunate men and women suffering from fears of persecution or from delusions. Generally, these strangers cause no harm and are forgotten almost as soon as they have departed. One man who approached me, however, gave me good reason to remember him later on. His name was William Kaiser. He was a retired Capitol policeman. It was in July 1947. Stopping me in the Capitol, he spoke about some money he had lost in bank failure in Columbus, Ohio. Of course, there was nothing I could do about it, and the brief conversation led nowhere.

Perhaps an hour or so afterward Kaiser, armed with a .22-caliber pistol, followed Senator Bricker into the subway that ran from the old Senate Office Building to the Capitol. (A new subway has been built recently.) Bricker had been Attorney General of Ohio at the time of the bank failure. As the Senator was walking to the monorail car, Kaiser fired at him and missed. Bricker and a companion leaped aboard and shouted to the operator to get going. As the car rolled along with Bricker ducking behind a seat, Kaiser fired—and missed—again. Frustrated, he put up his pistol and left, only to be arrested a short time later.

On March 1, 1954, when I was again Speaker in the Eighty-third Congress, I was presiding over what was, until a few seconds after 2:30 P.M., an uneventful session of the House. The measure we were about to consider was the "wetback" bill to permit federal supervision of migrant Mexican farm workers. At about two-thirty I called for a standing vote on a rule to bring it up. Two hundred forty-three members were present.

As I was counting the vote, starting with the Republicans on the left-hand side of the aisle as I faced them, a firecracker— or so I thought—was set off up in Gallery 11 at the extreme end of the chamber to my left. Too busy to take note of the disturbance at the moment, the thought flashed through my mind that I would order the sergeant-at-arms up to deal with the pranksters as soon as I had completed the count. When a second and third report followed in rapid succession, I swung around in exasperation.

Instead of seeing firecrackers, as I had expected, I found myself looking, at a distance, at the muzzle of a pistol. As I gaped, I saw three assailants—a woman and two men (I later learned that there was a third man whom I could not see)— and they all seemed to be aiming German pistols at me.

Bullets whistled through the chamber in the wildest scene in the entire history of Congress. Pandemonium spread so fast that control of the House was wrenched from my hands.

White plaster came sifting down from two bullet holes in the ceiling. Two more bullets struck the wall of Gallery 4, and one ripped into the door of that gallery. The walnut paneling behind the Democratic seats was pierced. A chair on the Democratic side and another on the Republican side were struck. Two bullets hit the majority table with such impact that a splinter flew into the face of Leo Allen, who was standing beside it.

Seconds before, the young woman, who was dressed in gray and whose name I later learned was Mrs. Lolita Lebron, had been waving a flag and screaming. Now she was holding a Luger in both hands, firing indiscriminately into the panic-stricken House. One of the men was shooting from a crouch; another was standing and aiming over his head.

The three looked to me like Mexicans, and I had a fleeting thought that they must have been driven to this madness by some grotesque misconception of the wetback bill. It was not until later that I learned that they were Puerto Rican nationalists conducting a fanatical demonstration on behalf of Puerto Rican independence, very much as Oscar Collazo and Griselio Torresola had done at Blair House when they tried to assassinate President Truman on November 1, 1950.

In the Press Gallery above me C. P. Trussell, of *The New York Times,* was struck on the cheek by plaster from the ceiling. William Belcher, a sixty-year-old doorkeeper, collapsed in the excitement. As on the earlier occasion of Mr. Kemmerer's visit, some members simply stood or sat at their desks, frozen in surprise and horror, while others dived to the floor and scrambled under desks and chairs.

"The House stands recessed," I declared, unhindered by any parliamentarian.

"That was the greatest understatement of all time," one of my colleagues told me later. Understatement or not, I darted clear of my chair and ducked behind a marble pillar behind the Speaker's desk. From there, protected against the firing, I could command a clear view of what was happening on the floor.

On the Democratic side, Representative Kenneth Roberts of Alabama had just resumed his seat after I had counted his vote. He crossed his left leg over his right knee, and suddenly gasped, "I'm hit!" Blood was seeping from his left leg. On hands and knees he crawled to the end of his row of seats where Representative Percy Priest of Tennessee removed his own necktie and applied it above the wound as a tourniquet.

Representative George H. Fallon of Maryland was shot in the hip. He tried to stand, but his leg gave way, toppling him to the floor behind some seats where he lay helpless until the shooting ended.

At the sound of shots, Representative Clifford Davis of Tennessee began sliding off his chair to take cover under his desk. He was too late. A bullet passed through the calf of his leg.

On the Republican side, Representative Alvin M. Bentley of Michigan was walking down the aisle when the firing started. Dropping to his knees, he crawled between the first and second rows of desks in a desperate search for protection, which he never found. A bullet struck him underneath the right armpit and tore clear through his body, penetrating two lobes of his right lung, opening a hole in his diaphragm, shattering his liver and traversing his stomach.

Representative Ben F. Jensen of Iowa, still waiting to be counted by me, was standing at his seat in the fifth row. He had just turned to speak to his Iowa colleague, Representative Thomas E. Martin, when a bullet hit him between his neck and right shoulder and ripped through the back muscles to lodge near his left shoulder blade.

"He got me!" Jensen cried, believing that he had been the victim of someone bearing a personal grudge. Jensen steadied himself against a chair and then staggered for an exit. Just as he reached a door, his strength gave out, and he collapsed across the threshold to the floor of the Speaker's Lobby.

Another member, rushing for the same door, saw Jensen fall and supposed that he had been shot from the lobby.

"My God, they're in here too!" he yelled. "They're in the corridor!"

At another exit two large men, Representatives Martin Dies of Texas and Frank W. Boykin of Alabama, arrived together at the same moment on their flight from the floor. Unheeding one another, they became wedged together in the doorway as they tried to scramble through simultaneously. Later, after they had frantically struggled free, Boykin said to Dies, "Say who was that guy who got caught between us in the doorway?"

While some were struck and others felled, Representative James E. Van Zandt of Pennsylvania, a decorated Navy veteran of both world wars, managed to break from the chamber, as La Guardia had done twenty-two years earlier, and race up to Gallery 11. He pinned one of the assailants to the floor, while the others were seized by attendants or fled, soon to be captured.

In the bedlam on the floor two members of the House who were physicians, Representatives Walter H. Judd of Minnesota and A. L. Miller of Nebraska, had rushed to the aid of Bentley, who lay moaning, the most seriously wounded of the five who had been struck. Happily, he and the others recovered from their wounds in the hospital.

There had never been such a scene since Sergeant Boston Corbett, the religious crank who claimed to be the slayer of John Wilkes Booth, shot up the Kansas House of Representatives in 1887. One of our members who was wounded had, as chance would have it, taken the pledge the day before. As he was being carried out to an ambulance, an old colleague of his looked at him sadly.

"I told you something would happen if you did that," he said.

After this episode all sorts of schemes were brought to me for increasing the protection of members of the House against similar attacks. We did indeed tighten up the security arrangements a good deal. Nevertheless I rejected the most ambitious proposal, one that called for installation of bullet-proof glass around the front of the galleries. For one thing, I was advised that the weight of this glass would be too great for the galleries to support. For another, I felt that, danger or not, Americans do not want their Congress walled off from the people by glass.

15

THE TWENTIETH of January 1953 was a memorable day for the Republican Party, yet one that in certain respects never altogether lived up to its promise. On that unseasonably mild afternoon we witnessed the inauguration of the first President to have been elected by our party since Herbert Hoover took the oath of office on March 4, 1929. The disheartening trail that began with Hoover's downfall in 1932 and descended through the defeats of Landon, Willkie, and Dewey had at last wound its way up again to the bright high ground of victory.

After twenty years of Democratic rule we Republicans were back in control of the White House and both houses of Congress. Eisenhower had received an immense popular vote. The country was united to a very high degree behind him.

People of both parties were confident that the country would have a good administration under Eisenhower, and, all things considered, I believe their hopes have been justified by events of the last eight years.

For Republicans, however, the 1953 inauguration held particular expectations. The party had been borne to power on strength contributed by every section of the national life. Votes had poured in from business, from the professions, from the farm, the city, the suburbs, the Negro community, the campus and even, in large number, from labor unions.

Millions of Democrats had deserted their own ticket to vote for Eisenhower. Though defeat had not reduced the Democratic Party to anything like the wreckage of the Republican Party in the mid-Thirties, it had nevertheless left the Democrats routed and practically leaderless.

221

The reversal of fortunes of the two parties, as dramatized by the inauguration, placed the new administration in a position to begin building the Republican organization up to a point where the Republican Party would be the dominant party in the United States for the next generation, just as the Democratic Party had been in the generation preceding.

This was the promising prospect of January 20, 1953, that somehow never quite materialized. Only twenty-two months later, in November 1954, the Democrats recaptured control of both houses of Congress and progressively strengthened their hold in the elections of 1956 and 1958. The election of 1956 was the first since Zachary Taylor defeated Lewis Cass in 1848 that a presidential candidate won while his party lost both the House and the Senate.

To blame this failure on any single person or group of persons or to attribute it to any one set of circumstances would be unrealistic and unfair. Perhaps it was too much to expect that one great victory, particularly when to a large extent it was a personal triumph for a war hero, could alter the fundamental balance existing between the two parties. The Democratic Party has such a tremendous reservoir of strength in its alliance with union labor in the North that it is able to survive defeats periodically and still return to the battlefield in force when the next campaign rolls around. Furthermore, the causes of the deficiencies in Republican power go back a long way in many instances. And, not excluding some old hands in Congress who may not always have painted the best possible face on the party, every Republican is in some measure responsible for the failure to capitalize on the opportunity that came our way with the victory of 1952.

At the same time it is true that from the beginning the new administration did not concentrate as it should have on the task of expanding and strengthening the party. In his early years in office the President seemed too much absorbed in other matters to grapple with party problems as such. Engaged as he was in general political conciliation, he did not make a strong show of Republicanism. *Republican* was a word that was not on the tip of his tongue.

Although his political instincts have been very sure, Eisenhower was not a professional politician experienced in the operation of party machinery. For him this was a source of strength with the voters, who welcomed a President who stood above the rumbles and machinations of partisan politics. For the party, on the other hand, it had obvious disadvantages. The President did not have an active interest in the technical aspects of party organization. He found many of the day-to-day troubles of the party tedious and, in particular, he loathed the problem of patronage, regarding it as something that did not deserve to occupy the time of the President of the United States. One can sympathize with and even admire this point of view, yet be compelled nevertheless to conclude that it does not stimulate the growth of a party at the grass roots.

One cannot expect to have a strong party unless there is complete cooperation from the Governor's office in the case of a state organization, or from the White House in the case of the national organization. The Governor or the President, as the case may be, must reach many decisions with the thought in mind of strengthening the party. Too often this consideration has been lacking in our own administration.

When it comes to making appointments, the mere fact of giving consideration to the political organization does not of itself mean that an appointment will be an unsatisfactory one. On the contrary, almost invariably the organization will agree to the man the administration desires. However, the organization wants to be consulted beforehand, to be given a sense of what is going on and of having a part in it. This cooperation strengthens the organization.

In this administration members of the House rarely have had any influence whatever in patronage, except for the postmasters in various districts. And politically, these appointments have become meaningless, more trouble than they are worth in fact, because they are controlled so tightly by civil-

service regulations and veterans' preference. To the extent
that the administration has allowed Senators an influence in
patronage, the privilege has come slowly and tardily.

I remember that to my surprise one day rather early in
the administration I picked up a newspaper in my district and
read that a Wellesley lawyer had been appointed Assistant
Attorney General. A man from my own district had been given
this important federal post, and reading it in a local paper
was the first I knew of it! What a way this was to go about
strengthening the local Republican organization! How many
times it must have been repeated!

Time and again I was struck by the social, Ivy League background of men who were appointed to office by the new administration. It was not that I doubted their qualifications, but I
was troubled over the fact that too many sons of rich families
were getting the jobs. For the good of the party I wanted to
see more of them go to the boys who were mining the coal and
sawing the wood for the Republican organization. How was
the party being strengthened by passing *them* by?

When I entered politics long ago the Republicans were much
more effectively organized than the Democrats. Prohibition,
the Depression, war, Al Smith, Franklin Roosevelt, and various other persons and events conspired to reverse this order.
All the more reason, one would have supposed, why we should
have striven when we were back in power to regain the old
supremacy. Of course, patronage was only one factor. It is
often said that politicians exaggerate its importance, and I
am aware of the thesis of some political scientists that, because
of the merit system, veterans' preference, and the availability
of jobs in the market place, patronage is no longer the life
blood of a party that it was, say in the days of the great immigration or the Depression. But as one who lived through the
Republican reaction to our own new administration day by
day, I can testify that it is still a vital instrument for practical
politicians concerned with the strength of their own organizations.

For the drudging work that develops political organizations at their foundations there must be incentive. While intangible rewards may suffice for some, there are others, as F.D.R. and party-buliders of the past realized, for whom the concrete incentive of patronage is a necessity. Not much of this incentive is to be found in the Republican organization today.

From the beginning, patronage was handled in a haphazard manner by the new administration. I do not remember that the subject was even brought up by anyone in the administration during any meeting that I attended in the White House. I do, however, remember very well an occasion on which it was brought up by our people from the Hill at one of Eisenhower's weekly conferences with legislative leaders.

"Mr. President," Leo Allen said, "for a year now I have been the chairman of the Rules Committee, and I haven't got a single job. How can a fellow get a job around here?"

I heard what he said all right, but it was such music to my ears that I asked, "What's that, Leo?"

"How can a fellow get a job around here?" he repeated across the Cabinet table. "I've been chairman of Rules for a year, and I haven't got a single job."

"Well you're not so bad off," I said. "I am *minus* two jobs."

"How can that be?" the President inquired.

"Easy," I explained. "The Democrats were kind to me, but when the Crusade came along, they took away two jobs and the Republicans didn't give me any. Doesn't that make minus two?"

When the meeting ended the President grabbed me by the coat and drew me aside, "You don't think I'd do anything like that to you, Joe, do you?" he asked. "We'll have to see about these two jobs right away." I am sure he asked one of his legion of liaison men to do something about the matter, but, of course, nothing ever was done. I am still minus two.

A corresponding deficiency lay in the inadequate stress placed upon electing Republican majorities of Congress, starting in 1952. It is not that the President himself has been loath to campaign for Republican candidates. On the contrary, he has done about as much in this field as one could expect a President to do, and in 1954 he outdid all his predecessors, I imagine, in getting about and trying to bring out the vote for Republican candidates for House and Senate.

However, a campaign is, in a sense, a last-minute undertaking. A party cannot win on its campaign alone. There needs to be continuous effort between elections to build up individual members of Congress, to single them out when occasion warrants and to strengthen the organizations that stand behind them. This is the kind of unending endeavor that has not been made. The organizations have not been kept happy and functioning. Their enthusiasm has not been aroused. As succinctly as I can sum it up, they have not been given a feeling of being in it with this administration.

In 1952 and 1956 a disproportionate amount of money for television and other campaign activities was devoted to the presidential race at the expense of the Congressional campaign. Candidates for the Senate and House were largely neglected. Our party sometimes tends to be smug: Republicans believe that they are doing a good job and just assume that everybody knows it and let it go at that. The Madison Avenue crowd that has attached itself to this administration has displayed little interest in electing a Congress. It's the presidency they are concerned about.

Except in the case of certain members who happened to be proficient golfers, there has not been any true comradeship between the White House and the Republicans in Congress. The rank and file on the Hill always found it extremely difficult, if not impossible, to see the President and hard enough to get an appointment with his top assistants.

This state of affairs was no wellspring of party harmony. Sherman Adams was an able and powerful official, and whoever had any dealings with him must have concluded that he was an honest man. He received a great deal of criticism that found its way to him only for lack of another eligible target.

Curiously, the kind of criticism that in other administrations fell on the President descended on the lieutenants in this one. For all his ability and prerogatives, however, Adams was limited in what he could do for the party.

The President, so far as I could observe, never surrounded himself with assistants who could solve political problems with professional skill. There were exceptions, like Thomas E. Stephens, the White House appointments secretary, who combines a wealth of experience with authentic political talent. Also Leonard Hall, while he was still Republican National Chairman, tried to open the administration's eyes to the political facts of life, with occasional success. But these exceptions were not enough to right the balance.

To a greater extent than other Presidents, Eisenhower has worked through subordinates in dealing with Congress, with results often the reverse of what he has desired. Men and women in Congress arrived there by their own wits and exertions, and they know they have got to be reelected on their own. They are inclined to resent having some young fellow who was picked up by the White House without ever having been elected to office himself coming around and telling them "The chief wants this" or "The chief wants that." The members would like to hear it from the chief himself once in a while. They feel that they hold positions important enough to be entitled to this consideration.

In the interest of building the party the administration never made use of many Republicans of consequence, whose services in one form or another would have been available for the asking. One of the principal contributors to the party in this generation was not invited to the first Eisenhower inauguration until Bridges and I discovered the omission and took it upon ourselves to get him an invitation.

In that same January of 1953 Sam Rayburn and I again changed places in our game of musical chairs over the Speakership. I had, it will be recalled, first replaced him in 1947. At that time the Texas flag hung in the Speaker's room, and although many of my Massachusetts friends wanted me to displace it with an emblem dearer to their hearts, I declined. Sam was proud of that flag, and beside, a lot of Republicans were starting to come to the fore in Texas. We needed all the Republicans we could get wherever we could find them. So I left the Texas flag hanging for Rayburn to return to some day, which, to my surprise—and Tom Dewey's—came in January 1949.

On reclaiming the office in 1953, I thanked Sam for having kept the chair warm and assured him that I would try to maintain the Speaker's limousine in good repair in case it should revert to him in 1955. Which it did. When we swapped the Speakership again that year for what was, I presume, to be the last time, he suggested that we not change offices since we could not foretell what would happen in 1957 or thereafter.

"I'm tired of all this shifting around," he said. So rather than to go to all the trouble of making a move that might have lasted only two years, although it did not turn out that way, Speaker Rayburn kept the minority leader's office, while I, as minority leader, remained in the Speaker's suite.

This continued to be my office until I was defeated as minority leader in 1959, whereupon I ascended to my present homy perch under the Capitol dome and settled comfortably among my collection of gavels, photographs, and GOP elephants.

Incidentally, one of these beasts, a surprisingly agile creature standing on its hind legs, came to me from the man who is least identified with such elephants of any person in the United States. Harry Truman gave it to me after someone had sent it to him in the White House.

"Take this up to Joe Martin," he told a secretary. "I don't want any damned dancing elephants around here."

16

In many ways my second term as Speaker was less an adventure than the first because in the Eightieth Congress, when the Democrats controlled the White House, I was the ranking Republican in Washington and enjoyed the excitement of leading the opposition. In the Eighty-third Congress, by contrast, a new Republican administration was in power. Instead of charging along at the head of the opposition, I had loyally to follow President Eisenhower and assume the responsibility of getting his program through the House. This was in almost all respects more exacting and less exhilarating than fighting the Truman administration.

For one thing the Republicans, after having been out of power for twenty years, had a difficult time shedding the psychology of opposition. Moreover, many of them had hoped to see Taft rather than Eisenhower in the Presidency. It was a great wrench for them to accept the Eisenhower program because they regarded it altogether too similar to the Roosevelt and Truman policies they had been accustomed to opposing. In the early days, in fact, there was no great difference, fundamentally, between the approach of Eisenhower and that of his Democratic predecessors.

When Eisenhower came in and asked for extension of the Reciprocal Trade Agreements Act, probably two thirds of the Republicans in the House were opposed to this program. In fact, it was none too easy for me, who had been one of the original opponents in the 1930s, to support it. Although I had voted for its extension after the war as a means of keeping

229

the channels of trade open, in the 1950s the manufacturers in my district were smarting under renewed foreign competition. My decision to support the President was less than a popular one in Massachusetts. One of my old friends, a textile man who had contributed liberally to Republican campaigns over the years, wrote me an angry letter advising me to pack my things and return home.

I do not believe the President could have got that program through the House if I had not drawn heavily on my store of good will with Republican members to get them to back him. I had continually to resist pressure from old and influential friends in the House to oppose Eisenhower on a range of issues from public housing to taxes.

The unhappiest of these conflicts found me caught between loyalty to Eisenhower and devotion to Dan Reed, a dear friend for many years. Reed not only had twice nominated me for Speaker, but had administered the oath of office after my election that January. In 1948, he had boomed me for the Republican presidential nomination. A Republican of tremendous conviction, he became chairman of the House Ways and Means Committee in 1953 and, without delay, set about to cut the income tax six months before it was due to drop and, in addition, to terminate the excess-profits tax. Eisenhower, newly installed in office, opposed both of these measures on the ground that spending must decline before any drop in the tax rate.

Under any other circumstances my inclination might well have led me to support Reed, but there I was in a position in which I felt that I had to fight my old friend in order to stand by the new President. This is precisely the kind of trial I had in mind when, earlier in the book, I mentioned the services that I had rendered to the President as his leader in the House.

We defeated Reed by stranding his tax-reduction bill in the House Rules Committee and then forcing his own Ways and Means Committee to report out an excess-profits-tax bill, which we accomplished by threatening to take the measure up on the floor without committee action.

During one of the critical moments in this fight the President was entertaining General MacArthur in the White House and asked me to drop down for a chat. I had scarcely arrived, it seemed, when I had to rush back to the Hill again. "As the general has said," I apologized, "there is no substitute for victory." Victories of this sort, however, did me no great good in the long run. Gradually they weakened my standing with the body of Republicans in the House who had once been my closest allies but who never really liked the Eisenhower program and did not in the least relish having it rammed down their throats.

I am not speaking here of Dan Reed. He remained my loyal friend to the end. Indeed after the tax fight I got Eisenhower and him together at a luncheon where they buried the hatchet. Inviting the President up for luncheon with Republican Congressmen was one device I tried for warming up this relationship. I remember arranging a luncheon in 1957 only to find that the House restaurant for some reason or other was unable to serve the luncheon, so we turned to a caterer, who offered to provide box lunches for $2 apiece.

"That seems a bit high to me," I told my assistant, Jim Milne. "You'd better see what some of these other caterers charge."

My New England instinct for thrift was never surer, because as a result of shopping around we got box lunches for $1.19 apiece, and the President and all the rest of us wound up having a capital time.

Shortly before Eisenhower took office I fell into a conversation at a party one evening with Senator Richard B. Russell, a Democrat from Georgia, who made a point to me that I was constantly to make to members of our own party after the new President began sending up recommendations that many of them opposed.

"Joe," Russell said, "we've got to make the Eisenhower administration a success. We've all got to cooperate to this end, because if it fails, the next administration will be a radical one."

Throughout those early months of 1953 I pleaded with disgruntled Republicans that the best chance for the conservative cause in the United States lay in supporting Eisenhower. Essentially, his program was a moderate one, and if it did not make the country strong and prosperous, the people would insist on moving to something more extreme. Then those Republicans who thought that their new President was going too far would find themselves up against someone whose course would make Eisenhower's seem dyed-in-the-wool conservative by comparison. In rounding up votes for the Eisenhower bills I tried tirelessly to make the point with my colleagues that since we no longer were the party of the opposition, we had to produce a record that would appeal to the voters at the next election or reconcile ourselves to defeat.

Bob Taft, who was the Republican leader of the Senate, shared this view. It was something that he and I discussed many times in those tragically few months left to him between the inauguration and his death the following July. Wounded though he had been by the loss of the nomination to Eisenhower the year before, he told me that he was going to give the administration every possible chance to succeed for the good of the party. Yet Taft was none too optimistic about the course the President was following. He did not believe that Eisenhower was surrounding himself with the right kind of Republicans, and he took exception to various appointments, particularly that of the late Martin P. Durkin as Secretary of Labor. Durkin, president of the Plumbers Union, was a Democrat who had committed what the Senator from Ohio deemed the ultimate folly of opposing the Taft–Hartley act.

The New Deal tendencies of the administration in its early days also aroused Taft's suspicion. At a legislative leader's conference in the White House on April 30 he startled everyone, including the President, with a vehement denunciation of continued heavy spending and deficits.

"The primary thing we promised the American people," he fairly shouted across the Cabinet table to the President, "was reduction of expenditures. Now you're taking us right down the road Truman traveled. It's a repudiation of everything we promised in the campaign."

Although the President composed himself and patiently explained why conditions in the world necessitated heavy outlays by the government, he did not change Taft's mind, nor did the explanation readily satisfy many other Republicans in Congress.

Happily, at least, these differences were largely ideological. Of course, there were one or two cases of personal animosity between the President and some Republicans in Congress, like the conflict between Eisenhower and the late Senator Joseph R. McCarthy of Wisconsin. Such instances were rare; furthermore, McCarthy was not one of the leaders. Between the Republican leadership of the House and Senate on the one hand and the President on the other, there were almost no serious grievances.

While the President's military background restrained him from the kind of familiarity with politicians that we had enjoyed with Roosevelt and Truman, we liked him personally and admired him as a good and an honest man.

As the years passed, even the ideological gap between the President and his Republican critics in Congress narrowed. Most Republicans gradually came to accept a large part of his program, while the President brought the mutual accommodation a great stride forward in 1959 by turning on the "radicals" and the "spenders" and launching his stout and effective fight for conservatism and a balanced budget. Eisenhower rarely, if ever, fought on the earlier issues the way he did on this one. My own view is that his course toward the end of his administration has reflected his philosophy of government more truly than the path he followed in the beginning.

One of the few times when, as Speaker, I felt compelled to desert the President, despite his personal solicitation, was on the St. Lawrence Seaway bill in 1954. Strong opposition to the project thrived in my district and throughout Massachusetts because the seaway threatened, we all believed, to divert business from the Port of Boston. From my earliest days in Congress I had been against it. Eisenhower himself had at first approached it with a lack of enthusiasm because of its great cost. However, the businessmen in his administration told him that it was necessary for the cheap transportation of Canadian iron ore to the United States. This, plus a threat by the Canadians to build the seaway by themselves, finally swung Eisenhower in favor of the bill for joint Canadian–United States construction. He promptly applied friendly pressure on me to go along with him.

At the legislative leaders' meetings I used to sit at his left hand at the Cabinet table, and one day he slid a paper along the polished mahogany surface, saying, "Joe, I've got a nice statement here on the St. Lawrence Seaway you may be interested in."

Almost before it left his fingertips I slid it right back to him with the comment, "No, Mr. President, I've been hearing about that problem for thirty-five years. I'm afraid that's one you can't convert me on."

"You're unchangeable," he lamented.

"Yes, on that particular subject I am, Sir," I replied.

Even when one is the President's leader in the House of Representatives, one has to consider the interests of one's own people now and then. After all, I knew perfectly well that the Eisenhower crowd was not going to reelect me that year. This was one time I had to look out for myself.

Eventually, the bill was passed without my backing. Now that six years have elapsed, I must say frankly that the seaway is not hurting New England the way we feared. On the contrary, we can see signs that it may prove helpful.

I used to ask the President why he did not draw upon the

strength residing in his influential friends around the country to bring pressure on Congress for various bills he was especially interested in. I was struck, for example, by the influence he could have generated in Georgia alone where he spent so many vacations at the Augusta National Golf Club with men like Bobby Jones and the Coca-Cola Company executives.

"Why don't you organize these people?" I would ask. "They're with you. Get them so that they can build up a local organization to contact their Congressmen. With that kind of help we can win these fights."

He listened courteously, but nothing ever seemed to come of my suggestions.

Instead of helping the President, his liberal-minded friends occasionally managed to undermine his relations with Republicans in Congress. I happened to be in the Senate dining room one day during the 1956 campaign when Senator William E. Jenner, a Republican from Indiana, entered, furious over an article in *Collier's* by Paul G. Hoffman, a sometime host and companion of the President's. The article was highly critical of certain Republican conservatives on Capitol Hill, including Jenner. The Senator showed me the draft of a bitter retort he intended to make public that would have exacerbated the feelings between the President and the conservatives about whom the President so often complained, privately, in those days.

"If I were you, Senator," I urged, "I would not do it. It won't do the party any good. You're not running this year, so it can't help you, but putting it out in the middle of the campaign would be bad for the party."

He refrained from issuing that particular statement and later thanked me for my advice. On another unrelated matter I had somewhat less success in an undertaking with Jenner, though it was no fault of his.

During Truman's final years in office Senator McCarthy had kept up the most aggressive attacks upon the administration, but most of us assumed that after a President of McCarthy's own party had taken office, these attacks would subside. To the consternation of many of us they did not. McCarthy assailed the Eisenhower administration with much the same hostility which he had taken out after the Democrats. The effect was deplorable not only for the administration but for McCarthy himself. The Democrats he could attack and get away with it, but when he made a Republican President his target he drew the line on an issue that he never could win. Republicans might support McCarthy on this question or that, but it was inconceivable that they could have stood behind him when he challenged their own President. This was his nemesis.

His lamentable quarrels with the President in the early months of the Eisenhower administration brought back to my mind some advice given me by Representative Thomas S. Butler, a Republican from Pennsylvania, when I first came to Congress. Tom Butler, who was the father of Smedley Butler, the Marine general, had been in Congress twenty-eight years when I turned up in 1925.

"You're a young man, Joe," he said, "and I hope you'll stay here a long time. But let me give you a bit of advice: don't talk too much. The fellows that talk, talk their way out of Congress."

In time I came to see ample proof of this. I recall in particular a certain Representative from the West years ago who succumbed to religious prejudice and allowed it to creep into his speeches. The first time I heard the note I warned him. When he persisted, I begged him to cut it out.

"If you don't stop now," I told him, "people will think you're a fanatic, and you won't have anybody with you."

This is exactly what happened, of course, and it cost him his seat. However, long afterward I happened to meet him on a western trip, and I could not help but wonder whether I had given him such good advice after all. I had tried to help him stay in Congress, but after he was defeated, he made a million dollars in real estate. If he had followed my advice he might have remained a Congressman of modest means.

Coming back to my mention of Jenner, I had little to do

personally with McCarthy, who served in the Senate while I was in the House, but his controversies with Eisenhower were becoming a matter of rising concern to us all. Mindful of old Tom Butler's advice, I broached the subject one day to Jenner, who was a friend of McCarthy's.

"McCarthy is making a great mistake," I said. "He's talking too much. He has great influence in the country, but he won't have it long if he keeps this up. Can't you do something about it?"

Jenner agreed to do what he could, but when I saw him again he was despairing.

"I talked to him about it," he said, "and the other day he assured me he wouldn't make any more speeches for a while. Thirty minutes later, while I was having lunch in the Senate restaurant, I heard someone saying, 'McCarthy's up' "—meaning he was making a speech on the Senate floor. "How can you keep a fellow like that quiet?"

And sometimes the things others say with the best of intentions can bring a politician as much grief as the things he says himself.

Early in 1958 the late William Francis, an Assistant Secretary of Defense, who was a Texan, invited me to a $100-a-plate dinner his friends were giving in Houston to raise money for the Republican National Committee. Jack Porter, the Republican National Committeeman from Texas, followed up Francis' invitation with an appeal to me to speak at the dinner. He said that I could help bring out a good crowd, and as I had an engagement the same week in Albuquerque, I agreed to go and do what I could to wipe out the national committee's deficit.

By sheer coincidence there was pending in the House a bill to relax federal regulation of the price of natural gas. Generally the conservatives were for it and the liberals were hotly opposed. A similar measure had been enacted by Congress two years earlier, but the President had vetoed it when it was dis-

covered that two oil-company lawyers had contributed to a Senator's campaign fund. Justly or not, the issue had long been
surrounded by an aura of big-money influence, lobbying, and
skullduggery, but that did not change the fact that this was
a sound bill. I was for it. There was, however, no connection
whatever between the fund-raising dinner in Houston and the
natural gas bill. Or, rather, I should say that there was no
reason for any connection. But in inviting a certain few of
his friends among the 1500 who bought tickets, Porter
unthinkingly wrote on a letterhead of the Republican National
Committee:

Joe Martin . . . has always been a friend of Texas, especially of
the oil and gas-producing industries. He mustered two-thirds of the
Republican votes in the House each time the gas bill passed. . . .

It will be up to Joe Martin to muster at least 65 per cent of the
Republican votes in order to pass the gas bill this year. . . . He has
put Republican members from northern and eastern consuming areas
on the spot politically because the bill is not popular due to the distortion of facts by newspaper columnists and others.

The dinner must raise substantial amounts of money for the Republican party, as part of these will go towards the election of Republican Congressmen and Senators. . . . Even though we may not
approve of everything Eisenhower has done . . . the Republican
party is the party of private enterprise and free economy. . . .

Totally unaware of this letter, whose tactless wording
painted an image of Houston money gushing up in support
of a Congressman who might be able to put through a bill
which Texas wanted, I addressed the dinner. The evening was
a plush affair with beefsteak and good companionship—and a
badly needed harvest of nearly $150,000 for the Republican
National Committee. My speech was well received in spite of
the fact that the natural gas bill was not even mentioned. And
when I retired later, I felt that I had passed a few hours that
had been pleasant enough for me and profitable for the Republican treasury.

The next morning I was at Porter's house quietly preparing

to leave for Albuquerque when reporters came clattering down on me, frothing with questions about the Porter letter and my role in the natural gas legislation. This was the first I knew of the existence of the letter, and it took some bewildered minutes for me to piece together a realization that I was caught in the middle of a situation that opponents of the gas bill back in Washington were trying to pump up into a great scandal.

What had happened was that the Washington *Post* had obtained a copy of the letter. As I have come to understand it, a liberal employed by one of the wealthy Texans who received one of the letters made a copy and sent it to the editor of the *Post*, who promptly dispatched his Pulitzer Prize-winning reporter, Edward T. Folliard, to Houston to report the whole affair.

When Folliard's story hit the front page in Washington the next morning, it killed the natural gas bill like a bolt of lightning. The gushers were spouting in the liberal camp now, with Democratic National Chairman Paul M. Butler proclaiming that "it is shocking that the name of the Republican leader of the House was used to give prestige and authority to this shoddy exercise in mass bribery held under the guise of a Republican fund-raising dinner." Even Sam Rayburn had to say, tartly, "If Porter had set out to defeat the gas bill, he couldn't have done a better job."

The dooming of the gas bill was one of those accidents that was beyond my control or responsibility. All I could do was shrug it off. But I was infuriated by the reaction that occurred in the White House.

After reading the *Post* story, Meade Alcorn, who was then Republican National Chairman, telephoned General Persons, at the time Deputy Assistant to the President, and James C. Hagerty, the President's press secretary. These two went to Eisenhower, and, as I learned later, the President ordered the national committee not to accept the proceeds of the dinner, although Alcorn issued a statement making it appear that the initiative had been his, with the President lending approval.

The very suggestion that there was any scandal about the Houston dinner was so baseless that the decision to deprive the national committee of the $150,000 was as absurd as anything I had seen in politics in a long time. While I may have burned with anger, however, the Houston people did not weep over it. The Republican organization in Texas had contracted heavy debts on behalf of the Eisenhower campaign in 1956. As long as the President would not let the money be turned over to the national committee, the Texans were pleased to keep it and pay off their obligations from his last campaign.

In Albuquerque I spoke at a dinner that raised $40,000 for the national committee. The envious chairman told me that he wished the New Mexico organization could keep this money the way Texas was holding on to its bonanza. His lament gave me an idea. In years past I had done a good deal to advance the cause of legislation to develop water resources in the Southwest, as a result of which New Mexico had a more plentiful water supply.

"Here's what you do," I told my friend. "Let the word leak out that you gave me this dinner as a testimonial to my having got you people some water down here. That will shock the powers in Washington into refusing to take your money."

I never heard whether he followed my advice. Probably he abandoned it in the end on the theory that water is not as scandalous a substance as natural gas.

We had been out of power for so many years that after the victory of 1952 we looked forward to a Republican administration with excitement and high expectations. It is almost unbelievable that already these eight years are practically at an end. This evaporation of time reminds us how fleeting is the interval that any President has in which to accomplish his objectives against all sorts of obstacles and inertia. As in any great passage in human affairs, one looks back on this span with mixed emotions.

There is gratification about many of the things that President Eisenhower has done. Animosities and divisions were rife among our people before he took office. The President healed and conciliated and pacified, and when his second term ends, he will, in my opinion, leave the White House with a better spirit in the country than he found when he arrived. By and large the country has been more united under Eisenhower than it has been, except in moments of national crisis, like that of Pearl Harbor, under any President in a long time. He has represented the United States abroad with great credit, and he has done perhaps as much as anyone could do under the circumstances to check the drift toward socialism in this country. His critics to the contrary notwithstanding, he has kept the United States strong in military power.

Along with the gratifications there have been disappointments, especially over the failure of the administration to do what it might have done to strengthen the Republican Party. For me there was the irony that after having served for years as Republican leader of the House in the administrations of Franklin Roosevelt and Harry Truman I should have been cast aside under Eisenhower.

It is a commentary on the unpredictable workings of destiny that if the Democrats, whom I fought in 1952 and again in 1956, had won over Eisenhower, I would without doubt still be the Republican leader of the House today. The factors that brought about my overthrow—the panic over loss of a Congressional election, the encouragement given by the White House to a rival, the grievances born of my support of unpopular proposals of the President—would not have operated against me in the decisive way that they did if we had remained the party out of power. In other circumstances, moreover, I probably would not have been so complacent about my chances of reelection as I was on January 1959.

After he had treated me for my blood clot and had assured me that I was in sound health, Dr. Paul Dudley White told me, "I want to give you some advice: talk less, walk more."

"Doctor," I replied, "that's a hell of a piece of advice to give a politician."

If I had talked more and run instead of walked, I would have remained in the place I had occupied since Bert Snell abandoned his seat and his leadership of the House Republicans at the end of 1938.

Conclusion

BE THAT AS IT MAY, I begin my second half-century in politics with few regrets and no lasting animosities. My mother taught me as a child not to bear grudges, and this is a lesson I have lived by. When I was a young politician in Massachusetts, there was a man named George A. Sweeney, who was the only Democrat around who year after year used to defeat his Republican opponent for selectman in Attleboro. I asked Sweeney once what was the reason for his repeated success.

"Very simple, Joe," he explained, "I start with a new set of books every January first."

As best I could I made this advice a part of my own behavior. Every so often I have tried to wipe the slate clean of grievances against those who have done me harm. It is only natural to be hurt when men whom one had trusted through the years and whose careers one had done much to advance failed one at the moment when their help was needed most. But that is human. One has to accept the fact that men are apt to do what they think is in their own selfish interest when they are put to the final test.

I learned more about human nature in the fight that went against me than I had in many others that I won. Some of these new insights were rewardingly droll.

One of the Republican members who used to hound me for patronage when I was leader was Representative William H. Ayres, of Ohio. After scrounging around and drawing on my friendship with the Democrats, who controlled most of the patronage because they were in the majority, I arranged for him to appoint a man to the Capitol police force. And this was only one of the favors I had, gladly, been able to do for

243

my colleague from Akron. As minority leader, for example, I was entitled to a limousine and chauffeur, and when a blossom queen from Ohio was arriving in Washington, Ayres asked me to lend him the Cadillac and driver so he could meet her in style, which I did.

The next thing I knew he was active on Halleck's side in the fight to depose me. After he and the rest of them in that faction had brought about my defeat, the leaders in both parties graciously put through a resolution giving any former Speaker who was still a member of the House the perquisite of a limousine and chauffeur. Of this, Ayres was extremely critical. Whatever the principles that had guided him to this attitude, however, they were not so rigid but what, when he espied my chauffeur in front of the Capitol one afternoon, he asked him to drive him to a hotel downtown. When I heard of this, I opened the door a crack on my ban against grudges.

"If you ever give that fellow a ride in this car again," I told my chauffeur, "you'll be fired."

Someone reminded me recently that not long after I had become Republican National Chairman in the Willkie campaign, I declared that I would give ten thousand dollars to get out of the job. Now I would not take ten times ten thousand dollars to return to my job as Republican leader of the House. What had seemed a humiliating misfortune at the time has turned out to be a blessing, one that may well have preserved my life. The consequences of my returning to the ranks were more leisure, greater political independence, and a remarkable improvement in health.

Until the doctors told me to slow down when I was afflicted by the blood clot shortly before the leadership fight, it had never occurred to me that I was becoming an old man. Suddenly I had need of a cane. I asked my sister to look around the house in North Attleboro to see if we did not have one somewhere. In the attic she found a stick with a gold head. It had been presented to me by the citizens of Attleboro when I left for Congress in 1925. I had never used it in thirty-four years, but now I was grateful for it, and it helped me to get about until the clot cleared up.

After the votes had been counted against me in the Republican conference in 1959 I took it for granted that when the two-year term I was then commencing came to an end this year, I would hear the gavel fall on my career in Congress. I was, I must confess, silently appalled at how different an exit this would be from any that I had imagined.

As the months passed and my health returned, my perspective changed. While I never would be leader again, the experience that had come from nearly fifty years in politics had taught me a great deal that I could still do for people. Other assets than leather lungs are needed in government. Age may make its own valuable contribution—as we are seeing today in West Germany in the wise leadership of Chancellor Konrad Adenauer, who is over eighty.

Before long I decided that the time had not yet come for me to quit. New England is entering a promising new era. The old country, as we Americans might almost call it, went through hard times when we lost the textile mills to the South. Today New England is sprouting modern new industries, like plastics and electronics. Splendid research laboratories are rising in what were until recently forest and untillable fields. These industries and laboratories require workmanship of the highest skill and pay better wages than the textile plants ever did. To provide the brains to manage and staff these highly specialized enterprises, New England colleges are turning out talent unsurpassed in any other region. Having struggled through the long decline, I want to stay around to contribute out of a lifetime of intimate knowledge to this revival that is going to carry New England a long way forward.

The opportunity to make the lives of men and women easier and happier has been the greatest single reward of my sometimes hectic years in public office. There is no reason why I should not continue performing these services for others in the future just as I have in the past.

Nothing else in life has remained with me with anything like the glow of satisfaction that I have experienced in doing things for people. Countless examples crowd my memory—the soldier brought home for his mother's funeral. The notice of a pension for a veteran's widow (mailed special delivery to Fall River so she would get it on a Saturday and not have another week end of worry). The families reunited as a result of special immigration bills. The settlement for a couple injured in a collision with an Army truck. The ailing veterans accepted by hospitals. These are but the merest sampling. In our large and increasingly complex society people are often bewildered and frustrated in trying to obtain assistance that they are entitled to. It is not only one of the obligations but one of the privileges of public life to help them find their way.

In contrast to the great problems of government this service may loom small, yet I have found, at least where members of the House are concerned, that it is far more important on election day than national and international issues. The average person, while he is interested in the large questions, really knows rather little about them. He lets his Congressman and his Senator and his President grapple with these. But when it comes to voting for the man who will represent him in Congress, the thing that is most likely to impress him is the degree to which his Congressman has been helpful to him or to the people of his district.

High among the lessons I have learned since I first paid my nickel on the interurban to campaign for the Massachusetts House of Representatives in 1911 is that a Congressman must first of all speak for the interests of his own district. Either he does this, or he will soon be living back in his district for good, with the Capitol dome a mere memory.

Nevertheless the time will come for everyone who sits in Congress when the national interest will conflict to some degree or other with the interests of his district. As in my own case, for example, he may come from a district whose manufacturers, the employers of hundreds of his constituents, may genuinely

require a protective tariff for their products at the very moment
when it is in the broad interest of the United States of America
to reduce tariffs. Or he may represent a district whose people,
instead of raising the food they consume, buy it in a supermarket. Their immediate interest may be to oppose price supports for farmers, which tend to raise the retail price of food.
Yet in the wider view of national interest it may be imperative
to place a floor under farm prices to keep the economy from
sagging to the detriment not only of the farmer but of the urban
customer in the supermarket.

In such dilemmas every member of Congress has to be
guided by his own conscience. It seems apparent to me, however, that our federal system of government cannot prosper
unless enough members are willing to support the national
interest against the local interest, painful though the choice
may be for the individual.

I could, of course, proceed from here through a primer of
practical lessons I have learned in these first fifty years in
politics.

For example, although I myself do not drink, I always make
a point of shaking hands with bartenders whenever I come
across them, because their recommendations, voiced at that
moment when men's minds are highly receptive to ideas, carry
much weight in a community.

I think it is, generally speaking, a mistake for a member of
Congress, whether he be a Democrat or a Republican, to accept
the role of national chairman of his party, although I did so
reluctantly myself. The positions he may have to take on national
issues may conflict disastrously with the interests of his own
state or district.

White-tie dinners at the White House are tedious, but sometimes valuable politically.

"I know, Joe," President Eisenhower once told me when
I was Speaker, "that you don't like all these affairs any more
than I do. We have to invite you because of your position, but

don't think you will be hurting my feelings if you want to decline."

"Well, thank you, Mr. President," I replied. "I think I am going to take you up on that except when a dinner is for a Frenchman or an Irishman or an Italian or a Pole or a Portuguese or someone like that. There are a great many people from these groups in my district, and they appreciate it when I join in honoring a visitor from the land of their ancestors."

Another lesson that comes readily to mind is that, especially if a President of one's own party is in office, the position of minority leader of the House of Representatives is the most thankless job in Washington. If the President's program fails, the minority leader catches hell. If it passes, the majority leader gets all the credit.

Before ending this primer I do not want to omit mentioning the satisfaction that comes from magnanimity.

Twenty years ago a bill was introduced in the House to provide pensions for retired members of Congress. Federal economy was a big pitch with me in those days. Furthermore I had sufficient confidence in my own thrift and self-reliance to feel certain that I would never need retirement benefits from the government. I made a speech against the bill, and later it was defeated. After we had recessed on the day of my speech, Speaker Bankhead strolled out of the Capitol with me.

"I'm sorry you did that, Joe," he said. "That bill was needed badly. Take my own case. I've put in years in the House. I have no law practice left. If I lost my seat, I'd be broke without a pension. That would be my lot for serving the country."

On reflection I came to the conclusion that I had taken a rather selfish and narrow point of view. And when the bill came up again at the next session I supported it enthusiastically, and it passed. Without its benefits, many men and women who have worked hard in Congress at the sacrifice of their normal means of livelihood at home would have suffered unjustly.

A few years ago, when I was still the leader of the Republicans in the House, we had a somewhat similar case in the bill to provide a pension of $25,000 a year to former Presidents. All of us knew, of course, that whereas Herbert Hoover, a man of wealth, did not need the money, it would come in very handy to the only other living former President, Harry Truman, who had spent his life in politics, which put him somewhere under the high-income brackets.

Since Truman's unpopularity among highly partisan Republicans has been slow wearing off, most members on my side of the aisle were strongly opposed to the bill. They argued that Truman would take the money and go whooping off with it on a campaign to malign Republicans.

This was nonsense, I retorted. I recalled how, in order to realize an adequate income after leaving the White House, Grover Cleveland had become a director of a life insurance company and Calvin Coolidge had written a syndicated newspaper column.

In my opinion these instances reflected on the dignity of the presidential office. I believed that any man who had occupied the White House should be able to live independently. Although I received a great deal of criticism from my own followers, I fought for the bill. When it passed, I felt that I had done the right thing, and I was pleased to receive the following letter:

Harry S. Truman
Independence, Missouri

August 26, 1958

Dear Joe:

I am very grateful to you for your efforts in connection with the Presidential Retirement Bill.

It was a wonderful thing for you to do, and I am more than appreciative.

Sincerely yours,
Harry S. Truman

Finally, I must say that one of the compensations of public life has been the direction and advice I have been able to give younger men who have come to me for counsel. Of the numerous cases that I could cite, none has been more dramatic as far as I am concerned than that of a certain gentleman who called on me back around 1928 after his graduation from Harvard Law School.

When he dropped by my house in North Attleboro, he said that he was a Republican and was deeply interested in a political career. Inasmuch as he had ties in both Massachusetts and Maine, however, he was uncertain in which state to try his luck. He explained that former Governor Cox of Massachusetts had suggested that he seek my advice. After mulling over his problem, I advised him to go to Maine. Among several reasons I mentioned the fact that in any of the towns in that state a young lawyer would quickly become prominent. The State Assembly in Maine was large. It would be relatively easy for a bright young man to be elected to it. Once there, he could strike out on a possibly important political career.

The young lawyer thanked me for my advice and departed. I do not know whether I even heard him when he had told me his name. If I did, I soon forgot both it and the visit. Many years afterward, in the late 1940s, Senator Owen Brewster, a Republican from Maine, invited me to speak in Augusta, the state capital. During my visit he and I had dinner with Governor Horace A. Hildreth, who was later to become president of Bucknell University and then United States Ambassador to Pakistan.

For some reason that I could never possibly explain I happened to mention during dinner the case of the young Harvard law student who had asked my advice about entering politics in Maine. I wondered aloud what had happened to him and who he was.

"That was I," Governor Hildreth said.

As I embark on my second half-century in politics, or as much of it as is to be allotted me, I pause to say a word about the men and women in Congress. They are human. They err. Sometimes they are guilty of folly and mistakes. All too often they are held up unjustly to public ridicule. In spite of this they measure up in intelligence and character to any other group I have encountered in a long life. Few other persons in any field are subject to anything like the pressures and the unbelievably difficult questions that confront them almost every day of their lives.

For all of the faulty decisions that may be reached the members of Congress are not solely responsible. The people of the United States cannot, I believe, escape their share of the blame. All too often Senators and Representatives are abandoned by the people to fight alone against powerful and selfish groups that operate with the connivance of the voters for the interest of a few.

Congress can, in truth, be only as strong as the people who stand behind it. If the citizens of the United States would pay closer attention to public affairs and would give righteous support to their representatives in the House and Senate, fewer complaints would arise over the happenings on Capitol Hill. In England, service in the government is held in high esteem. In these times, particularly, it deserves no less a place in the United States.

Still, when I am asked by this young person or that whether one should aspire to a career in public life, I do not give a discouraging answer.

Of course, if one is simply seeking money or ease or an eight-hour day or a glamorous combination thereof in the occasional glitter of Washington, I say *No!* for God's sake, don't go into politics.

On the other hand, if one is willing to work half the night, to live on a modest income, to wear himself out doing things for others and yet be tolerant of the ridicule, misunderstanding and criticism he is likely to get for his pains, then let him enter public life. It offers deep personal fulfillment. It is seldom a bore. And though it often appears to be the very recipe for frenzy and neurosis, it can provide an extraordinary sense of achievement and contentment.

After years of living with the coldest realities I still believe that one reaps what one sows and that to sow kindness is the best of all investments.

INDEX

Abel, Mrs. George P., 173
Acheson, Dean, 55, 202, 206, 209
Adams, Sherman, 171, 227
Adenauer, Konrad, 245
Agricultural Adjustment Act, 75
Agriculture, subsidies for, 75
Air-conditioning, 49
Albuquerque, 239
Alcorn, Meade, 16–17, 239
Aldrich, Richard S., 47
Allen, Leo, 82, 86, 182, 217, 225
American Bankers Association, 74
American Commonwealth, The, Bryce, 174
American embassies, 62
Amherst College, 60
Anderson, Jack Z., 7, 10
Andrews, Walter G. (Ham), 82
Appropriation bills, 49, 85
    for atomic bomb, 100–101
    for defense, 50
Arends, Les, 189
Arms embargo, repeal of, 93–94
Ashurst, Henry, 47
Asia, 200
    communism in, 200–201
Associated Willkie Clubs of America, 107–108
Atomic bomb, 100–101, 176, 178
Attleboro, Massachusetts, 25–26, 36
Attleboro *Sun,* 25–26, 28
Attleboros, the, 54–56
Augusta, Maine, 250
Aviation, 64–65
Ayres, William H., 243–244

Baker, Frederick E., 133–135
Balanced budget, 194, 233
Baldwin, Raymond E., 159
Balfour, Lloyd, 135
Bank deposits, federal guarantee of, 74
Bankhead, Tallulah, quoted, 18
Bankhead, William B., 18, 47, 180, 248
Barkley, Alben W., 186, 210
Barron's magazine, 83
Barton, Bruce, 118–119
    quoted, 119
Baseball, 24

Belcher, William, 217
Bentley, Alvin M., 218–219
Berkley, Massachusetts, 42
Beveridge, Albert J., quoted, 48
Bingham, Hiram, 149
Bird, Mrs. Charles Sumner, 51
Blaik, Earl, 18
Blanton, Thomas L., 213
Bleakley, William G., 166
Block, Paul, 116
Bootleggers, 50
Borah, William E., 47, 63, 147, 149
    quoted, 48
Boston, 56
    city charter of, 32
    Port of, 234
Boston *Globe,* 26
Boykin, Frank W., 219
Bradley, Keith, 140
Brady, Diamond Jim, 140–141
Brannan plan, 176, 190
Brehaut, James W., 26
Bresnahan, Lawrence J., 79
Brewster, Owen, 250
Bricker, Senator, 157–158, 161, 166–167, 216
Bridges, Styles, 189, 202, 208–209, 227
Brockton, Massachusetts, 76
Brooklyn, 199, 202–203
Brookshire, Harry L., 11
Brown, Albert E., 141
Brownell, Herbert, 167
Bryce, James, quoted, 174
Budge, Hamer H., 15
Bull Moose party, 35, 138
Bureaucracy, 68, 77
Burton, Marion L., 145
Burton, Theodore Elijah, 47, 145
Business, government and, 74
    taxation and, 77
Butler, Nicholas Murray, 146
Butler, Paul M., 239
Butler, Thomas S., quoted, 236
"Buy American" campaign, 76
Byrnes, James F., 177

California, 34
Cannon, Clarence, 77, 101

253

ABOUT ROBERT J. DONOVAN

Robert J. Donovan, chief of the Washington Bureau of the New York *Herald Tribune,* has covered the national and world scene since 1947. He is a past president of the White House Correspondents Association. He covered President Truman's entire "whistle-stop" campaign in 1948 and his overseas trips, including his famous junket to Wake Island in 1950 to confer with General MacArthur. He covered President Eisenhower's 1952 and 1956 campaigns and most of his foreign trips to Paris, western Europe, India, and Formosa.

Mr. Donovan is author of *Eisenhower: The Inside Story,* and *The Assassins,* and has contributed frequently to *The Saturday Evening Post, Harper's,* and *The New Yorker.*

DATE DUE